Cooking Light

LIGHTEN UP, AMERICA!

Cooking Light

LIGHTEN UP, AMERICA!

*Favorite American Foods
Made Guilt-Free*

Allison Fishman Task

Oxmoor House

To the delicious Abraham Lee and Zevin Jones:
You've got big appetites like your mama—use them wisely.
Thank you for being the best travel partners
I could have hoped for.

We sent *Cooking Light's* ebullient and tireless contributing editor, Allison Fishman Task, on a mission: to crisscross this great land in search of favorite regional foods. The result of her road-tripping culinary anthropology is an almost dizzying collection of classic treats from the diners, county fairs, cocktail parties, and hotel dining rooms of our collective yore. Between the Reuben sandwiches, Waldorf salads, sweet-and-sour meatballs, red flannel hash, and apple pie, there's enough comforting nostalgia here to butter all of New England's lobster rolls. But while traveling and eating, Allison also had her eye on a bigger theme: to lighten these American classics for a country that is starting to think hard about what it eats, even as it reaffirms what it loves from its past.

At *Cooking Light*, it's been our mission for more than 25 years to honor the flavor values of traditional foods while coaxing a lot of fat and calories out. Nothing gives us more pleasure than a light cheesecake that has the same swoon-inducing, throat-catching effect of the Brooklyn original—and half the calories. We love eating and cooking, but we don't give indulgent treats like artichoke-spinach dip a nostalgia pass just because they remind us of the time we snuck big mouthfuls at Mom's bridge-party soirée. We see lightening up these dishes as a new sort of cultural preservation: classic flavors served up for a healthier generation. This is important because the recent push toward mega-burgers, bacon bombs, five-cheese pizzas, and other over-the-top glop isn't doing much to honor and advance our food culture, let alone our health. We much prefer Allison's approach—respect the traditions, but improve upon them. Love what you eat, but do so with a healthy future in mind. And keep an eye out, as Allison did on her road trips, for the new favorites—the Vietnamese bánh mì sandwiches, the Mexican fish tacos—that continue the evolution of our food through the inspirations of immigrant cooks.

This book moves our preserve-but-improve philosophy nicely down the road, serving up more than 150 recipes that American families can really dig into, happily and healthfully.

Scott Mowbray
Editor, *Cooking Light*

CONTENTS

Introduction *10*

Up and At 'Em *18*
Breakfast & Brunch

Lunch Fare *52*
Sandwiches, Salads & Soups

Between Meals *90*
Appetizers & Snacks

Main Course *122*
Entrées & One-Dish Meals

On the Side *198*
Casseroles & Veggies

Beloved Desserts *246*
Pies, Cakes, Cookies & More

Index *312*
Nutritional Analysis *318*
Ingredient Metric Equivalents *319*

Baked French Toast, p. 26

Grinder, p. 63

Five-Layer Dip, p. 121

Garlic-Parsley Steak "Fries," p. 242

Chicken Parmesan, p. 138

B.L.A.S.T Sandwich, p. 69

Magic Cookie Bars, p. 301

More than 200,000 miles on the road. Over a million calories consumed. And I'm here to share the whole story with you.

You may know me as the host of Yahoo!'s food show *Blue Ribbon Hunter*. I've traveled from Maine to Hawaii doing what I love—meeting new people and eating. Along the way, I've learned the history behind some of our most beloved American foods. Memphis barbecue. Iowa pork tenderloin sandwiches. Chicago hot dogs. I've also sampled some of the more, shall we say, unusual foods this great country has to offer. When it comes to food, well, I'll eat just about anything. *I'm thinking of you, West Virginia burgoo, wild boar nachos, and bear meat loaf.*

When I first joined *Blue Ribbon Hunter*, I was in a quandary. So many of the foods I found on the road were stuffed—literally stuffed—with butter, cream, cheese, and other decadent ingredients. Was there a way to enjoy them with gusto without constantly worrying about what it was doing to my waistline? And thus began my quest to re-create the American favorites I've grown to adore, but in a healthier way.

If you've seen the show, you know I can eat quite a bit in

one sitting. At the National Hamburger Festival in Akron, Ohio, I ate 15 burgers. As a judge of the San Diego Bay Wine and Food Festival, I consumed 26 plates of food. I even went head to head with Maria Edible, a competitive eater, in a Buffalo wing–eating contest. Thirteen wings. In two minutes. She won, but I certainly held my own.

But even though I love my job—and the incredible indulgence that comes with it—it's important to me to stay healthy, keeping my energy up and my weight stable. And after recently becoming a mom to two beautiful twin boys, my desire to enjoy a long, healthy, fun-filled life has only gotten stronger. There simply isn't any alternative.

My love of food was nurtured in me early by my parents. But they also instilled in me a deep appreciation for *good* food, the kind that sustains and nourishes you. I know that I'm not alone in my struggle to balance eating the foods I love with staying healthy. I've come across a lot of you who are passionate about what you cook for your friends and family, yet feel guilty eating these very same dishes. But it is possible to enjoy your favorite comfort foods every night of the week. A few smart cooking techniques and simple ingredient substitutions are all you need to make your dishes leaner. Being smart about portion sizes will help keep your calories in check.

I know what you're thinking. Too often, "leaner" equals "flavorless." And "smart about portion sizes" means eating like a rabbit. But I'm the gal who loves food, remember? And I'm also a chef, having trained my taste buds at one of the country's best cooking temples, the Institute of Culinary Education.

Iowa State Fair, Des Moines, IA

Meet Zev and Abe, my sons

The Original at
Mel's Burger Bar, New York, NY

SEAFOOD MARKET

Me eating deep-fried
butter on a stick

My entry for the apple pie baking contest at the
LaFayette Apple Festival

Corvette dining at The Varsity drive-in

Learning from the locals

You could say it's against my religion to create a flavorless plate of rabbit food.

The recipes here have all the creamy, cheesy, ooey-gooey goodness of the foods we Americans love to eat—pizza, burgers, shrimp and grits, cinnamon buns, macaroni and cheese, apple pie and so much more—but without the unnecessary fat and calories. And, often, with a little bit more nutrition. They're the prize-worthy dishes I've discovered in my *Blue Ribbon Hunter* travels, the comfort foods my mother made for me when I was a kid, the daily meals I serve my own family.

The way I see it, the food we prepare and eat with our friends and families is one of life's simple pleasures. It's something to be appreciated and thankful for, to enjoy with gusto. And never, ever with guilt.

With love,

Allison Fishman Task

Feeding chili to the camera

The crowd at the Iowa State Fair

MY TOP LIGHTEN-UP SECRETS

Flip through the pages of this book, and you would never imagine that these classic American favorites are lighter recipes. They've been re-envisioned so that they are lower in fat, sodium, and calories than their traditional preparations, but just as delicious as their guilt-laden namesakes—if not more so!

I begin with fresh, seasonal ingredients when possible. They tend to have the best flavor and therefore require the smallest amount of embellishment. Once the best ingredients are in hand, putting them together in lean variations of favorite dishes can be achieved if you stick to some easy guidelines.

1. Add flavor and texture with veggies.

People tend to bulk up lots of their favorite dishes with starches like rice, potatoes, or corn. Instead, I add vegetables. I'll toss broccoli into a mac and cheese, zucchini or peppers into chili, and mushrooms or spinach into breakfast casseroles. Vegetables are loaded with fiber and beneficial vitamins and they're oh-so low in fat and calories.

2. Switch to whole grains.

Whole grains provide energy with fiber, and they take longer for the body to digest, so they keep you full longer. They also add a chewy texture and nutty flavor to most dishes.

3. Choose healthy, protein-rich ingredients.

Proteins from eggs, dairy, meat, poultry, soy, nuts, and beans are more satisfying than carbohydrates and fats alone. Eating an adequate amount of protein keeps you full and helps you maintain muscle mass, which helps to burn calories. I try to incorporate a little protein into every meal and snack.

4. Make smart substitutions.

Some of my favorite all-American recipes are laden with fat and calories. Lobster rolls. Lasagna. Spinach dip. A few educated substitutions are usually all it takes to turn favorites into lighter versions. I use leaner cuts of meat and substitute reduced-fat or fat-free dairy for a portion of the full-fat whenever possible.

5. Keep refined ingredients, like sugar and flour, in check.

Refined sugars and flours are not everyday foods for me. But since I don't keep "never" lists, I call them "sometimes" foods. Dessert is a fabulous treat, but not something to have at the end of every meal.

6. Rely on portion control.

I eat what I want, but if it's not particularly good for me, I try not to eat too much of it. Balance is key.

Federal Donuts, Philadelphia, PA

UP AND AT 'EM
Breakfast & Brunch

Wafels + Dinges food truck New York NY

Some might say my grandfather's generation had it right. Every morning, he sat down to a full three-course meal. What luxury!

most of us are lucky if we can down more than a cup of coffee on the way out the door. Whenever I skimp on breakfast, I feel hungrier all day long and my brain's a little, well, less brainy. For everyday breakfasts, I try to eat some sort of protein, plus whole grains and vegetables or fruits. I find this combo gives me the right dose of oomph to greet the day with open arms.

On the weekends, my family often indulges in more leisurely breakfasts—pancakes or French toast, or eggs and bacon. These are memorable meals when we come together and reflect on the events of the past week, or get excited about what's coming up. Here, you'll find dishes that fit any morning routine, whether you're in need of a quick weekday smoothie or a more decadent weekend brunch. But each is made just a little bit healthier, and that feels just right.

aroma

Mini Donuts, p. 31

Federal Donuts,
Philadelphia, PA

Mushroom, Bacon, and Swiss
Strata, p. 35

All-American Granola, p. 50

Demetri's BBQ, Birmingham, AL,
where I tried my first Cat Head biscuit

CARAMEL-PECAN STICKY BUNS

HANDS-ON TIME: 50 MINUTES ★ TOTAL TIME: 2 HOURS 50 MINUTES

It's hard to resist the sweet smell of cinnamon buns—now you don't have to. Chopped pecans add richness and just the right amount of crunch to these sticky treats.

⅓ cup packed dark brown sugar
3 tablespoons butter
4 teaspoons light corn syrup
Cooking spray
2 tablespoons chopped pecans
1 package dry yeast (about 2¼ teaspoons)

1⅔ cups warm water (100° to 110°)
1½ teaspoons salt
23.5 ounces all-purpose flour, divided (about 5¼ cups)
⅓ cup granulated sugar
1 teaspoon ground cinnamon
2 tablespoons butter, softened

1. Combine first 3 ingredients in a saucepan over medium heat; stir frequently until butter melts. Continue cooking until mixture thickens and becomes smooth (about 1 minute), stirring constantly; remove from heat. Pour into the center of a 9-inch square metal baking pan; quickly spread caramel onto pan bottom using a spatula coated with cooking spray. Sprinkle with pecans; cool to room temperature. Lightly coat sides of pan with cooking spray.

2. Dissolve yeast in 1⅔ cups warm water in a large bowl; let stand 5 minutes. Stir in salt. Weigh or lightly spoon flour into dry measuring cups; level with a knife. Add 5 cups flour to yeast mixture; stir until a soft dough forms. Turn dough out onto a floured surface. Knead until smooth and elastic (about 8 minutes); add ¼ cup flour, 1 tablespoon at a time, to keep dough from sticking to hands. Place dough in a large bowl coated with cooking spray, turning to coat top. Cover and let rise in a warm place (85°), free from drafts, 1 hour or until doubled in size. (Gently press two fingers into dough. If indentation remains, the dough has risen enough.) Punch dough down; cover and let rest 5 minutes.

3. Combine granulated sugar and cinnamon in a small bowl; set aside.

4. Roll dough into a 16 x 12–inch rectangle on a lightly floured surface; spread 2 tablespoons softened butter over dough. Sprinkle with cinnamon-sugar mixture, leaving a ½-inch border. Roll up rectangle tightly, starting with long edge, pressing firmly to eliminate air pockets; pinch seam to seal (do not seal ends). Cut into 16 (1-inch-wide) slices. Place slices, cut sides up, in prepared pan (rolls will be crowded). Cover and let rise 30 minutes or until doubled in size.

5. Preheat oven to 375°. Bake at 375° for 20 minutes or until rolls are light golden brown. Cool in pan 5 minutes on a wire rack. Place a serving platter upside down on top of pan; invert onto platter. Serve warm. Serves 16 (serving size: 1 roll)

CALORIES 232; FAT 5.3g (sat 1.9g, mono 2.1g, poly 0.7g); PROTEIN 4.5g; CARB 41.7g; FIBER 1.4g; CHOL 9mg; IRON 2.1mg; SODIUM 249mg; CALC 14mg

MONKEY BREAD

HANDS-ON TIME: 45 MINUTES ★ TOTAL TIME: 3 HOURS 50 MINUTES

When I prepare this cinnamon-y, pull-apart loaf for my stepdaughter, I serve it along with a big glass of reduced-fat milk and a handful of berries. We love its eat-with-your-hands, sticky-fingers aspect, and the spiced and buttered rounds go a long way.

13.5 ounces all-purpose flour
(about 3 cups)

4.75 ounces whole-wheat flour
(about 1 cup)

1 teaspoon salt

1 package quick-rise yeast
(about 2¼ teaspoons)

1 cup very warm fat-free milk
(120° to 130°)

¼ cup very warm orange juice
(120° to 130°)

¼ cup honey

2 tablespoons butter, melted

Cooking spray

½ cup granulated sugar

½ cup packed brown sugar

2 teaspoons ground cinnamon

4½ tablespoons fat-free milk,
divided

2 tablespoons butter, melted

½ cup powdered sugar

1 tablespoon ⅓-less-fat cream
cheese

1 teaspoon vanilla extract

1. Weigh or lightly spoon flours into dry measuring cups; level with a knife. Combine flours, salt, and yeast in the bowl of a stand mixer with dough hook attached; mix until combined. With mixer on, slowly add 1 cup milk, juice, honey, and 2 tablespoons butter; mix dough at medium speed 7 minutes or until smooth and elastic. Place dough in a large bowl coated with cooking spray, turning to coat top. Cover and let rise in a warm place (85°), free from drafts, 1 hour or until doubled in size. (Gently press two fingers into dough. If indentation remains, the dough has risen enough.)
2. Combine granulated sugar, brown sugar, and cinnamon in a shallow dish. Combine 3 tablespoons milk and 2 tablespoons butter in a shallow dish, stirring with a whisk.
3. Punch dough down; divide into 8 equal portions. Working with one portion at a time (cover remaining dough to prevent drying), roll into an 8-inch rope. Cut each dough rope into 8 equal pieces, shaping each piece into a 1-inch ball. Dip each ball in milk mixture, turning to coat, and roll in sugar mixture. Layer balls in a 12-cup Bundt pan coated with cooking spray. Repeat procedure with remaining 7 dough ropes. Sprinkle any remaining sugar mixture over dough. Cover and let rise in a warm place (85°), free from drafts, 1 hour or until almost doubled in size.
4. Preheat oven to 350°.
5. Bake at 350° for 25 minutes or until golden. Cool 5 minutes on a wire rack. Place a plate upside down on top of bread; invert onto plate. Combine powdered sugar, 1½ tablespoons milk, and next 2 ingredients (through vanilla) in a small bowl, stirring with a whisk. Microwave at HIGH 20 seconds or until warm. Drizzle over bread. Serves 16 (serving size: 4 pieces and 1 teaspoon sauce)

CALORIES 234; FAT 3.4g (sat 2g, mono 0.8g, poly 0.3g); PROTEIN 4.5g; CARB 47.2g; FIBER 1.9g; CHOL 9mg; IRON 1.5mg; SODIUM 184mg; CALC 43mg

They got milk

Eating contests are often the centerpiece of regional food festivals. In my travels for *Blue Ribbon Hunter*, I've covered tamale-eating contests, bacon-eating contests, and even hamburger-bobbing contests where contestants bobbed for burgers in pools of ketchup.

One of the most memorable contests I've witnessed was a "Milk Chug-a-Lug" at the Iowa State Fair. Kids were selected from an eager audience, each waving and shouting, "Pick me! Pick me!" hoping to be picked to see who could finish a carton of milk first. I have never been one to encourage volume eating, but it did this mom's heart some good to see such enthusiasm for this calcium-rich drink.

BAKED FRENCH TOAST

HANDS-ON TIME: 21 MINUTES ★ TOTAL TIME: 41 MINUTES

It's not unusual for my family to wake up to the aroma of my husband making French toast on weekend mornings. He usually incorporates slices of challah left over from our Friday night family dinner into his signature breakfast dish. The variation that I like to make cuts calories by substituting French bread.

18 (½-ounce) slices diagonally cut French bread (about 1 inch thick)
2½ cups 2% reduced-fat milk
1 teaspoon vanilla extract
3 large eggs
1 large egg white
Cooking spray
½ teaspoon ground cinnamon
3 cups sliced strawberries
½ cup pure maple syrup
2 tablespoons powdered sugar

1. Preheat oven to 400°.
2. Place bread slices in a single layer in 2 (13 x 9–inch) glass or ceramic baking dishes.
3. Combine milk and next 3 ingredients (through egg white), stirring well with a whisk. Pour milk mixture over bread, turning slices until milk mixture is absorbed. Transfer bread slices to 2 large baking sheets coated with cooking spray.
4. Bake at 400° for 20 minutes or until browned and puffed, turning halfway through cooking time. Sprinkle with cinnamon.
5. Place 3 French toast slices on each of 6 plates. Top with strawberries, syrup, and powdered sugar. Serves 6 (serving size: 3 toast slices, ½ cup strawberries, 4 teaspoons syrup, and 1 teaspoon powdered sugar)

CALORIES 348; FAT 6.3g (sat 2.1g, mono 1.9g, poly 1.4g); PROTEIN 12.2g; CARB 60.5g; FIBER 3.3g; CHOL 101mg; IRON 2.5mg; SODIUM 455mg; CALC 209mg

LIGHTEN UP

A friendlier French toast

My lighter version uses 2% reduced-fat milk rather than heavy cream in the egg mixture—this small change saves 250 calories and 48 grams of fat per serving!

PEACH AND BLUEBERRY PANCAKES

HANDS-ON TIME: 28 MINUTES ★ TOTAL TIME: 28 MINUTES

Each third-cupful of this thick batter produces a pancake that is wonderfully fluffy and filled with fresh fruit. The combination of peaches and blueberries is one of my favorites, and I often use it in cobblers and pies.

6.75 ounces all-purpose flour (about 1½ cups)

2 tablespoons sugar

2 tablespoons flaxseed (optional)

1 tablespoon baking powder

½ teaspoon kosher salt

1½ cups nonfat buttermilk

1 teaspoon grated lemon rind

2 large eggs

1 cup fresh or frozen blueberries, thawed

1 cup chopped fresh or frozen peaches, thawed

2 tablespoons unsalted butter

Fresh blueberries (optional)

1. Weigh or lightly spoon flour into dry measuring cups; level with a knife. Combine flour, sugar, flaxseed, if desired, baking powder, and salt in a large bowl, stirring with a whisk.
2. Combine buttermilk, lemon rind, and eggs in a medium bowl, stirring with a whisk. Add buttermilk mixture to flour mixture, stirring just until moist. Gently fold in blueberries and peaches.
3. Heat a nonstick griddle or nonstick skillet over medium heat. Pour ⅓ cup batter per pancake onto pan. Cook over medium heat 2 to 3 minutes or until tops are covered with bubbles and edges look cooked. Carefully turn pancakes over; cook 2 to 3 minutes or until bottoms are lightly browned. Serve with butter. Top with blueberries, if desired. Serves 6 (serving size: 2 pancakes and 1 teaspoon butter)

CALORIES 238; FAT 2.8g (sat 0.7g, mono 0.7g, poly 0.8g); PROTEIN 8.1g; CARB 38g; FIBER 1.9g; CHOL 72mg; IRON 1.9mg; SODIUM 448mg; CALC 214mg

SLURP-WORTHY SMOOTHIES

Get your fruits and veggies on the go.

MOCHA JAVA

 Northwest

Place ½ cup 1% low-fat milk, 1½ cups plain fat-free Greek yogurt, and 2 tablespoons instant espresso granules in a blender; process until smooth. Combine 2 tablespoons fat-free chocolate syrup and ⅛ teaspoon instant espresso granules in a small bowl, stirring well. Using a spoon, drizzle syrup mixture around inside rim of 2 small narrow glasses. Pour 1 cup yogurt mixture into each of 2 glasses. Serve immediately. SERVES 2 (serving size: 1 cup) CALORIES 171; FAT 0.6g (sat 0.4g); SODIUM 100mg

POG

 West

Place 1 cup plain fat-free Greek yogurt in a blender. Add 1 cup passion fruit nectar, 1 cup guava nectar, and ⅔ cup fresh orange juice; process until smooth. Add 1 cup crushed ice; process until smooth. Pour into glasses. Serve immediately. SERVES 4 (serving size: about 1 cup) CALORIES 80; FAT 0g (sat 0g); SODIUM 25mg

CREAMY MANGO, AVOCADO & LIME

 Southwest

Place ¼ cup sliced avocado, 1 cup sliced mango, 1 tablespoon lime juice, 1 tablespoon fresh mint, 1 teaspoon honey, and 2 cups crushed ice in a blender; process until smooth. Pour into a glass. Garnish with mint sprig, if desired. Serve immediately. SERVES 1 (serving size: 1⅔ cups) CALORIES 184; FAT 6g (sat 0.9g); SODIUM 5mg

DARK CHERRY

 Midwest

Place 1½ cups plain fat-free yogurt in a blender. Add ¼ cup honey and 2 cups pitted dark sweet cherries to blender; process until smooth. Pour into glasses. Serve immediately. SERVES 4 (serving size: ¾ cup) CALORIES 173; FAT 0g (sat 0g); SODIUM 51mg

BLUEBERRY SOY

Northeast

Place 1 cup fresh or frozen blueberries, ⅔ cup fat-free milk, ½ cup reduced-fat firm silken tofu (about 4 ounces), 2 tablespoons raspberry spread, and 1 (6-ounce) carton raspberry low-fat yogurt in a blender; process until smooth. Pour into glasses. Serve immediately. SERVES 2 (serving size: 1¼ cups) CALORIES 202; FAT 1.3g (sat 0.6g); SODIUM 134mg

FRESH PEACH

Southeast

Empty 2 (5.3-ounce) cartons vanilla fat-free Greek yogurt into a blender. Add ¾ cup peach nectar, 1 table-spoon honey, and ⅛ teaspoon almond extract; process until blended. Add 3 cups sliced fresh peaches; process until smooth. Pour into glasses; gar-nish with mint sprigs, if desired. Serve immedi-ately. SERVES 4 (serving size: 1 cup) CALORIES 140; FAT 0.3g (sat 0g); SODIUM 37mg

SPICY BLOODY MARY

South

Place 1¾ cups chilled low-sodium tomato juice, ½ cup chopped English cucumber, 2 tablespoons fresh lemon juice, 2 teaspoons Worcestershire sauce, ¾ teaspoon Sriracha (hot chile sauce), and 5 ice cubes in a blender; process until smooth. Pour into glasses; garnish each serving with a 4-inch-long English cucumber spear, if desired. Serve immediately. SERVES 3 (serving size: 1 cup) CALORIES 37; FAT 0g (sat 0g); SODIUM 120mg

RUBY SLIPPER

East

Place ¼ cup plain fat-free Greek yogurt in a blender. Add 1 cup blueberries, ½ cup raspberries, ⅓ cup sliced and cooked beets, ¼ cup fresh orange juice, and 1 teaspoon honey to blender; process until smooth. Add 1 cup ice; process until smooth. Serve immediately. Garnish with berries, if desired. SERVES 3 (serv-ing size: 1½ cups) CALO-RIES 214; FAT 1g (sat 0g); SODIUM 59mg

Smoothie tip Choose ripe, in-season fruits and vegetables for the best-tasting beverage. If you prefer superthick fruit smoothies, freeze the fruit before blending.

MINI DONUTS

HANDS-ON TIME: 25 MINUTES ★ TOTAL TIME: 41 MINUTES

While visiting Federal Donuts in Philadelphia, I tasted wild flavors like Pink Lemonade and Carrot Cake. Inspired by these fun treats, my own version is dressed in a maple syrup glaze. Use a mini donut pan, available in most cookware stores.

Donuts:
Cooking spray
½ cup granulated sugar
¼ cup unsalted butter, softened
1 large egg
6.75 ounces all-purpose flour (about 1½ cups)
¾ teaspoon baking powder
¼ teaspoon baking soda
⅛ teaspoon kosher salt
⅛ teaspoon ground nutmeg
¾ cup 1% low-fat buttermilk

Glaze:
1 cup powdered sugar
2 tablespoons 2% reduced-fat milk
¼ teaspoon maple syrup
Colored sprinkles (optional)

Federal Donuts, Philadelphia, PA

1. Preheat oven to 350°. Coat 24 mini donut cups with cooking spray.

2. To prepare donuts, place granulated sugar and butter in a large bowl; beat with a mixer at medium speed until well blended (about 5 minutes). Add egg, beating well. Weigh or lightly spoon flour into dry measuring cups; level with a knife. Combine flour and next 4 ingredients (through nutmeg), stirring well with a whisk. Add flour mixture and buttermilk alternately to sugar mixture, beginning and ending with flour mixture.

3. Spoon dough into a heavy-duty zip-top plastic bag. Snip a small hole in 1 corner of bag. Squeeze dough into prepared donut cups, filling two-thirds full. (Do not cover centers of donut cups.) Bake at 350° for 8 minutes or until a wooden pick inserted in donuts comes out clean. Cool donuts in pans on a wire rack 1 minute. Remove from pans. Cool completely on a wire rack.

4. While donuts bake, prepare glaze. Combine powdered sugar, milk, and maple syrup in a small bowl, stirring with a whisk until smooth. Dip top of 1 donut in glaze; place donut, glazed side up, on a cooling rack. Immediately sprinkle colored sprinkles over glaze, if desired. Repeat procedure with remaining donuts and glaze. Let stand until glaze is set. Serves 8 (serving size: 3 donuts)

CALORIES 279; FAT 7g (sat 4.1g, mono 1.9g, poly 0.5g); PROTEIN 4.2g; CARB 50.1g; FIBER 0.7g; CHOL 40mg; IRON 1.2mg; SODIUM 143mg; CALC 63mg

MAINE BLUEBERRY CAKE

HANDS-ON TIME: 15 MINUTES ★ TOTAL TIME: 1 HOUR 42 MINUTES

This dish is often served as dessert after traditional Maine lobster bakes. I prefer to save it for breakfast the next day because after an evening of lobster, clams, corn, and potatoes, I seldom have room for anything else.

Cooking spray

1 cup plus 2 tablespoons sugar, divided

1 teaspoon ground cinnamon

2 tablespoons unsalted butter, melted

2 tablespoons canola oil

1 teaspoon vanilla extract

½ teaspoon grated lemon rind

1 teaspoon fresh lemon juice

1 large egg

1 large egg white

⅓ cup 2% reduced-fat milk

5 ounces all-purpose flour (about 1¼ cups)

1 teaspoon baking powder

½ teaspoon salt

12 cups fresh blueberries

1 ounce all-purpose flour (about ¼ cup)

1. Preheat oven to 350°.

2. Coat a 9-inch square metal baking pan with cooking spray. Combine 2 tablespoons sugar and cinnamon in a small bowl.

3. Combine butter and next 6 ingredients (through egg white) in a medium bowl, stirring with a whisk until blended. Gradually add 1 cup sugar, stirring with a whisk until blended. Stir in milk.

4. Weigh or lightly spoon 1¼ cups flour into dry measuring cups; level with a knife. Combine 1¼ cups flour, baking powder, and salt in a large bowl, stirring with a whisk.

5. Add milk mixture to flour mixture, stirring just until moist. Toss blueberries in ¼ cup flour; fold into milk-flour mixture. Spoon batter into prepared pan. Sprinkle cinnamon-sugar mixture over top of batter. Bake at 350° for 35 minutes or until a wooden pick inserted in center comes out clean. Cool completely in pan on a wire rack. Serves 9 (serving size: ⅑ of cake)

CALORIES 261; FAT 6.8g (sat 2.2g, mono 3.0g, poly 1.2g); PROTEIN 3.9g; CARB 47.1g; FIBER 1.5g; CHOL 28mg; IRON 1.2mg; SODIUM 171mg; CALC 50mg

CRANBERRY-ORANGE SCONES

HANDS-ON TIME: 10 MINUTES ★ TOTAL TIME: 21 MINUTES

Although scones are among the most quintessentially British teatime treats, the addition of cranberries, a fruit indigenous to America, keeps them firmly on our side of the pond. This recipe is courtesy of food writer Susan Axelrod.

7.9 ounces all-purpose flour (about 1¾ cups)

2 teaspoons baking powder

1 teaspoon sugar

½ teaspoon baking soda

½ teaspoon kosher salt

5 tablespoons unsalted butter, cut into pieces

¾ cup 1% low-fat buttermilk

½ cup sweetened dried cranberries

1 tablespoon grated orange rind

Cooking spray

1 tablespoon 1% low-fat buttermilk

1 tablespoon sugar

1. Preheat oven to 450°.
2. Weigh or lightly spoon flour into dry measuring cups; level with a knife. Combine flour and next 4 ingredients (through salt) in a bowl. Use fingertips to incorporate butter pieces into flour mixture until they are thoroughly distributed; pieces of butter about the size of peas should still be visible. Add buttermilk, cranberries, and orange rind, stirring just until moist.
3. Turn dough out onto a lightly floured surface; knead lightly 4 times with floured hands. Pat dough into an 8-inch circle on a baking sheet coated with cooking spray. Cut dough into 8 wedges. Place wedges 2 inches apart on an ungreased baking sheet. Brush wedges with 1 tablespoon buttermilk and sprinkle with 1 tablespoon sugar.
4. Bake at 450° for 11 minutes, or until golden. Serves 8 (serving size: 1 scone)

CALORIES 200; FAT 8g (sat 4.8g, mono 1.9g, poly 1.0g); PROTEIN 0.4g; CARB 31g; FIBER 1g; CHOL 21mg; IRON 1mg; SODIUM 238mg; CALC 93mg

For the love of bacon

a summertime bacon festival in Kansas City, Missouri, featured some of the most outrageous bacon dishes I've ever had (and I've consumed my share of bacon). A few of the standouts were a chocolate-covered cheesecake pop dipped in candied bacon, an Asian-style "pig wing" (pork shank) wrapped in bacon and dipped in spicy sambal, and my personal favorite, cornmeal-chile waffles with bourbon-cured jalapeño bacon. Interestingly, it was a riff on an American classic that took home the blue ribbon— a bacon Benedict made with a ground-bacon-and-sausage patty topped with a poached egg and drizzled with hollandaise.

Given the enthusiasm of the many American bacon lovers (as well as the number of bacon festival participants), it is no surprise to know that the average American consumes 18 pounds of bacon a year.

From my perspective, less is more when it comes to the wonderfully flavorful, fat-ribboned meat. I prefer using bacon as a flavor enhancer in dishes rather than using it as the main ingredient. I adore cooked bacon crumbled into casseroles and side dishes, or over plain vegetables, which gives recipes that hit of salty bacon flavor without adding tons of extra fat and calories.

It's no surprise that the average American eats 18 pounds of bacon per year. I know I've had my share.

MUSHROOM, BACON, AND SWISS STRATA

HANDS-ON TIME: 40 MINUTES ★ TOTAL TIME: 10 HOURS

This make-ahead breakfast casserole streamlines a morning routine like few other recipes can. Assemble it the night before, then pop it in the oven about an hour before you want to eat.

12 ounces ciabatta bread, cut into 1-inch cubes (about 7 cups)
2 tablespoons butter
2 cups chopped onion
2 (8-ounce) packages presliced mushrooms
Cooking spray
6 ounces reduced-fat Swiss cheese, shredded (about 1½ cups)
8 center-cut bacon slices, cooked and crumbled
3 cups 1% low-fat milk
1½ cups egg substitute
2 teaspoons chopped fresh thyme
½ teaspoon freshly ground black pepper
¼ teaspoon salt
Chopped thyme (optional)

1. Preheat oven to 350°. Arrange bread in a single layer on a jelly-roll pan. Bake at 350° for 20 minutes or until toasted. Place bread cubes in a large bowl.
2. Melt butter in a large nonstick skillet over medium-high heat. Add onion and mushrooms to pan; sauté 10 minutes or until liquid evaporates and vegetables are tender.
3. Add onion mixture to bread; toss well to combine. Arrange half of bread mixture in a 13 x 9–inch glass or ceramic baking dish coated with cooking spray. Sprinkle with half of cheese and half of bacon; top with remaining bread mixture, cheese, and bacon.
4. Combine milk and next 4 ingredients (through salt), stirring with a whisk. Pour milk mixture over bread mixture. Cover and refrigerate 8 hours.
5. Preheat oven to 350°.
6. Remove strata from refrigerator; let stand at room temperature 15 minutes. Bake strata, covered, at 350° for 30 minutes. Uncover and bake an additional 15 minutes or until set. Let stand 10 minutes before serving. Garnish with chopped thyme, if desired. Serves 8 (serving size: ⅛ of strata)

CALORIES 313; FAT 10.4g (sat 5g, mono 4.2g, poly 0.8g); PROTEIN 21.7g; CARB 35.5g; FIBER 2.7g; CHOL 25mg; IRON 1.9mg; SODIUM 737mg; CALC 318mg

L.E.O. SCRAMBLE

HANDS-ON TIME: 11 MINUTES ★ TOTAL TIME: 11 MINUTES

L.E.O. refers to the winning combination of lox, eggs, and onions in this savory scramble. It's a New York diner favorite that's easy to prepare at home.

6 large eggs
4 large egg whites
1 teaspoon canola oil
⅓ cup sliced green onions
4 ounces smoked salmon, cut into ½-inch pieces
2 ounces reduced-fat cream cheese (about ¼ cup), cut into 12 pieces

¼ teaspoon freshly ground black pepper
4 (1.1-ounce) slices pumpernickel bread, toasted

1. Place eggs and egg whites in a bowl; stir with a whisk until blended.
2. Heat a medium nonstick skillet over medium-high heat. Add oil to pan; swirl to coat. Add green onions to pan; sauté 2 minutes or until tender. Add egg mixture to pan. Cook without stirring until mixture sets on bottom. Draw a spatula across bottom of pan to form curds. Add salmon and cream cheese. Continue drawing spatula across bottom of pan until egg mixture is slightly thick but still moist; do not stir constantly. Remove from pan immediately. Sprinkle egg mixture with pepper. Serve with pumpernickel toast. Serves 4 (serving size: ¾ cup scramble and 1 toast slice)

CALORIES 297; FAT 14.5g (sat 5.1g, mono 5.3g, poly 2.8g); PROTEIN 22.8g; CARB 17.4g; FIBER 2.4g; CHOL 304mg; IRON 2.5mg; SODIUM 443mg; CALC 86mg

Less is more

In my lighter version of this New York favorite, I simply substitute egg whites for some of the whole eggs and reduced-fat cream cheese for the full-fat variety.

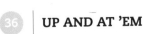

TEX-MEX MIGAS

HANDS-ON TIME: 12 MINUTES ★ TOTAL TIME: 12 MINUTES

"Migas" means "crumbs," and that's just what this dish is—small bits of tortilla, cheese, salsa, and eggs scrambled up into one of the Southwest's signature specialties. A staple of the Lone Star State, migas can also be found in Mexican breakfast spots across the country.

3 large eggs
3 large egg whites
1 tablespoon canola oil
4 (6-inch) corn tortillas, cut into ½-inch-wide strips
½ cup chopped onion
¼ cup chopped seeded jalapeño peppers (about 2 large)
⅔ cup lower-sodium salsa
1.3 ounces Monterey Jack cheese, shredded (about ⅓ cup)
½ cup sliced green onions
Hot sauce (optional)
Lower-sodium red salsa (optional)
Lower-sodium green salsa (optional)

1. Place eggs and egg whites in a bowl; stir with a whisk until blended.
2. Heat a medium nonstick skillet over medium-high heat. Add oil to pan; swirl to coat. Add tortilla strips to pan, and cook 3 minutes or until brown, stirring frequently. Add onion and jalapeño peppers to pan; sauté 2 minutes or until tender. Stir in ⅔ cup salsa, and cook, stirring constantly, 1 minute.
3. Add egg mixture; cook 2 minutes or until eggs are soft-set, stirring occasionally. Sprinkle egg mixture with cheese. Cook 30 seconds or until cheese melts. Top with green onions, and serve immediately. Serve with hot sauce, red salsa, or green salsa, if desired. Serves 4 (serving size: ¾ cup)

CALORIES 193; FAT 10.4g (sat 3.3g, mono 3.7g, poly 2.6g); PROTEIN 10.2g; CARB 13.7g; FIBER 1.7g; CHOL 148mg; IRON 0.9mg; SODIUM 237mg; CALC 113mg

RED FLANNEL HASH

HANDS-ON TIME: 23 MINUTES ★ TOTAL TIME: 2 HOURS 10 MINUTES

This hash is a Yankee tradition, so called, some say, for its colors, which resemble a red flannel shirt. It's customarily served the morning after a New England boiled dinner, when there's plenty of leftover corned beef and potatoes. My version combines roasted beets and potatoes with a small portion of corned beef for a lighter take on the original.

Topsham, VT

¾ pound Yukon gold potatoes (2 medium)
½ pound beets (4 medium)
1 tablespoon canola oil
1 cup vertically sliced red onion
¼ pound deli corned beef, cut into ½-inch cubes (about ¾ cup)
1 tablespoon ketchup
1 teaspoon Worcestershire sauce
¼ teaspoon salt
¼ teaspoon freshly ground black pepper
4 large eggs
Cooking spray
¼ cup chopped fresh parsley
Freshly ground black pepper

1. Preheat oven to 400°.
2. Place potatoes and beets in a metal baking pan lined with foil. Bake at 400° for 1 hour or until tender. Remove from oven, and cool 30 minutes. Peel potatoes and beets, and cut into ½-inch cubes.
3. Heat a large skillet over medium-high heat. Add oil to pan; swirl to coat. Add red onion; sauté 3 minutes or until tender. Add corned beef; cook 3 minutes. Stir in ketchup, next 3 ingredients (through pepper), potato, and beets. Cover and cook 3 minutes or until thoroughly heated. Keep warm.
4. Add water to a large skillet, filling two-thirds full; bring to a boil. Reduce heat; simmer. Break 1 egg into each of 4 (6-ounce) custard cups coated with cooking spray. Place custard cups in simmering water in pan. Cover pan; cook 8 minutes. Remove custard cups from water.
5. Divide hash evenly among 4 plates. Carefully loosen eggs from custard cups. Invert 1 egg over hash on each plate. Sprinkle parsley and black pepper evenly over each serving. Serve immediately. Serves 4 (serving size: 1 cup hash, 1 egg, and 1 tablespoon parsley)

CALORIES 243; FAT 9.7g (sat 2.5g, mono 4.5g, poly 2.0g); PROTEIN 14.1g; CARB 25.1g; FIBER 3.2g; CHOL 202mg; IRON 3.1mg; SODIUM 660mg; CALC 51mg

AMERICA LOVES: EGGS

Crackin' the incredible edible

WEST
Hangtown Fry

Hangtown is the nickname for Placerville, California, a town at the heart of the California gold rush. When the miners struck it rich, they ordered the town's most expensive dish—the Hangtown Fry. Featuring fried oysters, eggs, and bacon, the meal incorporated ingredients that were particularly hard to come by in the rugged Sierra Foothills at that time.

SOUTHWEST
Huevos Rancheros

"Ranchers' eggs" contains key south-of-the-border ingredients such as corn tortillas, beans, salsa, and eggs. Standard fare of Texas and throughout the Southwest, huevos rancheros is breakfast enough to satisfy those who work hard all day and need serious sustenance.

WEST
Loco Moco

Pronounced loh-koo moh-koo, this is Hawaii's original fast food breakfast. Although many variations exist, it commonly includes white rice topped with a hamburger patty, a fried egg, and brown gravy. In addition to the classic ingredients, you might also find it topped with ham, pork, sausage, teriyaki beef or chicken, or any fresh catch of the day.

MIDWEST
Savory Egg Muffins
Stove Top Stuffing Mix was introduced by General Foods in 1972 in Illinois, giving rise to a whole new generation of stuffing-based recipes. This breakfast classic—still a household favorite across the Midwest—features stuffing, either from the box or from scratch, baked with eggs, cheese, and sausage.

NORTHEAST
Eggs Benedict
In 1894, Mr. Benedict, a retired Wall Street broker, found himself at New York's Waldorf-Astoria hotel looking for a cure for his hangover. He asked for buttered toast, a poached egg, bacon, and a bit of hollandaise. The Waldorf's maître d', Oscar Tschirky, substituted Canadian bacon and an English muffin and put it on the menu.

SOUTH
Eggs Redneck
Eggs Redneck is a specialty of the Arcade Restaurant, a Memphis institution renowned for its hip '50s diner décor and down-home Southern cooking. The Redneck Plate features eggs, hash browns, and biscuits and sausage smothered in country-style gravy.

EAST
Pennsylvania Dutch Pickled Eggs
The Pennsylvania Dutch were German-speaking people who settled in Pennsylvania in the 17th and 18th centuries. They commonly pickled items such as eggs, fruits, and vegetables to preserve them so they could be eaten months later. Eggs were traditionally brined with beets, which give them their signature pinkish-red color. Today, they are a staple at Pennsylvania potlucks and picnics.

PHILLY SCRAPPLE

HANDS-ON TIME: 29 MINUTES ★ TOTAL TIME: 9 HOURS 39 MINUTES

There are many local variations of this breakfast staple, but it commonly includes various bits of pork, ground cornmeal or wheat, and seasonings. In Philadelphia, it's served with a sunny-side-up egg, and elsewhere it's served with everything from grape jelly to apple butter and honey to ketchup and mustard.

¾ pound ground pork
¾ pound ground turkey
1 cup finely chopped onion
¼ cup cornmeal
1 tablespoon chopped fresh sage
1 tablespoon chopped fresh thyme
1 teaspoon garlic powder
1 teaspoon dried savory
½ teaspoon kosher salt
½ teaspoon freshly ground black pepper
1 Granny Smith apple, peeled and grated (1 cup)
2 large eggs, lightly beaten
Cooking spray
1 teaspoon canola oil
Ketchup (optional)
Prepared horseradish (optional)

1. Preheat oven to 375°.
2. Combine pork, turkey, and next 10 ingredients (through eggs) in a bowl; gently mix just until combined. Transfer mixture to a 9 x 5–inch loaf pan coated with cooking spray.
3. Bake at 375° for 55 minutes or until a thermometer registers 165°. Cool to room temperature; cover and refrigerate overnight.
4. Remove from pan. Cut scrapple into 10 slices.
5. Heat a large nonstick skillet over medium-high heat. Add oil to pan; swirl to coat. Add scrapple slices to pan; sauté 1 to 2 minutes on each side or until browned.
6. Place 2 scrapple slices on each of 5 plates. Top each serving with ketchup and horseradish, if desired. Serve warm. Serves 5 (serving size: 2 scrapple slices)

CALORIES 262; FAT 10g (sat 2.8g, mono 4.5g, poly 1.9g); PROTEIN 27g; CARB 16g; FIBER 1g; CHOL 101mg; IRON 1mg; SODIUM 84mg; CALC 23mg

SHAKSHUKA

HANDS-ON TIME: 13 MINUTES ★ TOTAL TIME: 25 MINUTES

Shakshuka is an Israeli dish that is becoming increasingly popular across America. I love to serve spoonfuls of the spicy tomato-and-pepper sauce over rice.

1 tablespoon olive oil
1 cup (¼-inch-wide) strips red bell pepper
1 cup (¼-inch-wide) strips green bell pepper
2 cups (¼-inch-thick) vertically sliced red onion
¼ teaspoon kosher salt

2 garlic cloves, minced
2 cups lower-sodium marinara sauce
1 teaspoon smoked paprika
4 large eggs
2 cups cooked brown rice
¼ cup baby fresh basil
2 tablespoons crumbled feta cheese

1. Heat a 10-inch nonstick skillet over medium heat. Add oil to pan; swirl to coat. Add bell peppers, onion, and salt; cook 5 minutes, stirring occasionally. Add garlic; cook 30 seconds. Stir in marinara sauce and paprika. Bring to a boil; reduce heat, cover, and simmer 5 minutes.
2. Form 4 (2-inch) indentations in sauce, using the back of a spoon. Crack eggs, 1 at a time, into a small custard cup, and gently slip egg into an indentation. Cover and cook 6 minutes or until eggs are done.
3. Spoon rice evenly into 4 shallow bowls. Spoon egg mixture evenly over rice; sprinkle with basil and cheese. Serves 4 (serving size: ½ cup rice, 1 cup sauce, 1 egg, 1 tablespoon basil, and 1½ teaspoons cheese)

CALORIES 305; FAT 11.3g (sat 3g, mono 5.2g, poly 2.3g); PROTEIN 11.9g; CARB 39.5g; FIBER 5.2g; CHOL 190mg; IRON 3.4mg; SODIUM 354mg; CALC 108mg

CAJUN-STYLE SHRIMP AND GRITS

HANDS-ON TIME: 32 MINUTES ★ TOTAL TIME: 32 MINUTES

At Castaways Raw Bar and Grill on Holden Beach in North Carolina, they serve up huge portions of spicy shrimp and grits. My version is inspired by theirs—zesty with green onions and tasso ham, with a generous dose of Cajun spice.

1 tablespoon olive oil
2 ounces tasso ham, minced (½ cup)
1 cup chopped onion
1 garlic clove, minced
36 medium shrimp, peeled (about 1¼ pounds)
1 teaspoon Cajun seasoning
2¼ cups water, divided
1 tablespoon unsalted butter

1 cup fat-free milk
¼ teaspoon salt
1 cup uncooked quick-cooking grits
4 ounces sharp cheddar cheese, shredded (about 1 cup)
½ cup sliced green onions

1. Heat olive oil in a large skillet over medium-high heat. Add tasso; sauté 2 minutes or until edges are golden. Add onion; sauté 2 minutes. Add garlic; sauté 1 minute. Add shrimp to pan, sprinkle with Cajun seasoning, and cook 3 minutes, turning once. Add ¼ cup water, scraping pan to loosen browned bits. Remove from heat; add butter, stirring to melt. Cover and keep warm.

2. Bring milk, salt, and 2 cups water to a boil over medium-high heat. Reduce heat. Gradually add grits, and cook until thick and bubbly (about 5 minutes), stirring constantly with a whisk. Remove grits from heat; add cheese, stirring with a whisk until cheese melts.

3. Spoon grits evenly onto 6 plates. Top evenly with shrimp, ham mixture, and green onions. Serves 6 (serving size: ½ cup grits, 6 shrimp, about 3 tablespoons ham mixture, and 4 teaspoons green onions)

CALORIES 346; FAT 14g (sat 7.3g, mono 4.6g, poly 1g); PROTEIN 24g; CARB 29g; FIBER 1.8g; CHOL 153mg; IRON 1.2mg; SODIUM 870mg; CALC 299mg

My Carolina tradition

y parents retired from the New York suburbs to the small intracoastal community of Lockwood Folly in Supply, North Carolina, almost two decades ago. These two lifelong Yankees adapted well to their new environment and were happy to trade in last-minute trips to the grocery store for leisurely days when they can cast a fishing line off their dock and reel in dinner.

They live on the water and watch as shrimp boats go out to the ocean in the morning and return in the afternoon. Local shrimp are plentiful and delicious, and since the boats dock just minutes from my parents' house, my dad loves to purchase fresh catch. My parents have found many ways to prepare them. Plain shrimp cocktail is a favorite, of course, but nothing beats pairing shrimp with creamy grits. Grits are as common a side dish in the South as mashed potatoes are in the Northeast, but nowhere are they more common breakfast fare than in the lowlands of the Carolinas. There, creamy bowls of cheese grits, generally topped with plenty of fresh local shrimp, make the perfect start to a full day.

When my parents make the 13-hour drive to visit me up north, they pack a cooler full of Carolina shrimp, frozen in a block of ice that is thawed by the time they arrive. I consider a block of frozen shrimp to be just about the most perfect hostess gift ever. In addition to shrimp cocktail, I'll prepare grilled kebabs of shrimp and vegetables with a fresh chimichurri or a light dinner of shrimp, orzo, and feta cheese. Leftovers often remain after my parents have gone, a delicious reminder of their newfound lowcountry lifestyle.

> **In the lowcountry, creamy bowls of cheese grits topped with shrimp are standard breakfast fare.**

ALABAMA CAT HEAD BISCUITS
WITH SAUSAGE GRAVY

HANDS-ON TIME: 35 MINUTES ★ TOTAL TIME: 35 MINUTES

No, there's no cat in these biscuits; they've earned their name because of their size. This recipe is a riff on the Southern classic I had at Demetri's BBQ in Birmingham, AL.

9 ounces all-purpose flour (about 2 cups)

3¼ teaspoons baking powder

½ teaspoon baking soda

½ teaspoon kosher salt

¼ cup vegetable shortening

1 cup 1% low-fat buttermilk

Cooking spray

¼ pound reduced-fat pork breakfast sausage

1 teaspoon unsalted butter

1 cup chopped onion

2¼ cups 2% reduced-fat milk, divided

2 teaspoons minced fresh sage

¼ teaspoon kosher salt

1 teaspoon freshly ground black pepper

2½ tablespoons all-purpose flour

1. Preheat oven to 450°. Weigh or lightly spoon 2 cups flour into dry measuring cups; level with a knife. Combine flour and next 3 ingredients (through salt) in a bowl; cut in shortening with a pastry blender or 2 knives until mixture resembles coarse meal. Add buttermilk; stir just until moist.

2. Turn dough out onto a heavily floured surface; knead lightly 5 times. Roll dough to ½-inch thickness; cut with a 3¼-inch biscuit cutter. Place on a baking sheet coated with cooking spray. Bake at 450° for 10 minutes or until golden.

3. Cook sausage in a large nonstick skillet over medium-high heat 10 minutes or until browned; stir to crumble. Remove from pan, and drain on paper towels. Add butter to drippings; cook until butter melts. Add onion; cook 12 minutes, stirring frequently. Stir in sausage, 2 cups milk, sage, ¼ teaspoon salt, and pepper.

4. Combine 2½ tablespoons flour and ¼ cup milk, stirring with a whisk until well blended to form a slurry. Stir slurry into sausage mixture. Cook, stirring constantly, 3 minutes or until gravy is thick and bubbly. Cut biscuits in half. Spoon gravy evenly over biscuit halves. Serves 6 (serving size: 1 biscuit and about ½ cup gravy)

CALORIES 368; FAT 14.8g (sat 5.1g, mono 4.6g, poly 3g); PROTEIN 12.8g; CARB 44.4g; FIBER 1.8g; CHOL 22mg; IRON 2.3mg; SODIUM 761mg; CALC 303mg

EGG AND CHEESE ON A ROLL

HANDS-ON TIME: 7 MINUTES ★ TOTAL TIME: 7 MINUTES

This is a popular grab-and-go breakfast for New Yorkers on the run. Countless variations exist, and I've added one more with my own homemade favorite. I lighten up the cheese and eggs, swap the roll for an English muffin, and doctor the sandwich with ketchup and a healthy dose of hot sauce, just like they do in the Big Apple.

1 large egg
1 large egg white
Dash of salt
2 (0.66-ounce) slices
    reduced-fat cheddar
    cheese

1 English muffin, split
    and toasted
1 teaspoon canola oil
¾ teaspoon ketchup
⅛ teaspoon hot sauce
    (optional)

1. Preheat broiler.
2. Combine first 3 ingredients in a small bowl, stirring with a whisk.
3. Place 1 cheese slice on top of each muffin half. Place muffin halves on a baking sheet. Broil 1 minute or until cheese melts.
4. Heat a small nonstick skillet over medium heat. Add oil to pan; swirl to coat. Add egg mixture to pan; cook without stirring until mixture sets on bottom. Draw a spatula across bottom of pan to form curds. Continue drawing spatula across bottom of pan until egg mixture is slightly thick, but still moist; do not stir constantly. Remove from pan immediately and place on muffin bottom.
5. Spread ketchup over cheese on muffin top. Sprinkle egg with hot sauce, if desired, and cover with muffin top. Serve immediately. Serves 1 (serving size: 1 sandwich)

CALORIES 330; FAT 13g (sat 3.5g, mono 5.8g, poly 2.6g); PROTEIN 24g; CARB 27.6g; FIBER 1g; CHOL 194mg; IRON 2.9mg; SODIUM 630mg; CALC 186mg

The stuffing that Ruth built

Ruth Siems, a home economist from Evansville, Indiana, was working for General Foods when she created the famous Stove Top Stuffing Mix in 1972. The company's marketing department requested an easy mix for instant stuffing, and their research and development team got to work. Ms. Siems' stuffing was special because of the size of the crumb—too small and it would absorb water and turn into mush; too large and it would remain too dry. Her recipe was quickly patented, and today, more than 60 million boxes of the stuffing are sold during the Thanksgiving season alone.

SAVORY EGG MUFFINS

HANDS-ON TIME: 11 MINUTES ★ TOTAL TIME: 45 MINUTES

My husband has loved Stove Top Stuffing Mix since he was a kid, and my 12-year-old stepdaughter requests these muffins on school days. I make them the night before so she can pop two into the toaster oven for a quick—but filling—breakfast.

1½ cups water

2 tablespoons unsalted butter

1 (6-ounce) package Stove Top lower-sodium Stuffing Mix for chicken

3 ounces bulk pork sausage

Cooking spray

6 large eggs, beaten

1.3 ounces Monterey Jack cheese, shredded (about ⅓ cup)

½ cup finely chopped red bell pepper (optional)

¼ cup sliced green onions

1. Preheat oven to 400°.

2. Bring 1½ cups water and butter to a boil in a medium saucepan. Stir in stuffing mix. Cover, remove from heat, and let stand 5 minutes; fluff with a fork. Let stand, uncovered, 10 minutes or until cool enough to handle.

3. While stuffing cools, cook sausage in a small skillet over medium-high heat until browned; stir to crumble. Drain.

4. Coat fingers with cooking spray. Press about ¼ cup stuffing into bottom and up sides of each of 12 muffin cups heavily coated with cooking spray. Pour egg evenly into stuffing cups. Layer cheese, sausage, bell pepper, if desired, and green onions evenly over egg.

5. Bake at 400° for 18 to 20 minutes or until centers are set. Let stand 5 minutes before serving. Run a thin sharp knife around edges of muffin cups to loosen. Remove from pans. Serve immediately. Serves 6 (serving size: 2 muffins)

CALORIES 292; FAT 15.7g (sat 6.5g, mono 5.3g, poly 1.7g); PROTEIN 14.6g; CARB 22g; FIBER 1.2g; CHOL 214mg; IRON 2.3mg; SODIUM 476mg; CALC 80mg

ALL-AMERICAN GRANOLA

HANDS-ON TIME: 10 MINUTES ★ TOTAL TIME: 50 MINUTES

Sweetened with maple syrup and studded with dried cherries and sliced almonds, this pantry staple is easy to customize. Try dried blueberries, cranberries, or even apples, and maybe even a little flaxseed for fiber. Or toss with fresh berries before serving.

3 cups uncooked
    old-fashioned rolled oats
1½ cups sliced almonds
½ cup coarsely chopped
    dried cherries
½ teaspoon ground
    cinnamon
¼ teaspoon salt
½ cup pure maple syrup
Cooking spray

1. Preheat oven to 300°.
2. Combine first 5 ingredients in a large bowl. Drizzle syrup over oat mixture, stirring to coat completely.
3. Spread mixture on a baking sheet coated with cooking spray. Bake at 300° for 35 minutes or until golden and crisp, stirring every 10 minutes. Transfer to a wire rack, and cool completely in pan. Store in an airtight container for up to 1 week. Serves 12 (serving size: about ½ cup)

CALORIES 197; FAT 7.3g (sat 0.7g, mono 4.1g, poly 1.9g); PROTEIN 5.3g; CARB 29.4g; FIBER 4g; CHOL 0mg; IRON 1.4mg; SODIUM 43mg; CALC 48mg

Granola, circa 1863

What we now know as granola was the brainchild of Dr. James Jackson of upstate New York. In 1863, he developed a healthy, whole-grain cereal he called "granula."

Graham flour (a whole-grain wheat flour that had a health-food reputation) was formed into sheets that were baked until dry, broken up, baked again, and then crumbled into small pieces. In the 1880s, Dr. John Harvey Kellogg developed a similar cereal of baked and ground grains, also calling it "granula" then changing the name to granola after being sued by Dr. Jackson. Granola as we know it wasn't popularized until the 1960s when the health-food movement revived interest in whole-grain cereals.

LUNCH FARE

Sandwiches, Salads & Soups

Grabbing a fish taco in Carpinteria, CA

Provision Company, Holden Beach NC

WE'RE OPEN

For too many of us, the midday meal is, sadly, a boring afterthought. But lunch can be one of the more exciting meals of the day if you break out of your routine.

When I'm in a new city, one of my favorite things to do is seek out the local food-truck scene. Food trucks have exploded in popularity over the past couple of years, and I think they've given the classic American lunch a much-needed twist. Even in small cities, you can find an expert rendition of the light but satisfying Vietnamese bánh mì sandwich or a super-fresh grilled fish taco that takes you to a beach in Southern California. There's a lot to be said for leaving the office to experience the lunch trip of a lifetime with your tastebuds. The recipes here—some old-school lunch counter favorites mixed with more contemporary options—reflect the American mixing bowl of flavors and cultures.

Shrimp Po' Boy, p. 70

Deluxe Town Diner, Watertown, MA

B.L.A.S.T. Sandwich, p. 69

Lobster Rolls, p. 77

REUBEN SANDWICH

HANDS-ON TIME: 15 MINUTES ★ TOTAL TIME: 18 MINUTES

Some people assume the Reuben was created by the owner of Reuben's Restaurant, a celebrity hot spot in New York City where the sandwich was popular. But the truth is that it was invented by Reuben Kulakofsky in Omaha, Nebraska, as a late-night snack for poker-playing friends.

Dressing:
¼ cup canola mayonnaise
1 tablespoon chili sauce
2 teaspoons finely minced
   dill pickle
1 teaspoon Worcestershire
   sauce
½ teaspoon grated onion

Sandwiches:
8 (¾-ounce) slices rye bread
3 ounces Swiss cheese,
   shaved (about ¾ cup)
4 ounces lower-sodium
   corned beef, thinly sliced
1 cup organic sauerkraut,
   drained well

1. Preheat broiler.
2. To prepare dressing, combine first 5 ingredients in a small bowl, stirring well.
3. To prepare sandwiches, place bread slices in a single layer on a heavy baking sheet. Broil bread 1½ minutes or until toasted. Turn bread over; broil 1 minute or until lightly toasted. Remove 4 slices. Divide cheese evenly among remaining 4 slices, sprinkling it over lightly toasted sides. Broil 1 minute or until cheese melts. Spread about 1½ tablespoons dressing over the cheese-coated side of each bread slice; top each serving with 1 ounce corned beef, ¼ cup sauerkraut, and remaining bread slices. Serve immediately. Serves 4 (serving size: 1 sandwich)

CALORIES 280; FAT 12.9g (sat. 4.3g, mono 4.9g, poly 1.9g); PROTEIN 13.8g; CARB 26g; FIBER 2g; CHOL 35mg; IRON 0.1mg; SODIUM 804mg; CALC 170mg

Reuben's Restaurant, circa 1930s

LIGHTEN UP

A lower-sodium Reuben

Thin slices of rye, low-sodium corned beef, and a prudent amount of well-drained sauerkraut all contribute to a healthier variation that saves you 200 calories, 15 grams of fat, and 600 milligrams of sodium.

PHILLY CHEESESTEAK

HANDS-ON TIME: 30 MINUTES ★ TOTAL TIME: 30 MINUTES

It's meaty, gooey, and delightfully messy—but eating it shouldn't make you tip the scale in the wrong direction. I keep my Philly in check by using equal parts portobello mushrooms and steak.

1 (12-ounce) flank steak, trimmed
¼ teaspoon kosher salt
¼ teaspoon freshly ground black pepper
2 teaspoons extra-virgin olive oil, divided
1 cup thinly sliced onion
2 (5-inch) portobello mushroom caps, sliced
1½ cups thinly sliced green bell pepper
2 teaspoons minced garlic
½ teaspoon Worcestershire sauce
½ teaspoon lower-sodium soy sauce
2 teaspoons all-purpose flour
½ cup 1% low-fat milk
1 ounce provolone cheese (about ¼ cup), torn into small pieces
2 tablespoons grated fresh Parmigiano-Reggiano cheese
¼ teaspoon dry mustard
4 (3-ounce) hoagie rolls, toasted

1. Cut beef into thin slices; sprinkle with salt and pepper.
2. Heat a large nonstick skillet over medium-high heat. Add 1 teaspoon oil to pan; swirl to coat. Add beef to pan; sauté 2 minutes or until beef loses its pink color, stirring constantly. Remove beef from pan. Add 1 teaspoon oil to pan. Add onion; sauté 3 minutes. Add mushrooms, bell pepper, and garlic; sauté 6 minutes. Return beef to pan; sauté 1 minute or until thoroughly heated and vegetables are tender. Remove from heat. Stir in Worcestershire and soy sauce; keep warm.
3. Place flour in a small saucepan; gradually add milk, stirring with a whisk until blended. Bring to a simmer over medium heat; cook 1 minute or until slightly thick. Remove from heat. Add cheeses and mustard, stirring until smooth. Keep warm (mixture will thicken as it cools).
4. Hollow out top and bottom halves of hoagie rolls, leaving a ½-inch-thick shell; reserve torn bread for another use. Divide beef mixture evenly among bottom halves of hoagie rolls. Drizzle sauce evenly over beef mixture; replace top halves. Serves 4 (serving size: 1 sandwich)

CALORIES 397; FAT 13.8g (sat 4.6g, mono 6.7g, poly 1.6g); PROTEIN 32.8g; CARB 54g; FIBER 4.8g; CHOL 61mg; IRON 4.2mg; SODIUM 773mg; CALC 258mg

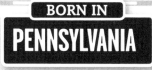
Home of the Philly Original

Rocky Balboa may not have trained on a diet of cheesesteaks, but Philly landmark Pat's King of Steaks did achieve some notoriety when the Hollywood-imagined prize fighter shot a scene there for *Rocky*. Pat's has another claim to fame: The Philly cheesesteak was invented here in the 1930s.

Initially, Pat's was a modest hot dog stand near the Italian market in South Philly. One day while working at the stand, Pat made himself a lunch of thinly sliced rib-eye steak, placed in an Italian roll, and dressed with some cooked onions. When a cabbie stopped in for a bite and smelled the aroma of hot beef on the griddle,

> **The Philadelphia cheesesteak is an icon right up there with the Liberty Bell.**

he requested the same lunch that the counter guys were having. "Forget 'bout those hot dogs!" he said. "You guys should be making these." Just like that, the Philly steak was born.

Yes, the Philly steak—interestingly, there was no cheese in the original sandwich. Cheese was added in the 1960s, and today, the most popular cheese to use is Cheez Whiz, but provolone is also a Pat's favorite.

In 1966, Pat's King of Steaks received some friendly rivalry from Geno's Steaks, located across the street. Some believe that owner Joey Vento was the first to put cheese on the cheesesteak. For over 40 years the two shops have waged a pleasant competition for the title of best cheesesteak in town.

These days, Pat's is a Philadelphia institution and, for some, ranks right up there with the Liberty Bell on Philly's list of go-to tourist destinations. It still occupies the same central location in the city's oldest Italian neighborhood, almost like a town square, and repeat patrons joke that "all roads lead to Pat's." Locals and out-of-towners alike gather on Pat's outdoor patio on warm days to talk and munch on the meaty, cheese-drenched sandwiches now known as "Philly Originals."

GYROS

HANDS-ON TIME: 28 MINUTES ★ TOTAL TIME: 35 MINUTES

Widely served in Greek communities across America in the 1970s, gyros have since become a beloved grab-and-go lunch. This homemade variation starts with a loaf of ground lamb and beef. The meat is broiled, thinly sliced, and then tucked into pitas with a lightened-up yogurt sauce.

Lamb Loaves:
1 teaspoon onion powder
1 teaspoon garlic powder
1 teaspoon dried oregano
2 teaspoons fresh lemon juice
¼ teaspoon salt
3 garlic cloves, minced
6 ounces ground lamb
6 ounces ground sirloin
Cooking spray
⅛ teaspoon ground red pepper

Sauce:
1 cup peeled shredded cucumber
¼ cup vertically sliced red onion
1 tablespoon chopped fresh mint
½ teaspoon garlic powder
½ teaspoon fresh lemon juice
⅛ teaspoon salt
⅛ teaspoon freshly ground black pepper
1 (8-ounce) carton plain fat-free yogurt

Remaining Ingredient:
4 pocketless pitas

1. Preheat broiler.
2. To prepare loaves, combine first 8 ingredients (through ground sirloin), stirring well. Divide mixture in half, forming each half into a 6 x 3–inch loaf. Place each loaf on a broiler pan coated with cooking spray; broil 7 minutes on each side or until done.
3. Sprinkle loaves with red pepper. Cut each loaf crosswise into ⅛-inch slices.
4. To prepare sauce, place cucumber and onion onto several layers of heavy-duty paper towels. Cover with additional paper towels; let stand 5 minutes.
5. Combine cucumber mixture, mint, and next 5 ingredients (through yogurt), stirring well. Divide meat slices evenly among pitas; top each serving with about ¼ cup sauce. Serves 4 (serving size: 1 gyro)

CALORIES 379; FAT 11.3g (sat. 4.4g, mono 4.5g, poly 1.1g); PROTEIN 27.5g; CARB 42.2g; FIBER 2.1g; CHOL 65mg; IRON 3.4mg; SODIUM 597mg; CALC 155mg

Don't call it "jy-ro"

I grew up on Long Island, where the locals aren't exactly celebrated for their elocution— sorry, guys. So I suppose it's no wonder that when I used to order gyros from my favorite Greek restaurant, I asked for the sandwiches with a hard "j" as in "jelly." It wasn't until years later that I discovered I'd been mispronouncing the name. It's pronounced "YEER-oh," the "g" pronounced like a soft "y." If you love this sandwich as much as I do, give it the respect it deserves and call it by the right name. Unless, of course, you're on Long Island. They'll have no idea what you're talking about.

KENTUCKY HOT BROWN

HANDS-ON TIME: 11 MINUTES ★ TOTAL TIME: 11 MINUTES

Hailing from The Brown Hotel in Louisville, this dish was created during the roaring '20s as a wee-hours-of-the-morning, post-dancing snack. In this lightened version, I've kept the bacon, thick toast, and cheese sauce, which will surely put a smile on your face, any time of the day or night.

Sauce:

1 tablespoon butter

1 tablespoon all-purpose flour

1 cup fat-free milk

¼ teaspoon freshly ground black pepper

⅛ teaspoon salt

¼ cup (1 ounce) grated fresh Parmigiano-Reggiano cheese

Sandwiches:

3 ounces sliced oven-roasted turkey breast, warmed

2 (1½-ounce) slices white bread, toasted

¼ teaspoon paprika

2 bacon slices, cooked and drained

2 tablespoons chopped fresh parsley

1 plum tomato, cut into 4 wedges

1. To prepare sauce, melt butter in a medium saucepan. Add flour, stirring well with a whisk. Gradually add milk, pepper, and salt, stirring constantly with a whisk until blended. Place over medium heat; cook until thick (about 5 minutes), stirring constantly. Remove from heat; stir in cheese.

2. To prepare sandwiches, layer turkey slices evenly on toast slices; pour sauce evenly over turkey, and sprinkle evenly with paprika. Top with bacon, and sprinkle with parsley. Serve warm with tomato wedges. Serves 2 (serving size: 1 open-faced sandwich)

CALORIES 331; FAT 12g (sat 6.5g, mono 3.2g, poly 2.2g); PROTEIN 24g; CARB 31g; FIBER 1.6g; CHOL 48mg; IRON 2.2mg; SODIUM 868mg; CALC 409mg

GRINDER

HANDS-ON TIME: 25 MINUTES ★ TOTAL TIME: 25 MINUTES

The grinder is a specialty served at the Iowa State Fair, home to some of the nation's richest and most waist-expanding treats. Still a hefty meal-in-one, my rendition takes a lighter approach. I cut the size in half (always a good place to start) and substitute fresh mushrooms for some of the fatty meat.

½ pound cremini mushrooms, trimmed

1 teaspoon canola oil

½ pound ground sirloin

½ pound 50%-less-fat breakfast sausage

1 cup chopped red onion

¼ teaspoon crushed red pepper flakes (optional)

2 cloves garlic, minced

1½ cups lower-sodium pasta sauce

2 top-split white-wheat hot dog buns

4 ounces reduced-fat mozzarella cheese, shredded (about 1 cup)

1. Place mushrooms in a food processor, and pulse until finely ground. Reserve.

2. Heat canola oil in a medium nonstick skillet over medium-high heat. Add sirloin and sausage. Cook until golden brown, breaking up meat with a spoon, about 5 minutes; remove with a slotted spoon and reserve. Add onion to pan and reduce heat to medium-low; cook until soft, about 4 minutes.

3. Preheat broiler.

4. Add mushrooms and red pepper, if desired, to the pan, and mix well. Cook until mushrooms are darker in color, about 5 minutes. Add garlic, and cook 30 seconds until fragrant. Add pasta sauce; stir to blend. Return cooked sirloin mixture to pan; bring sauce to a simmer and cook 2 minutes.

5. Divide mixture among buns and top with mozzarella cheese. Broil in oven or toaster oven until cheese melts. Serve warm. Serves 4 (serving size: 1 sandwich)

CALORIES 322; FAT 17.4g (sat 6g, mono 4.1g, poly 6.5g); PROTEIN 23.6g; CARB 22.7g; FIBER 3.8g; CHOL 57mg; IRON 3.7mg; SODIUM 740mg; CALC 567mg

BÁNH MÌ

HANDS-ON TIME: 20 MINUTES ★ TOTAL TIME: 1 HOUR 20 MINUTES

Although the bánh mì may have originated in the markets of Saigon, in bigger cities in the U.S. it is now as much of an American lunchtime staple as the burrito or panini. There are as many variations of the bánh mì as there are cooks who make it. My version combines pork, cucumber, and a pickled slaw of radish, carrot, and onion.

Pickles:

½ cup rice vinegar

⅓ cup granulated sugar

⅓ cup water

2 teaspoons sambal oelek

½ cup shredded carrot

⅓ cup matchstick-cut radishes

⅓ cup thinly sliced red onion

Sandwiches:

6 (2-ounce) boneless pork breakfast cutlets

¼ teaspoon kosher salt

Cooking spray

1 (12-ounce) French bread baguette (16 inches long)

¼ cup light mayonnaise

1 teaspoon sambal oelek

¼ cup thinly sliced peeled cucumber

½ cup cilantro leaves

1. To prepare pickles, combine first 4 ingredients (through sambal oelek) in a small saucepan. Bring to a boil, stirring until sugar dissolves. Remove from heat. Add carrot, radishes, and onion. Let stand, uncovered, at room temperature 1 hour.

2. Preheat broiler.

3. Place pork between 2 sheets of plastic wrap; pound to ⅛-inch thickness using a meat mallet or small heavy skillet. Sprinkle pork evenly with salt, and place on a broiler pan coated with cooking spray. Broil 5 minutes. Remove from pan.

4. Cut bread in half lengthwise. Hollow out bottom half of bread, leaving a ½-inch-thick shell; reserve torn bread for another use. Place bread halves, cut sides up, on a baking sheet. Broil 1 minute or until toasted.

5. Combine mayonnaise and 1 teaspoon sambal oelek in a small bowl. Spread mayonnaise mixture on cut side of bread top. Layer pickled vegetables, pork slices, cucumber, and cilantro evenly on bread bottom. Cover with bread top. Cut sandwich into 4 equal portions. Serves 4 (serving size: 1 sandwich)

CALORIES 416; FAT 11.6g (sat 2.6g, mono 4.4g, poly 4.1g); PROTEIN 22g; CARB 55.5g; FIBER 3.3g; CHOL 55mg; IRON 2.5mg; SODIUM 691mg; CALC 76mg

An Iowan's food fair favorite

*t*hat's one crazy-looking sandwich, right? Tiny bread and a piece of breaded pork the size of a dinner plate—that's how they do it in the Midwest. I've visited dozens of food festivals and state fairs across America and sampled lots of fair food along the way. There's a striking similarity in the culinary offerings from one state to the next and I've certainly had my share of chili dogs, corn dogs, corn cobs, turkey drumsticks, barbecued ribs, and fried chicken. But go to a fair in Iowa, any fair, and you'll try something you won't find outside the Midwest; the pork tenderloin sandwich is an Iowan's go-to, hands-down fair food favorite.

Nowhere in America is pork more exalted than in Iowa (one in three hogs raised in the States is from Iowa), and it can often seem as if much of it is served at the Iowa State Fair, which attracts over 1 million visitors each summer. Although Midwestern fair concessioners flirt with other pork preparations (such as pork chops, pork bellies, bacon, and sausages), breaded pieces of pork loin are the star ingredient in the immensely over-sized sandwiches sold at fairs and carnivals

Nowhere in America is pork more exalted than in Iowa.

across the region. To make a pork tenderloin sandwich, vendors cut a generous chunk of pork loin (the sandwich's name is a bit of a misnomer) into slices, pound it until it's the size of your head, bread it, fry it, and put it inside a hamburger bun. The meal is not complete until it's doctored up with gobs of ranch dressing, mustard, ketchup, pickles, and onions.

PORK TENDERLOIN SANDWICH

HANDS-ON TIME: 25 MINUTES ★ TOTAL TIME: 25 MINUTES

My version is about half the size of the original, because it uses a pork tenderloin rather than the larger cut of pork loin. It is pan-fried instead of deep-fried, but offers the same whole-hearted flavor that has made this sandwich an Iowan classic.

1.1 ounces all-purpose flour (about ¼ cup)

1 tablespoon water

1 large egg

¾ cup panko (Japanese breadcrumbs)

1 tablespoon dried parsley

1 (1-pound) pork tenderloin, trimmed

¼ teaspoon kosher salt

¼ cup canola oil, divided

4 romaine lettuce leaves

4 (1.25-ounce) slider buns, toasted

8 dill pickle slices

Ranch dressing, mustard, ketchup, chopped onions (optional)

1. Weigh or lightly spoon flour into a dry measuring cup; level with a knife. Place flour in a shallow bowl. Combine 1 tablespoon water and egg in a second shallow bowl, stirring with a whisk. Combine breadcrumbs and parsley in a third shallow bowl.

2. Cut pork crosswise into 4 pieces. Place pieces between 2 sheets of heavy-duty plastic wrap; pound to ¼-inch thickness using a meat mallet or small heavy skillet. Sprinkle both sides of pork evenly with salt.

3. Heat a large nonstick skillet over medium-high heat. Add 2 tablespoons oil to pan; swirl to coat. Dredge half of pork in flour; dip in egg mixture, and dredge in breadcrumb mixture. Cook pork in hot oil 3 minutes on each side or until tender. Repeat procedure with remaining oil and pork.

4. Place 1 lettuce leaf on each bun bottom. Top each with 1 piece of pork and 2 pickle slices; add ranch dressing, mustard, ketchup, or chopped onions, if desired. Cover with bun top. Serves 4 (serving size: 1 sandwich)

CALORIES 390; FAT 12.8g (sat 1.7g, mono 5.8g, poly 3.7g); PROTEIN 31.9g; CARB 36.1g; FIBER 2g; CHOL 120mg; IRON 2.6mg; SODIUM 474mg; CALC 67mg

CHIMICHURRI FISH TACOS

HANDS-ON TIME: 25 MINUTES ★ TOTAL TIME: 2 HOURS 25 MINUTES

In Southern California, fish tacos often feature fillets that are grilled and then flaked into pieces, rather than breaded and fried as in other regional preparations. I prefer grilling—it saves about half the calories and delivers a fresher fish flavor. If wild-caught Alaskan halibut is not available, substitute striped bass or U.S. line-caught cod.

2 cups fresh flat-leaf parsley leaves
2 tablespoons oregano leaves
¾ teaspoon ground cumin
¼ teaspoon ground red pepper
5 garlic cloves, crushed
⅓ cup extra-virgin olive oil
5 (6-ounce) halibut fillets
1 teaspoon kosher salt
½ teaspoon freshly ground black pepper
Cooking spray
12 (6-inch) corn tortillas
1½ cups shredded lettuce
½ cup thinly sliced red onion

1. Place first 5 ingredients in a food processor; process until finely chopped. Slowly pour oil through food chute; process until smooth. Place fish in a shallow dish; rub mixture over fish. Cover and chill 2 hours.
2. Preheat grill to high heat.
3. Sprinkle fish with salt and black pepper. Place fish on grill rack coated with cooking spray, and grill 3 to 4 minutes on each side or until fish flakes easily when tested with a fork. Remove from grill. Break fish into chunks. Heat tortillas according to package directions. Divide fish evenly among tortillas. Top evenly with lettuce and onion. Serves 6 (serving size: 2 tacos)

CALORIES 396; FAT 16.7g (sat 2.2g, mono 10.9g, poly 2.9g); PROTEIN 29.2g; CARB 30.6g; FIBER 2.9g; CHOL 69mg; IRON 1.6mg; SODIUM 499mg; CALC 51mg

B.L.A.S.T. SANDWICH

HANDS-ON TIME: 8 MINUTES ★ TOTAL TIME: 8 MINUTES

A B.L.A.S.T. is a blue-ribbon version of a classic BLT. Here's the lineup as I see it: Classic tomato and mayo win a delicious bronze. Bacon, lettuce, and tomato are a strong silver. But combine bacon, lettuce, avocado, and sweet tomato, and the sandwich becomes a bona fide blue-ribbon winner.

3 (1-ounce) slices Canadian bacon
2 (1-ounce) slices whole-wheat bread, toasted
2 teaspoons reduced-fat mayonnaise

1 large romaine lettuce leaf
2 (¼-inch-thick) slices beef-steak tomato
5 peeled avocado slices (about ¼ medium avocado)

1. Cook bacon in a small nonstick skillet over medium heat 2 minutes on each side, or until golden. Remove from pan.
2. Spread 1 side of each toast slice with 1 teaspoon mayonnaise. Layer lettuce, bacon, tomato, and avocado over mayonnaise on 1 toast slice. Cover with remaining toast slice, mayonnaise side down. Serves 1 (serving size: 1 sandwich)

CALORIES 296; FAT 11.1g (sat 2.5g, mono 4.8g, poly 2.7g); PROTEIN 18.9g; CARB 32.1g; FIBER 6.3g; CHOL 32mg; IRON 2.2mg; SODIUM 870mg; CALC 71mg

SHRIMP PO' BOY

HANDS-ON TIME: 34 MINUTES ★ TOTAL TIME: 34 MINUTES

Seasonal gulf shrimp is a natural for this classic NOLA sandwich. (That's New Orleans, Louisiana, for those of us from north of the Bayou.) Oysters are another traditional ingredient and often the locals' choice.

1 (12-ounce) French bread baguette (16 inches long)

¼ cup canola mayonnaise

1½ tablespoons chopped fresh flat-leaf parsley

1½ tablespoons fresh lemon juice

1 tablespoon capers, chopped

2 teaspoons whole-grain Dijon mustard

1 teaspoon minced garlic

¼ cup cornstarch

¼ cup cornmeal

1¼ pounds large shrimp, peeled and deveined

4 teaspoons canola oil

3 romaine lettuce leaves

¼ cup thinly sliced red onion

1. Cut baguette in half horizontally. Hollow out top and bottom halves of bread, leaving a ½-inch-thick shell; reserve torn bread for another use. Combine mayonnaise and next 5 ingredients (through garlic) in a small bowl; stir well. Spread mayonnaise mixture evenly over cut sides of bread.

2. Combine cornstarch and cornmeal in a shallow dish. Dredge shrimp in cornmeal mixture; shake off excess cornmeal mixture.

3. Heat a large nonstick skillet over medium-high heat. Add oil to pan; swirl to coat. Add shrimp; cook 3 minutes on each side or until done.

4. Arrange lettuce, shrimp, and onion on bottom half of baguette; cover with top half of baguette. Cut loaf into 4 pieces. Serve immediately. Serves 4 (serving size: 1 sandwich)

CALORIES 381; FAT 8.5g (sat 0.4g, mono 4.1g, poly 2.4g); PROTEIN 25.9g; CARB 49.6g; FIBER 2.2g; CHOL 179mg; IRON 2.9mg; SODIUM 831mg; CALC 90mg

Cajun comfort food

According to legend, the Po' Boy, short for "Poor Boy," dates back to New Orleans in 1929. At that time, there was a streetcar conductor strike that lasted for four long months. A downtown restaurant owned by brothers Bennie and Clovis Martin—both former streetcar conductors—provided sandwiches free of charge for the strikers. When one of the strikers would come in for a sandwich, the call would go out in the restaurant, "Here comes another po' boy!" The name stuck and the sandwich, featuring shrimp or oysters in extra-long loaves, remains a Big Easy favorite today.

TASTY DOGS

Build a seriously delicious frank with a regional twist.

SEATTLE CREAM CHEESE

 | *Northwest*

Preheat grill to medium heat. Place 4 (97% fat-free) beef franks on grill rack coated with cooking spray; grill, covered, 10 to 15 minutes, turning frequently until done. Spread 1 tablespoon reduced-fat cream cheese on bottom half of each of 4 toasted white-wheat hot dog buns. Place franks in buns. Sprinkle ½ cup sauerkraut, ¼ cup pickle relish, and ¼ cup chopped onions evenly over franks. SERVES 4 (serving size: 1 dog) CALORIES 160; FAT 5g (sat 2.4g); SODIUM 840mg

SO-CAL BAJA

 | *West*

Preheat grill to medium heat. Thinly slice 1 radish. Pit, peel, and chop 1 avocado. Chop fresh cilantro, if desired. Place 4 (97% fat-free) beef franks on grill rack coated with cooking spray; grill, covered, 10 to 15 minutes, turning frequently until done. Place franks into each of 4 toasted white-wheat hot dog buns; spoon 1 cup pico de gallo evenly over top of dogs. Sprinkle evenly with radishes, avocado, and cilantro, if desired. SERVES 4 (serving size: 1 dog) CALORIES 145; FAT 3g (sat 1g); SODIUM 740mg

HAWAIIAN

 | *West*

Preheat grill to medium heat. Place 4 (97% fat-free) beef franks on grill rack coated with cooking spray; grill, covered, 10 to 15 minutes, turning frequently until done. Place 1 ounce thinly sliced low-sodium ham into each of 4 toasted white-wheat hot dog buns; top with beef franks. Spoon ½ cup chopped pineapple and ¼ cup chopped green onions evenly over dogs. SERVES 4 (serving size: 1 dog) CALORIES 160; FAT 3.5g (sat 1g); SODIUM 812mg

CHICAGO

 | *Midwest*

Preheat grill to medium heat. Place 4 (97% fat-free) beef franks on grill rack coated with cooking spray; grill, covered, 10 to 15 minutes, turning frequently until done. Place 3 strips tomato, 1 thin slice cucumber, and 1 frank in each of 4 toasted white-wheat hot dog buns. Top each frank with about 2 tablespoons diced white onion, about ½ tablespoon sweet pickle relish, and about 2 teaspoons mustard. SERVES 4 (serving size: 1 dog) CALORIES 135; FAT 3g (sat 1g); SODIUM 734mg

MEMPHIS BBQ

South

Preheat grill to medium heat. Place 4 (97% fat-free) beef franks on grill rack coated with cooking spray; grill, covered, 10 to 15 minutes, turning frequently until done. Place 1 thinly, vertically sliced cucumber spear in 4 toasted white-wheat hot dog buns; add 1 frank to each bun. Spoon ½ cup warm shredded barbecue pork and ¼ cup prepared coleslaw evenly over top of dogs. SERVES 4 (serving size: 1 dog) CALORIES 210; FAT 8.7g (sat 2.9g); SODIUM 742mg

CONEY ISLAND

Northeast

Preheat grill to medium heat. Place 4 (97% fat-free) beef franks on grill rack coated with cooking spray; grill, covered, 10 to 15 minutes, turning frequently until done. Place franks in 4 toasted white-wheat hot dog buns; spoon ½ cup cooked chili over dogs. Top evenly with ½ cup chopped onion and 1 tablespoon mustard. SERVES 4 (serving size: 1 dog) CALORIES 150; FAT 4.2g (sat 2g); SODIUM 716mg

PHILLY

East

Preheat grill to medium heat. Place 4 (97% fat-free) beef franks on grill rack coated with cooking spray; grill, covered, 10 to 15 minutes, turning frequently until done. Place franks in 4 toasted white-wheat hot dog buns. Spread ¼ cup Cheez Whiz evenly over franks. Place ½ cup grilled yellow, red, and green bell pepper slices and ½ cup onion slices evenly over dogs. SERVES 4 (serving size: 1 dog) CALORIES 188; FAT 6.6g (sat 3.2g); SODIUM 860mg

CUBAN

Southeast

Preheat grill to medium heat. Place 4 (97% fat-free) beef franks on grill rack coated with cooking spray; grill, covered, 10 to 15 minutes, turning frequently until done. Place 1 (½-ounce) thin slice reduced-fat Swiss cheese and 1 (½-ounce) thin slice reduced-sodium ham in each of 4 toasted white-wheat hot dog buns; add 1 frank to each bun. Spoon 2 tablespoons chopped dill pickle evenly over top of dogs. Top with mustard, if desired. SERVES 4 (serving size: 1 dog) CALORIES 180; FAT 6g (sat 2.4): SODIUM 837mg

Hot dog tip Make your dogs a little healthier by choosing 97% fat-free beef franks. You'll save 10 times the fat and four times the calories over traditional beef franks.

SHRIMP BURGER

HANDS-ON TIME: 43 MINUTES ★ TOTAL TIME: 43 MINUTES

My recipe was adapted from my friend Barbara Esposito's low-fat version of a menu favorite at Provision Company in North Carolina.

Provision Company, Holden Beach NC

Burgers:

2 slices high-quality whole-wheat bread

2 pounds raw large shrimp, peeled, deveined, and divided

1 egg white

1 tablespoon grated onion

¾ tablespoon Old Bay seasoning

¼ teaspoon freshly ground black pepper

¼ cup chopped parsley

Sauce:

¼ cup light mayonnaise

¼ cup light sour cream

1½ teaspoons lemon zest

1 tablespoon lemon juice

2 teaspoons capers, chopped (optional)

1 teaspoon prepared horseradish

1 teaspoon chopped parsley

Remaining Ingredients:

3 teaspoons canola oil, divided

6 hamburger buns, toasted

6 romaine lettuce leaves

6 (¼-inch-thick) slices tomato

1. To prepare burgers, pulse bread in a food processor to coarse crumbs, about 4 pulses. Transfer to a bowl. Place 1½ pounds shrimp into food processor; add egg white, onion, Old Bay, and pepper, and pulse until there is a mix of finely minced pieces and coarsely chopped pieces, about 7 pulses. Add mixture to breadcrumbs.

2. Chop remaining ½ pound shrimp into ½-inch pieces; add to breadcrumb-shrimp mixture. Add ¼ cup chopped parsley, and mix until combined. Shape mixture into 6 (⅓-cup) balls. To prepare sauce, combine mayonnaise, sour cream, lemon zest, lemon juice, capers, if desired, horseradish, and 1 teaspoon parsley. Reserve.

3. Heat 1½ teaspoons oil in a medium nonstick skillet over medium-high heat until oil begins to shimmer, about 1 minute. Place 3 shrimp balls in pan, flattening to ½-inch thickness. Reduce heat to medium; cook until edges turn pink, and burger looks golden, about 3 to 4 minutes. Turn over and cook 3 minutes or until done. Repeat with remaining oil and shrimp balls.

4. Spread about 2 tablespoons sauce on each bun bottom. Top each with shrimp burger, lettuce leaf, and tomato slice. Cover with bun tops. Serves 6 (serving size: 1 burger)

CALORIES 319; FAT 10g (sat 2g, mono 3g, poly 5g); PROTEIN 27.2g; CARB 28g; FIBER 1.6g; CHOL 194mg; IRON 2mg; SODIUM 818mg; CALC 319mg

LOBSTER ROLLS

HANDS-ON TIME: 11 MINUTES ★ TOTAL TIME: 11 MINUTES

The key to a perfect lobster roll is to do as little as possible to the lobster meat itself. Have your grocer or fishmonger steam the lobsters for you—most will do it free of charge.

¼ cup finely chopped celery
1½ tablespoons canola mayonnaise
5 ounces cooked lobster meat, cut into bite-sized pieces (about 1 [1¼-pound] Maine lobster)

1 tablespoon unsalted butter, softened
2 top-split hot dog buns
2 lemon wedges

1. Place first 3 ingredients in a bowl. Mix gently to combine.
2. Spread butter evenly on outsides of buns (the part that won't be filled with lobster meat). Place buns in a skillet and toast each side until golden, about 3 minutes.
3. Spoon lobster salad evenly into buns. Serve immediately with lemon wedges. Serves 2 (serving size: 1 sandwich)

CALORIES 275; FAT 11.2g (sat 4g, mono 3.8g, poly 2g); PROTEIN 18.9g; CARB 23.3g; FIBER 1.4g; CHOL 66mg; IRON 2mg; SODIUM 559mg; CALC 137mg

Fisherman in Chatham, MA

Don't skip the butter or mayo

In some lobster roll preparations, the outside of the toasted bun is buttered (to give the sandwich an extra layer of flavor) and heaps of mayonnaise are added to the dressing (to keep it creamy). These techniques make a delicious sandwich but also drive up the calories. This version uses butter on the rolls and mayonnaise in the dressing, but in reduced amounts, which saves around 1,000 calories.

WALDORF SALAD

HANDS-ON TIME: 30 MINUTES ★ TOTAL TIME: 30 MINUTES

There are, of course, many variations on this American classic. I like to dress mine with a combination of fat-free Greek yogurt and light mayonnaise. I also take some liberties with the ingredients, adding matchstick-sized pieces of celery root and a bed of mildly peppery arugula.

¼ cup plain fat-free Greek yogurt

2 tablespoons light mayonnaise

1 tablespoon fresh lemon juice

1 teaspoon walnut oil

⅜ teaspoon kosher salt

¼ teaspoon freshly ground black
   pepper

5 cups julienne-cut Gala apple
   (2 apples)

1 cup julienne-cut celeriac
   (celery root)

½ cup sliced celery

1 cup seedless red grapes, halved

3 cups baby arugula

⅓ cup coarsely chopped walnuts,
   toasted

1. Combine first 6 ingredients in a large bowl, stirring with a whisk. Add apple, celeriac, and celery; toss to coat. Add grapes; toss.

2. Place ½ cup arugula on each of 6 plates. Spoon 1 cup fruit mixture over arugula on each plate. Sprinkle evenly with walnuts. Serves 6 (serving size: 1 salad and about 1 tablespoon walnuts)

CALORIES 117; FAT 5.9g (sat 0.7g, mono 1g, poly 4g); PROTEIN 2.9g; CARB 15.4g; FIBER 2g; CHOL 0mg; IRON 0.7mg; SODIUM 203mg; CALC 48mg

A Waldorf-Astoria classic

Swiss immigrant Oscar Tschirky worked at the legendary Waldorf-Astoria hotel in New York City for 50 years. He was hired as a busboy in 1893 and worked his way to maitre d' in less than a decade. Though never a chef, he was able to inspire many of the hotel's signature dishes, chief among them the iconic Waldorf Salad. Because of its lavish elegance, the hotel was frequently visited by wealthy guests such as movie stars, government dignitaries, and oil barons who dined on this classic dish. The initial combination included only slices of apple and celery with creamy, homemade mayonnaise. Over the years, walnuts were added, as were grapes.

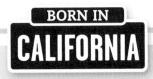
A star is born

The origins of the Cobb salad are hotly debated, but one story says that late one night in 1937, Bob Cobb, then owner of Hollywood's famous Brown Derby Restaurant, searched the restaurant's refrigerator for a little midnight snack. He found some romaine, tomato, avocado, hard-boiled egg, blue cheese, chicken, and a few strips of leftover fried bacon. He created a masterful salad, then sat down to eat with pal Sid Grauman of Grauman's Chinese Theatre across the street. Sid loved the salad so much that the next day, he asked for a "Cobb" salad for lunch. The salad was put on the menu and a star was born.

The salad became the restaurant's signature dish and a hit with Hollywood celebrities, studio executives, and regular folks like you and me. More than 4 million Cobb salads were served at the original Brown Derby before it closed its doors in 1985. The Brown Derby name has since been licensed to Walt Disney Company, which opened a reproduction of the original bowler-shaped restaurant at Disney World in Orlando, Florida, in 1989. The Cobb salad remains the most popular item on the Brown Derby menu.

COBB SALAD
WITH GREEN GODDESS DRESSING

HANDS-ON TIME: 20 MINUTES ★ TOTAL TIME: 25 MINUTES

I like to dress my Cobb salad with Green Goddess dressing instead of the traditional blue cheese. I think the fresh herbs add another dimension of flavor.

2 cups water

2 garlic cloves, smashed

1 (6-ounce) skinless, boneless chicken breast half, cut into ¾-inch cubes

1 (5-ounce) package baby romaine lettuce

2 cups grape tomatoes, halved

2 ounces blue cheese, crumbled (about ¼ cup)

2 hard-cooked large eggs, peeled and chopped

2 bacon slices, cooked and crumbled

1 peeled avocado, cut into ⅓-inch pieces

Green Goddess Dressing

1. Bring 2 cups water and garlic to a boil in a medium saucepan. Add chicken; remove from heat, and let stand 8 minutes or until done. Remove chicken from pan, using a slotted spoon; pat dry with paper towels. Place on a plate, and cool completely.

2. While chicken cooks, prepare Green Goddess Dressing.

3. Place lettuce on a platter. Arrange chicken, tomatoes, and next 4 ingredients (through avocado) over lettuce, alternating ingredients. Serve with dressing. Serves 4 (serving size: ¼ of salad and ¼ cup dressing)

CALORIES 317; FAT 20.8g (sat 5.1g, mono 10.2g, poly 3.3g); PROTEIN 21.4g; CARB 12g; FIBER 5.4g; CHOL 134mg; IRON 2mg; SODIUM 676mg; CALC 164mg

GREEN GODDESS DRESSING

HANDS-ON TIME: 5 MINUTES ★ TOTAL TIME: 5 MINUTES

1 small garlic clove, peeled

1 cup basil leaves

½ cup fat-free Greek yogurt

⅓ cup parsley leaves

¼ cup canola mayonnaise

2 tablespoons fresh lemon juice

½ teaspoon kosher salt

1. With food processor on, drop garlic through food chute; process until minced. Add basil and remaining ingredients; process until smooth. Serves 4 (serving size: ¼ cup)

CALORIES 59; FAT 3.8g (sat 0g, mono 2.4g, poly 1.4g); PROTEIN 3g; CARB 2.5g; FIBER 0.4g; CHOL 0mg; IRON 0.7mg; SODIUM 361mg; CALC 47mg

NORTHWEST
Baked Potato Soup
America's potato capital serves up soup with all the traditional baked potato fixin's. Cheddar cheese, sour cream, bacon, and green onions add familiar flavor to the potato soup, which is commonly pureed with broth but can also be served chunky.

AMERICA LOVES: SOUP
Bowled over with local flavor

WEST
Green Chile Stew
Chiles are New Mexico's largest agricultural crop and, especially when harvested green, are the state's most notable culinary offering. There are many varieties of green chile stew, but most include pork or beef and potatoes in addition to the chiles.

SOUTHWEST
Tortilla Soup
This is a savory broth-based soup showcasing many of the region's celebrated ingredients and Mexican heritage: tortillas, corn, beans, tomatoes, onions, and meat (usually chicken). Salsa and avocado are also commonly added.

MIDWEST
Cheddar Cheese & Beer Soup

Wisconsin still accounts for the majority of the cheddar cheese produced in America today. Combine that with the golden carbonated beverage that's another of the state's most popular exports and you have a true Wisconsin classic. Popcorn is often the preferred garnish.

NORTHEAST
New England Clam Chowder

Known in many parts of the state as Boston clam chowder, this milk- or cream-based chowder is commonly made with potatoes, onions, and clams. It originated as a working-class one-pot meal among the fishermen of colonial-era Boston.

EAST
Pepper Pot

In Philadelphia, pepper pot is hailed as the fortifying dish that revitalized George Washington's troops during the long, cold winter when they were encamped at Valley Forge during the heart of the American Revolution. The soup, a mixture of tripe, vegetables, and peppercorns, may have been brought north by slaves or traders from West Africa, where it originated.

SOUTH
Pot Likker Soup

Pot likker, also known as pot liquor, is the flavorful broth that remains in the pot after cooking down a "mess" of collard, mustard, or turnip greens. The greens are typically seasoned with a smoked ham hock or smoked turkey wings that gives the liquor deep rich flavor. During the colonial days, this liquid was drained and often served as a broth. Today, folks in the South don't separate the collards from their liquor and instead make a hearty soup by bulking up the broth with a variety of ingredients such as celery, onion, carrots, black-eyed peas, and rice.

SOUTHEAST
Brunswick Stew

There are several accounts of the origin of this hearty pot stew made with a variety of meats, corn, tomatoes, lima beans, and sometimes okra. But a plaque on an old iron pot in Brunswick, Georgia, says the first Brunswick stew was made in 1898 on St. Simons Island in Georgia. Early versions may have contained rabbit or squirrel, although contemporary variations often feature chicken.

GRILLED VEGETABLE CAPRESE WITH PESTO

HANDS-ON TIME: 45 MINUTES ★ TOTAL TIME: 45 MINUTES

The original Caprese salad consists of mozzarella, tomato, and basil, but my take adds grilled vegetables and homemade pesto for a hearty twist.

Pesto:

2 large garlic cloves

¼ cup walnuts, toasted

1 (1-ounce) package fresh basil, stems removed

½ cup (2 ounces) grated fresh Parmesan cheese

¼ cup extra-virgin olive oil

¼ cup white balsamic vinegar

2 tablespoons water

Salad:

1 (1-pound) eggplant, cut diagonally into ½-inch-thick slices

1 large red onion, cut into ½-inch slices

Cooking spray

1 pound zucchini, diagonally cut into ½-inch-thick slices

1 pound yellow squash, diagonally cut into ½-inch-thick slices

2 cups cherry tomatoes

2 (12-inch) metal skewers

5 ounces bocconcini mozzarella cheese, sliced

¼ teaspoon kosher salt

1. To prepare pesto, drop garlic through food chute with food processor on; process until minced. Add walnuts and basil; process until finely ground. Add cheese and next 3 ingredients (through water); process until smooth. Transfer to a small bowl; cover and chill.

2. To prepare salad, preheat grill to medium-high heat.

3. Place eggplant and onion on grill rack coated with cooking spray; cover and grill 6 to 8 minutes or until tender. Remove from grill.

4. Place zucchini and yellow squash on grill rack; cover and grill 4 to 6 minutes or until tender. Remove from grill.

5. Thread tomatoes evenly onto skewers; coat with cooking spray. Place skewers on grill rack; cover and grill 5 to 7 minutes or until tender. Remove tomatoes from skewers.

6. Arrange vegetables, tomatoes, and cheese on a large platter; drizzle ½ cup pesto over salad, and sprinkle with salt. Serve with remaining pesto. Serves 6 (serving size: ⅙ of salad and about 3 tablespoons pesto)

CALORIES 295; FAT 21.2g (sat 6.4g, mono 10g, poly 3.7g); PROTEIN 14.6g; CARB 17.0g; FIBER 5.3g; CHOL 21mg; IRON 1.3mg; SODIUM 389mg; CALC 330mg

SHE-CRAB SOUP

HANDS-ON TIME: 42 MINUTES ★ TOTAL TIME: 42 MINUTES

This Carolina lowcountry soup gets its name from the generous dollop of crab roe that customarily garnishes the top. Crab roe is available in season (May–August), but this creamy soup is just as delicious without it.

1 tablespoon canola oil
1 cup finely chopped onion
½ cup finely chopped carrot
1 tablespoon tomato paste
6 garlic cloves, minced
2 tablespoons all-purpose flour
1¼ cups water
¾ cup half-and-half
2 (8-ounce) bottles clam juice

6 ounces ⅓-less-fat cream cheese (about ¾ cup)
¼ cup dry sherry
1 tablespoon chopped fresh chives
1 teaspoon chopped fresh thyme
8 ounces lump crabmeat, drained and shell pieces removed
Chopped chives (optional)

1. Heat a large saucepan over medium-high heat. Add oil to pan; swirl to coat. Add onion, carrot, and tomato paste. Cook 10 minutes, stirring occasionally. Add garlic; cook, stirring constantly, 1 minute. Stir in flour; cook 1 minute, stirring frequently.

2. Stir in 1¼ cups water, half-and-half, and clam juice. Bring to a boil; reduce heat, and simmer, uncovered, 10 minutes, stirring occasionally. Remove from heat; add cheese, stirring until melted. Stir in sherry, chives, and thyme. Ladle soup into bowls; top evenly with crab. Garnish with chopped chives, if desired. Serves 6 (serving size: about ¾ cup soup and ¼ cup crab)

CALORIES 214; FAT 12.4g (sat 6.4g, mono 4.2g, poly 1.1g); PROTEIN 12.2g; CARB 11.2g; FIBER 1.1g; CHOL 60mg; IRON 0.8mg; SODIUM 505mg; CALC 105mg

TOMATO SOUP AND GRILLED CHEESE

HANDS-ON TIME: 35 MINUTES ★ TOTAL TIME: 1 HOUR 15 MINUTES

Just like Mom used to make, only better, because the soup doesn't come out of a can, which means you can control the sodium. Keep the sandwich old-school with American cheese.

2 tablespoons unsalted butter
1 cup chopped onion
2 tablespoons minced fresh tarragon (optional)
½ teaspoon sugar
1 garlic clove, chopped
1 (28-ounce) can Italian-style whole tomatoes, undrained
1 (28-ounce) can Italian-style whole tomatoes, drained

3 cups lower-sodium organic vegetable broth
3 tablespoons tomato paste
½ cup half-and-half
½ cup heavy cream
6 (1¾-ounce) slices country white bread
6 (¾-ounce) slices American cheese
1 tablespoon unsalted butter, softened

1. Melt 2 tablespoons butter in a Dutch oven over medium heat. Add onion; cook 10 minutes, stirring occasionally. Add tarragon, if desired, sugar, and garlic; sauté 2 minutes. Add tomatoes, broth, and tomato paste. Increase heat to medium-high, and bring to a boil; partially cover, reduce heat to medium-low, and simmer 30 minutes.
2. Remove from heat; cool 5 minutes. Place half of soup mixture in blender; process until smooth. Return mixture to pan. Repeat procedure with remaining soup mixture.
3. Add half-and-half and heavy cream, stirring with a whisk over low heat. Set aside; keep warm.
4. While soup simmers, place 3 bread slices on a work surface; arrange 2 cheese slices on each of 3 bread slices. Top with remaining 3 bread slices. Spread softened butter on sides of sandwiches. Heat a large nonstick skillet over medium heat. Add sandwiches to pan; cook 4 minutes or until lightly browned. Turn sandwiches over; cook 2 minutes or until cheese melts. Cut each sandwich in half diagonally.
5. Ladle soup into bowls; serve with sandwiches. Serves 6 (serving size: about 1⅓ cups soup and ½ sandwich).

CALORIES 302; FAT 12g (sat 6.9g, mono 2.3g, poly 1.4g); PROTEIN 10.5g; CARB 37.1g; FIBER 4g; CHOL 34mg; IRON 1.9mg; SODIUM 681mg; CALC 106mg

Après-ski Soupsköl

Nothing warms better on a brisk winter's day than a steaming hot bowl of really tasty soup. So goes the thinking behind the Aspen, Colorado, festival called Soupsköl, held each year during the January chill in the Rocky Mountain resort town's snow-bound streets. Soupsköl ("Toast to Soup") is part of Aspen's annual Wintersköl festival, which celebrates the ski town's bracing and energetic Nordic lifestyle with all types of winter frivolity, from torchlight parades and broomball to canine fashion shows and snow sculpture. Soupsköl is at the steaming heart of the midwinter festival, held the second weekend of January after the tourists have gone home. It's the part I like the best. Two dozen of the city's restaurants offer up generous bowls of their very best soup to vie for nothing more than bragging rights. Tastes are free and voting encouraged. No fancy judging here. The bowl that takes top honors is 100% people's choice.

The restaurant Aspen Square Grouper took home a recent trophy for their chunky jackalope gumbo. What? Jackalopes do exist? No, silly. The "jackalope" portion of this soup is a sausage made from a mixture of rabbit and antelope. The "gumbo" portion is a classic Creole mixture of shrimp, chicken, and okra, all topped with a cornbread crouton.

Another recent winner was Ute City

> **Soupsköl is the steaming heart of Aspen's annual midwinter festival.**

for a red bell pepper–Parmesan soup with duck confit grilled cheese. Clearly most Aspenites are interested in more than run-of-the-mill chicken noodle or split pea varieties.

My hands-down favorite? A baked potato soup I only reluctantly tasted, thinking it would be thick and heavy. What a nice surprise to find a bowl of flavorful broth laden with small chunks of bite-sized potatoes, bacon, cheddar, and scallions in a pleasantly light and satisfying soup.

CREAMY DANDELION SOUP

HANDS-ON TIME: 29 MINUTES ★ TOTAL TIME: 29 MINUTES

Dandelion greens are best during the spring, when the small pale green leaves are most tender. If you can't find them, substitute an equal amount of any other bitter green. My favorite is broccoli rabe, but beet greens, arugula, watercress, or baby spinach can also be substituted.

1 pound dandelion greens, trimmed

1 tablespoon canola oil

1 tablespoon unsalted butter

½ cup finely chopped onion (½ medium-sized)

1.1 ounces all-purpose flour (about ¼ cup)

2 cups fat-free, lower-sodium chicken broth

1½ cups fat-free milk

½ cup half-and-half

½ teaspoon kosher salt

¼ teaspoon freshly ground black pepper

Reduced-fat sour cream (optional)

8 lemon wedges

Dandelion Cook-Off, Dover, OH

1. Separate 1 dandelion leaf from the bunch; thinly slice, and set aside. Fill a large Dutch oven half full with water; bring to a boil. Add remaining greens to boiling water; cover and cook for 2 minutes. Drain. Place greens in a food processor; process 30 seconds or until smooth.

2. Place oil and butter in a 3-quart saucepan. Cook over medium heat until butter melts. Add onion; sauté 3 minutes or until tender. Sprinkle flour over onion mixture, stirring to coat. Add broth and next 4 ingredients (through pepper), stirring with a whisk. Stir in pureed greens. Bring to a boil; reduce heat, and simmer, uncovered, 5 minutes, stirring occasionally. Garnish servings evenly with reserved sliced greens. Top with sour cream, if desired. Serve with lemon wedges. Serves 6 (serving size: 1 cup)

CALORIES 155; FAT 7.4g (sat 3.2g, mono 2.7g, poly 1.1g); PROTEIN 6.9g; CARB 17.3g; FIBER 3.3g; CHOL 15mg; IRON 2.7mg; SODIUM 299mg; CALC 244mg

Corn on the go at the Iowa State Fair

BETWEEN MEALS

Appetizers & Snacks

Holden Brothers Farm Market, Shallotte, NC

Anyone who's ever tried to lose weight knows that snacks can be a dieter's best friend or worst enemy. The key is choosing snacks that satisfy without unwanted calories.

*d*iet-y snacks are particularly problematic because they're often not as crunchy or creamy or tasty as the full-fat version. I love to nibble—and most of my favorite snacks are loaded with excess calories and fat. Think deep-fried stuffed jalapeños, pigs in a blanket, and artichoke-spinach dip. Not one to shrink from a challenge, I set to work transforming them from foes to friends. The result was a radical, but incredibly successful, renovation. I love these lighter recipes so much, it's easy for me to turn down the old deep-fried, fat-packed, and too-creamy snacks I used to crave. I hope you will, too.

Five-Layer Dip, p. 121

Crab Cakes with Cajun Rémoulade, p. 105

Texas Caviar, p. 120

Blue Cheese Ball, p. 114

BAKED MOZZARELLA BITES

HANDS-ON TIME: 14 MINUTES ★ TOTAL TIME: 18 MINUTES

The plump little love children of battered fresh cheese and a deep fryer, fried cheese curds are a midwinter favorite of beer-and-cheese states from Iowa to Wisconsin. This recipe, which substitutes string cheese for the curds and baking for the frying, is a lighter variation.

⅓ cup panko (Japanese breadcrumbs)
3 (1-ounce) sticks part-skim
    mozzarella string cheese
3 tablespoons egg substitute
Cooking spray
¼ cup lower-sodium marinara sauce

1. Preheat oven to 425°.
2. Heat a medium skillet over medium heat. Add panko to pan, and cook 2 minutes or until toasted, stirring frequently. Remove from heat, and place panko in a shallow dish.
3. Cut mozzarella sticks into 1-inch pieces. Working with 1 piece at a time, dip cheese in egg substitute; dredge in panko. Place cheese on a baking sheet coated with cooking spray. Bake at 425° for 3 minutes or until cheese is softened and thoroughly heated.
4. Pour marinara sauce into a microwave-safe bowl. Microwave at HIGH 1 minute or until thoroughly heated, stirring after 30 seconds. Serve with mozzarella pieces. Serves 4 (serving size: 3 mozzarella bites and 1 tablespoon sauce)

CALORIES 91; FAT 5.1g (sat 2.8g, mono 1.3g, poly 0.3g); PROTEIN 7.2g; CARB 6.7g; FIBER 0.1g; CHOL 12mg; IRON 0.3mg; SODIUM 162mg; CALC 162mg

I ♥ cheese curds

If you haven't been to the International Eelpout Festival in Walker, Minnesota, put it on your bucket list. It's where I first ate and fell in love with cheese curds, the small, tasty chunks of cheese solids that are a natural by-product of cheesemaking. The winter festival actually has little to do with cheese, focusing instead on the region's most celebrated midwinter ice-fishing catch, the half-eel, half-fish eelpout (otherwise known as the ugliest fish in the world). A party of 10,000 people gathers on a frozen lake to fish, eat, and engage in all kinds of winter frivolity. Fried cheese curds are the festival-goer's snack of choice, and the salty, scrumptious, teeth-squeaking cheese had me at first bite.

GRILLED JALAPEÑO POPPERS

HANDS-ON TIME: 25 MINUTES ★ TOTAL TIME: 33 MINUTES

The rich and creamy combination of bacon, cream cheese, and cheddar nicely contrasts the muted spice of the grilled jalapeños in these poppers. You'll never guess these are lightened up! That's why this recipe—a healthy, fresh alternative to the popular breaded and fried snack—is one of my favorite appetizers to make.

2 center-cut bacon slices
4 ounces cream cheese (about ½ cup), softened
4 ounces fat-free cream cheese (about ½ cup), softened
1 ounce extra-sharp cheddar cheese, shredded (about ¼ cup)
¼ cup minced green onions
1 teaspoon fresh lime juice
¼ teaspoon kosher salt
1 small garlic clove, minced
14 jalapeño peppers, halved lengthwise and seeded
Cooking spray
2 tablespoons chopped fresh cilantro
2 tablespoons chopped seeded tomato

1. Preheat grill to medium-high heat.
2. Cook bacon in a skillet over medium heat until crisp. Remove bacon from pan, and drain on paper towels. Crumble bacon. Combine crumbled bacon, cheeses, and next 4 ingredients (through garlic) in a bowl, stirring to combine. Divide cheese mixture evenly, and fill pepper halves. Place peppers, cheese side up, on grill rack or grill grate coated with cooking spray. Cover and grill peppers 8 minutes or until bottoms of peppers are charred and cheese mixture is lightly browned. Place peppers on a serving platter. Sprinkle with cilantro and tomato. Serves 14 (serving size: 2 pepper halves)

Note: If making these poppers for a party, you can stuff the peppers, cover, and chill. Then grill just before your guests arrive.

CALORIES 56; FAT 4.1g (sat 2.2g, mono 1.1g, poly 0.2g); PROTEIN 2.9g; CARB 2.1g; FIBER 0.5g; CHOL 13mg; IRON 0.2mg; SODIUM 157mg; CALC 55mg

PIGS IN A BLANKET

HANDS-ON TIME: 18 MINUTES ★ TOTAL TIME: 60 MINUTES

Brooklyn Piggies, a food stand in Brooklyn, NY, serves up a version of this 1950s American cocktail appetizer that's parallel to none. Light, flaky puff pastry encases quality sausage to create one of my favorite indulgences. At home, I substitute pizza dough for the puff pastry and turkey dogs for the sausage.

1 (6-ounce) portion fresh
  pizza dough
1½ ounces part-skim
  mozzarella cheese,
  shredded (about ⅜ cup)
4 turkey hot dogs, halved
  crosswise

Cooking spray
2 tablespoons ketchup
1 tablespoon barbecue
  sauce
1 teaspoon prepared
  mustard

1. Preheat oven to 425°.
2. Let dough stand, covered, 20 minutes. On a lightly floured surface, roll dough into a 12 x 4–inch rectangle. Cut rectangle into 4 (4 x 3–inch) rectangles; cut each rectangle in half diagonally to form 8 triangles. Divide cheese evenly among triangles; place in center of wide ends. Place ½ hot dog at the wide end of each triangle; roll up, pinching ends to seal. Arrange rolls on a baking sheet coated with cooking spray. Bake at 425° for 12 minutes. Combine ketchup and next 2 ingredients (through mustard). Serve with rolls. Serves 8 (serving size: 1 roll and about 1 teaspoon sauce)

CALORIES 108; FAT 3.2g (sat 1g, mono 0.3g, poly 0.4g); PROTEIN 6.8g; CARB 13.8g; FIBER 0.4g; CHOL 16mg; IRON 0.7mg; SODIUM 413mg; CALC 43mg

COCKTAIL REMIX

Have a really happy hour at home with these low-cal boozy beverages.

MAI TAI

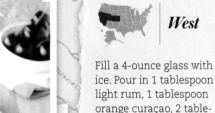

West

Fill a 4-ounce glass with ice. Pour in 1 tablespoon light rum, 1 tablespoon orange curaçao, 2 table-spoons orange juice, ½ tablespoon fresh lime juice, 1 dash orgeat, and 1 dash simple syrup. Drizzle ½ tablespoon dark rum on top. Garnish with mint, pineapple slice, and paper umbrella, if desired. SERVES 1 (serving size: 1 cocktail) CALORIES 114; FAT 0g (sat 0g); SODIUM 3mg

MONTANA SKY

Northwest

Combine 1 ounce bourbon, ½ ounce tawny port, and 1 dash Angostura bitters over ice in a small glass. Stir to combine, and garnish with brandied cherries, if desired. SERVES 1 (serving size: 1 cocktail) CALORIES 89; FAT 0g (sat 0g); SODIUM 2mg

MARGARITA

Southwest

Rub rim of a chilled small margarita glass with lime wedge, and dip rim in margarita salt to coat, if desired. Fill cocktail shaker with ¾ cup ice. Add 2 tablespoons lime juice, 1 tablespoon orange liqueur, and 2 tablespoons premium tequila; cover with lid, and shake until thoroughly chilled. Strain into prepared glass. Garnish with a lime wedge, if desired, and serve immediately. SERVES 1 (serving size: 1 cocktail) CALORIES 120; FAT 0g (sat 0g); SODIUM 1mg

CHICAGO ATTACK

Midwest

Rub rim of an old-fashioned glass with a lemon slice, and dip in powdered sugar. Add cracked ice to glass. Stir in 2 ounces brandy, a dash of Angostura bitters, and ¼ teaspoon curaçao or triple sec over cracked ice. Garnish with lemon wedge, if desired. SERVES 1 (serving size: 1 cocktail) CALORIES 70; FAT 0g (sat 0g); SODIUM 0mg

SAZERAC

South

Fill cocktail shaker with 1 cup ice. Add 3 tablespoons rye whiskey, 1 teaspoon simple syrup, and 2 dashes Peychaud's bitters; cover with lid, and shake until thoroughly chilled. Coat inside of a chilled 3½-ounce glass with ¼ teaspoon anise liqueur; pour out excess. Rub lemon rind strip over rim, and place in glass. Strain whiskey mixture into prepared glass. SERVES 1 (serving size: 1 cocktail) CALORIES 106; FAT 0g (sat 0g); SODIUM 0mg

OLD FASHIONED

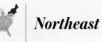

Northeast

Place 1 brown sugar cube on a cocktail napkin. Sprinkle 2 to 3 drops orange bitters and 2 to 3 drops Angostura bitters over sugar cube. (Napkin will soak up excess bitters.) Transfer cube to a 10-ounce old-fashioned glass. Add 1 orange slice and a few drops bourbon to glass. Mash sugar cube and orange slice, using a muddler, until sugar is almost dissolved. (Avoid mashing the rind; doing so will release a bitter flavor.) Add 3 tablespoons bourbon, and fill glass with ice cubes. Stir until well chilled. SERVES 1 (serving size: 1 cocktail) CALORIES 110; FAT 0g (sat 0g); SODIUM 1mg

LONG ISLAND ICED TEA

East

Fill cocktail shaker with crushed ice. Add 4 tablespoons sweet-and-sour mix, 2 tablespoons vodka, 2 tablespoons gin, 2 tablespoons orange liqueur, 2 tablespoons light rum, and 2 tablespoons tequila. Cover with lid, and shake until thoroughly chilled. Strain into 4 chilled small martini glasses. Pour 2 tablespoons sugar-free cola into each glass. Garnish with lemon slices, if desired. SERVES 4 (serving size: 1 cocktail) CALORIES 105; FAT 0g (sat 0g); SODIUM 9mg

MOJITO

Southeast

Combine 1 cup fresh mint leaves, ¾ cup white rum, ⅓ cup agave nectar, and 1 cup ice cubes in pitcher. Mash mint leaves, rum, and agave together; stir in 1 cup fresh lime juice (about 10 limes) and 1 cup sparkling water. Pour into 4 glasses. SERVES 4 (serving size: 1 cocktail) CALORIES 190; FAT 0g (sat 0g); SODIUM 5mg

Cocktail tip Sidestep the extra calories by making cocktails with fresh fruit juices and calorie-free beverages rather than mixes, which are loaded with sugar.

FRIED GREEN TOMATOES
WITH GARLICKY RÉMOULADE

HANDS-ON TIME: 22 MINUTES ★ TOTAL TIME: 22 MINUTES

Buttermilk is the key ingredient in this recipe; it helps the cornmeal coating adhere to the tomatoes. These are served with a garlicky rémoulade just as they would be in New Orleans.

12 (¼-inch-thick) slices green tomato (about 3 medium tomatoes)

¼ teaspoon kosher salt

¼ teaspoon freshly ground black pepper

1 cup plus 2 tablespoons 1% low-fat buttermilk, divided

1 large egg

2.25 ounces all-purpose flour (about ½ cup)

⅔ cup yellow cornmeal

2 tablespoons canola oil

Cooking spray

2½ tablespoons canola mayonnaise

1½ teaspoons chopped fresh chives

2 teaspoons fresh lemon juice

1 teaspoon minced garlic

1. Sprinkle both sides of tomato slices evenly with salt and pepper. Combine 1 cup buttermilk and egg in a shallow dish, stirring with a whisk. Place flour in a shallow dish. Place cornmeal in a shallow dish.

2. Dredge tomato slices lightly in flour; shake off excess flour. Dip tomato slices in egg mixture; dredge in cornmeal. Heat a large nonstick skillet over medium-high heat 2 minutes. Add 1 tablespoon oil to pan; swirl to coat. Cook 6 tomato slices 2 to 3 minutes or until lightly browned on bottom. Spray tops with cooking spray; turn tomatoes, and cook 3 minutes or until lightly browned. Remove from pan; place on a wire rack. Repeat procedure with remaining oil and tomato slices.

3. Combine 2 tablespoons buttermilk, mayonnaise, and next 3 ingredients (through garlic), stirring with a whisk. Serve with tomatoes. Serves 6 (serving size: 2 tomato slices and about 1 tablespoon sauce)

CALORIES 165; FAT 7g (sat 0.7g, mono 3.7g, poly 1.9g); PROTEIN 3.9g; CARB 23.8g; FIBER 1.1g; CHOL 32mg; IRON 1.1mg; SODIUM 155mg; CALC 34mg

DEVILED EGGS

HANDS-ON TIME: 12 MINUTES ★ TOTAL TIME: 27 MINUTES

To keep these portable snacks from turning on their sides when serving, use a deviled egg tray. Especially in vogue during the 1940s and '50s, when specialized serving dishes could be found in a variety of china patterns, deviled egg plates are still quite common today.

6 large eggs

3 tablespoons canola mayonnaise

2 teaspoons Dijon mustard

½ teaspoon fresh lemon juice

¼ teaspoon freshly ground black pepper

2 teaspoons coarsely chopped fresh chives

⅛ teaspoon hot paprika

1. Place eggs in a large saucepan. Cover with water to 1 inch above eggs; bring just to a boil. Remove from heat; cover and let stand 15 minutes. Drain and rinse with cold running water until cool.

2. Peel eggs; cut in half lengthwise, and remove yolks. Place yolks in a bowl; mash with a fork. Stir in mayonnaise and next 3 ingredients (through pepper).

3. Spoon yolk mixture evenly into egg white halves. Sprinkle evenly with chives and paprika. Serves 6 (serving size: 2 egg halves)

CALORIES 95; FAT 7g (sat 1.6g, mono 3.1g, poly 1.7g); PROTEIN 6.3g; CARB 0.6g; FIBER 0g; CHOL 186mg; IRON 0.9mg; SODIUM 129mg; CALC 29mg

BAKED CLAMS

HANDS-ON TIME: 52 MINUTES ★ TOTAL TIME: 52 MINUTES

Clams are a low-tide favorite on any American coast. Buy them as fresh as possible and discard any whose shells don't close when touched. Keep them well chilled and use within a day of purchase.

½ cup dry white wine

32 littleneck clams in shells, scrubbed

1½ tablespoons unsalted butter, divided

1 (1-ounce) slice French bread baguette

1 applewood-smoked bacon slice

2 teaspoons minced shallots

1½ teaspoons chopped fresh thyme

1. Bring wine to a boil in a large skillet over medium-high heat. Add clams; cover and cook 4 minutes or until shells open. Remove clams from pan, reserving cooking liquid. Discard any unopened shells. Strain cooking liquid through a cheesecloth-lined sieve into a medium bowl. Cool clams. Discard top shells. Place clams, still in bottom shell halves, in a single layer on a baking sheet.

2. Return reserved cooking liquid to pan; bring to a boil over medium-high heat. Cook until reduced to ¾ cup (about 3 minutes). Remove from heat; remove 6 tablespoons cooking liquid from pan, and reserve for another use. Add 1½ teaspoons butter to cooking liquid in pan; stir until butter melts. Spoon about ½ teaspoon cooking liquid back into each clam shell.

3. Preheat broiler.

4. Place bread in a food processor; pulse 10 times or until fine crumbs measure about ½ cup. Cook bacon in a small skillet over medium heat until crisp. Remove bacon from pan; finely chop. Add shallots to drippings in pan; sauté 30 seconds. Add 1 tablespoon butter to pan, stirring until melted.

5. Remove pan from heat; stir in breadcrumbs and bacon. Divide breadcrumb mixture evenly among clam shell halves, pressing mixture gently into shells. Broil 1 minute or until golden brown. Sprinkle with thyme. Serves 8 (serving size: 4 clams)

CALORIES 80; FAT 3g (sat 1.5g, mono 0.6g, poly 0g); PROTEIN 6.5g; CARB 4.8g; FIBER 0.2g; CHOL 33mg; IRON 2mg; SODIUM 79mg; CALC 29mg

BEER-STEAMED CLAMS AND MUSSELS

HANDS-ON TIME: 10 MINUTES ★ TOTAL TIME: 20 MINUTES

Be sure to use a large, wide pot so the shellfish can cook evenly, then serve them straight from the pot with crusty Italian bread to soak up the broth.

1 tablespoon butter
1 tablespoon olive oil
1 cup sliced shallots
5 sprigs thyme
2 garlic cloves, thinly sliced
1 cup pale ale

2 pounds fresh littleneck
  clams in shells
  (about 18)
1 pound mussels in shells,
  scrubbed and
  debearded (about 30)
6 lemon wedges

1. In a large pot or Dutch oven, heat butter and oil over medium heat. Add shallots, thyme, and garlic; cook until shallots begin to soften, about 3 minutes. Add beer, and bring to a simmer. Add clams and mussels; return to a gentle simmer.
2. Cover pot with a lid, and reduce heat to medium-low. Cook until shells open, about 10 minutes. Discard unopened shells. Serve with lemon wedges and a bowl for the shells. Serves 6 (serving size: about 3 clams, 5 mussels, about 2 tablespoons broth, and 1 lemon wedge)

CALORIES 144; FAT 5.7g (sat 1.8g, mono 2.6g, poly 1.2g); PROTEIN 10.9g; CARB 9.5g; FIBER 1g; CHOL 27mg; IRON 2.8mg; SODIUM 327mg; CALC 36mg

Cooking the day's catch

food always tastes better when you catch and cook it yourself. Over the years, my parents have become quite adept at baiting and catching fresh crabs near their home in Lockwood Folly in Supply, North Carolina. They enjoy a reliable supply throughout the year. I've learned a few things from my parents, and their great tips on catching the hard-shelled critters have come in handy.

My parents drop their baited trap into the calm, muddy-bottomed waterway (working at night if they're really serious about it) and pull up the trap teeming with crabs a few hours later. Their trick? A bait of chicken bones and an uncanny knack for finding the right spot at which to lower their trap. Now for the tricky part—what to do with the crabs after catching them. Shake them out of the trap, using tongs to place them in a pot or basin. Next, slow their movement by chilling them over ice or in the refrigerator before using the tip of a knife to pierce the ventral nerve between their eyes (as for lobsters) before steaming them.

It might seem like a lot to go through for a simple meal, but the subtly sweet flavor of fresh-caught crab makes it all worthwhile.

After a day of catching crab, I love to make crab cakes. I often make a version that was inspired by my visits to G & M Restaurant and Lounge in Linthicum Heights, Maryland. My brother lives there and when I visit him, I like to stop by for an order of their award-winning crab cakes. They make them just the way I like them, with a higher amount of crabmeat than breadcrumbs so the crab is the star of the dish.

CRAB CAKES
WITH CAJUN RÉMOULADE

HANDS-ON TIME: 30 MINUTES ★ TOTAL TIME: 30 MINUTES

Numerous variations of crab cakes exist, and this one takes its cue from Cajun cuisine. A quick sauté on the cooktop crisps them on the outside without saturating them in oil.

Crab Cakes:
¼ cup finely diced red bell pepper
2 tablespoons finely chopped green onions
½ teaspoon dry mustard
¼ teaspoon celery seeds
¼ teaspoon paprika
⅛ teaspoon ground red pepper
1 large egg, beaten
1 cup panko (Japanese breadcrumbs)
1 pound lump crabmeat, drained and shell pieces removed
2 tablespoons canola oil

Cajun Rémoulade:
1 cup plain fat-free Greek yogurt
2 tablespoons chopped green onions
2 tablespoons finely chopped fresh flat-leaf parsley
2 teaspoons drained capers, finely chopped
2 teaspoons Worcestershire sauce
½ teaspoon paprika
¼ teaspoon ground red pepper

Remaining Ingredient:
Lemon slices

1. To prepare crab cakes, combine first 7 ingredients (through egg). Add panko and crab, tossing gently to combine.
2. Fill a ¼-cup dry measuring cup with crab mixture. Invert onto work surface; gently pat into a 1-inch-thick patty. Repeat procedure with remaining crab mixture, forming 12 cakes.
3. Heat a large nonstick skillet over medium-high heat. Add oil to pan; swirl to coat. Add crab cakes to pan; cook 2 minutes or until bottoms are golden. Carefully turn crab cakes; cook 2 minutes or until bottoms are golden and crab cakes are thoroughly heated. Remove crab cakes from pan; keep warm.
4. To prepare rémoulade, combine 1 cup yogurt and next 6 ingredients (through red pepper) in a small bowl; stir with a whisk. Serve crab cakes with rémoulade and lemon slices. Serves 12 (serving size: 1 crab cake and about 2 teaspoons rémoulade)

CALORIES 95; FAT 3g (sat 0.4g, mono 1.7g, poly 0.9g); PROTEIN 9.7g; CARB 6.5g; FIBER 0.4g; CHOL 52mg; IRON 0.5mg; SODIUM 198mg; CALC 55mg

Shrimp sense

Despite the fact that much of the shrimp we consume in the U.S. is imported, America's coastal waters are abundant with many varieties. Perhaps best known are the Gulf shrimp, consisting of rock, brown, pink, and white species, fished in coastal waters from Florida to Texas. Gulf shrimp are flavorful and sweet with little taste variation between the species.

The wild-caught shrimp of colder, Northern waters are predominantly smaller than their warm-water cousins. The shrimp from Maine and Oregon are both known as bay shrimp, notable for their diminutive size. Prawns, the largest species of shrimp from the Pacific Northwest, are less plentiful but a local favorite.

COCONUT SHRIMP
WITH FIERY MANGO SAUCE

HANDS-ON TIME: 55 MINUTES ★ TOTAL TIME: 67 MINUTES

This dish is a happy-hour favorite. I keep it lean by baking instead of frying the shrimp. Stand them upright on the baking sheet so they brown and cook evenly—and so you don't have to worry about turning them.

Sauce:
1¼ cups chopped peeled ripe mango
¼ cup no-sugar-added apricot
   preserves
1½ tablespoons finely chopped
   seeded jalapeño pepper
2 teaspoons honey
¾ teaspoon grated lime rind
2 tablespoons fresh lime juice
1 teaspoon Dijon mustard

Shrimp:
24 large shrimp (about 1½ pounds)
1.1 ounces all-purpose flour (about
   ¼ cup)
½ teaspoon salt
¼ teaspoon ground red pepper
2 large egg whites
2 tablespoons water
¾ cup panko (Japanese breadcrumbs)
½ cup flaked sweetened coconut
2 tablespoons canola oil
Cooking spray

1. Preheat oven to 375°.
2. To prepare sauce, place all sauce ingredients in a food processor; pulse 3 times or to desired consistency. Transfer to a serving bowl.
3. To prepare shrimp, peel and devein shrimp, leaving tails intact. Combine flour, salt, and red pepper in a large zip-top plastic bag. Combine egg whites and 2 tablespoons water in a shallow dish, stirring with a whisk. Combine panko, coconut, and oil in a separate shallow dish.
4. Place shrimp in zip-top plastic bag; seal and shake to coat. Dip shrimp in egg white mixture; dredge in coconut mixture. Stand coated shrimp on their ends on a wire rack coated with cooking spray set on a baking sheet.
5. Bake at 375° for 12 minutes or until shrimp are done. Serve with sauce. Serves 8 (serving size: 3 shrimp and about 2 tablespoons sauce)

CALORIES 143; FAT 5.5g (sat 1.7g, mono 2.4g, poly 1.1g); PROTEIN 5.3g; CARB 19.7g; FIBER 1.3g; CHOL 26mg; IRON 0.4mg; SODIUM 200mg; CALC 17mg

THAI LETTUCE WRAPS

HANDS-ON TIME: 42 MINUTES ★ TOTAL TIME: 42 MINUTES

An increase in immigration from Southeast Asia over the past 20 years has made dishes like this more popular, especially in urban centers. The ingredients for this dish can be easily purchased at your local market. Lean pork, low-sodium soy sauce, and plenty of fresh vegetables make these a great low-carb, low-calorie snack at any time of the day.

Dressing:
4 teaspoons fresh lime juice
2 teaspoons dark sesame oil
2 teaspoons lower-sodium soy sauce
1 teaspoon sambal oelek (ground fresh chile paste)
1 teaspoon fish sauce

Filling:
½ teaspoon canola oil
½ pound 80% lean ground pork
1 tablespoon grated peeled fresh ginger

1 cucumber, halved lengthwise, seeded, and grated (1 cup)
1 carrot, grated (1 cup)
¼ cup cilantro leaves
¼ cup chopped fresh mint
3 tablespoons thinly sliced green onions
2 tablespoons chopped dry-roasted peanuts

Remaining Ingredient:
8 Boston lettuce leaves

1. To prepare dressing, combine all dressing ingredients in a small bowl; stir well.

2. To prepare filling, heat a large nonstick skillet over medium-high heat. Add oil to pan; swirl to coat. Add pork and ginger; cook 6 to 8 minutes or until pork is browned, stirring to crumble. Drain well; return to pan. Stir in 4 teaspoons dressing.

3. Spoon 2 tablespoons pork mixture, 2 tablespoons cucumber, 2 tablespoons carrot, 1½ teaspoons cilantro, 1½ teaspoons mint, about 1 teaspoon onions, and about ¾ teaspoon peanuts into each lettuce leaf; drizzle each with ½ teaspoon dressing. Serves 8 (serving size: 1 wrap)

CALORIES 85; FAT 5.2g (sat1.4g, mono 2.4g, poly1.2g); PROTEIN 6.7g; CARB 1g; FIBER 1g; CHOL 21mg; IRON 0mg; SODIUM 148mg; CALC 17mg

The sweet-and-sour spark

My introduction to sweet-and-sour meatballs, a quintessential party hors d'oeuvre, came in the third grade, on the occasion of my school's International Day festival. I was partnered with twin sisters, and their mother helped us prepare a tray of the glistening treat to bring into our class to share with the rest of the kids. This was my first experience actually preparing a dish with Asian-inspired flavors. Although the meatballs weren't an authentic Chinese dish, I was impressed by their taste and wanted to learn more about cuisines from other cultures. This experience sparked my curiosity—a curiosity that has lasted a lifetime.

SWEET-AND-SOUR MEATBALLS

HANDS-ON TIME: 13 MINUTES ★ TOTAL TIME: 28 MINUTES

Look for sweet chili sauce on the ethnic aisle at most supermarkets, or in Asian grocery stores. Dark sesame oil and lower-sodium soy sauce deliver tremendous flavor with less sodium and saturated fat.

¼ cup bottled sweet chili sauce, divided

¼ cup lower-sodium soy sauce, divided

3½ teaspoons dark sesame oil, divided

1 tablespoon thinly sliced green onions

3 tablespoons minced shallots

3 large garlic cloves, minced

1 pound ground sirloin

1. Preheat oven to 450°.

2. Combine 1 tablespoon chili sauce, 2 tablespoons soy sauce, ½ teaspoon oil, and green onions in a small bowl. Set aside.

3. Combine 3 tablespoons chili sauce, 2 tablespoons soy sauce, 1 tablespoon oil, shallots, and garlic in a medium bowl. Add beef, stirring gently to combine. Shape meat mixture into 24 (1-inch) meatballs. Arrange meatballs in a single layer on a jelly-roll pan.

4. Bake at 450° for 10 minutes or until done. Remove from oven and let stand 5 minutes. Serve meatballs with dipping sauce. Serves 8 (serving size: 3 meatballs and 1½ teaspoons sauce)

CALORIES 90; FAT 4.5g (sat 1.3g, mono 1.8g, poly 1.2g); PROTEIN 11.5g; CARB 0.9g; FIBER 0g; CHOL 30mg; IRON 1mg; SODIUM 210mg; CALC 4mg

AMERICA LOVES: CHEESE

The goes-with-everything go-to snack

NORTHWEST
Oregon Tillamook Cheddar

Since 1851, Oregon's wet Tillamook Valley has been producing some of the West's finest cheeses. Known primarily for their medium cheddar, the co-op of Oregon farmers that contributes to the Tillamook brand also makes yogurt, sour cream, butter, and ice cream.

WEST
San Francisco Teleme

This is a creamy, semi-soft cheese originally produced on the windy coastline north of San Francisco in the 1940s. It's a fresh, rindless cheese prized for its milky flavor and for a soft texture that makes it excellent for melting.

SOUTHWEST
Arizona Cotija

This hard cow's- or goat's-milk cheese is sometimes referred to as the "Mexican Parmesan" for the way it's crumbled over finished dishes of Hispanic origin. It is a dry, firm, salty cheese with a slightly granular, crumbly consistency. Originally produced only in Mexico, where it was named after the Michoacán town of Cotija de la Paz, it is now produced in the States as well.

NORTHEAST
Vermont La Luna
La Luna, an aged cheese made from organic, raw goat's milk, is produced by Blue Ledge Farms in Salisbury, Vermont. This semi-firm cheese is a Vermont original that's akin to Gouda and Havarti. It has a milky flavor with mild herbal notes reminiscent of fresh grass.

MIDWEST
Iowa Maytag Blue
Since 1941, Maytag Dairy Farms has been producing world-acclaimed blue cheese with the milk from its prize-winning herd of Holstein cattle. They still use a time-honored process for making blue cheese that was developed at Iowa State University in the 1940s.

EAST
Philadelphia Cream Cheese
This fresh, high-fat cheese is not native to Philadelphia, but to New York, where it was first produced in the 1870s when cream was added to Neufchâtel cheese. It wasn't sold under the brand name "Philadelphia Brand Cream Cheese" until the 1880s.

SOUTH
Alabama Goat Cheese
Belle Chevre, a French-style goat's milk cheese, is made in a small creamery in rural Elkmont, Alabama. The soil and climate of the Southern terroir is believed to be the key factor in the cheese's award-winning indulgent texture and distinctive flavors. Great care goes into the production and packaging of this fine cheese since both are done by hand.

SOUTHEAST
Pimiento Cheese
A mixture of shredded cheddar cheese, diced pimientos, and mayonnaise, this Southern staple has its origins in North Carolina. Southeast states account for 80% of all pimiento cheese spread sold in the U.S., but most Southern cooks maintain that the best is always homemade.

BLUE CHEESE BALL

HANDS-ON TIME: 15 MINUTES ★ TOTAL TIME: 8 HOURS 15 MINUTES

Cheese balls were originally the tangy result of a collection of leftover cheeses. Modern riffs have since become more selective, adding high-quality cheeses, herbs, and even dried fruits to the mix. My recipe is a lighter interpretation of the retro-chic dish.

4 ounces blue cheese, crumbled (about 1 cup)

1 tablespoon nonfat buttermilk

5 ounces fat-free cream cheese, softened (about ⅔ cup)

3 ounces ⅓-less-fat cream cheese, softened (about ⅓ cup)

3 tablespoons minced pitted Medjool dates (2 to 3 dates)

1 tablespoon minced shallots

½ teaspoon grated lemon rind

¼ teaspoon kosher salt

¼ teaspoon freshly ground black pepper

¼ cup minced fresh flat-leaf parsley

2½ tablespoons finely chopped walnuts, toasted

1. Place first 4 ingredients in a large bowl; beat with a mixer at medium speed 2 minutes or until smooth and creamy. Add dates and next 4 ingredients (through pepper); beat at medium speed until well blended, scraping sides of bowl as necessary.

2. Spoon cheese mixture onto a large sheet of plastic wrap. Form into a ball, using a rubber spatula. Wrap cheese ball in plastic wrap; chill overnight.

3. Combine parsley and walnuts in a shallow dish. Unwrap cheese ball; gently roll in nut mixture, coating well. Place on a serving plate. Serve immediately, or cover and refrigerate until ready to serve. Serves 14 (serving size: 2 tablespoons)

CALORIES 78; FAT 4.8g (sat 2.6g, mono 1.2g, poly 0.7g); PROTEIN 4.2g; CARB 5.3g; FIBER 0.5g; CHOL 12mg; IRON 0.2mg; SODIUM 229mg; CALC 74mg

HONEY-GLAZED ALMONDS

HANDS-ON TIME: 5 MINUTES ★ TOTAL TIME: 25 MINUTES

Spiced nuts are usually slowly baked; this stovetop version speeds up the process. The smoky-spicy snack will store well in an airtight container for several days.

1½ cups raw, unblanched almonds

1 tablespoon sugar

1½ tablespoons honey

½ teaspoon ground chipotle chile powder

¼ teaspoon ground cumin

¼ teaspoon salt

1. Line a large baking sheet with parchment paper.
2. Place almonds in a medium nonstick skillet; cook over medium heat 6 minutes or until lightly toasted, shaking pan frequently. Combine sugar and next 4 ingredients (through salt) in a 2-cup glass measure. Microwave at HIGH 30 seconds. Add honey mixture to pan, and cook 2 minutes, stirring constantly. Arrange almond mixture on prepared baking sheet in a single layer; let stand 10 minutes. Break apart any clusters. Store in an airtight container for up to 3 days. Serves 10 (serving size: about 16 almonds)

CALORIES 138; FAT 10.6g (sat 0.8g, mono 6.6g, poly 2.6g); PROTEIN 4.6g; CARB 8.5g; FIBER 2.6g; CHOL 0mg; IRON 0.8mg; SODIUM 63mg; CALC 57mg

GUACAMOLE

HANDS-ON TIME: 9 MINUTES ★ TOTAL TIME: 9 MINUTES

Guacamole was concocted by the Aztecs over 400 years ago. Since then it has become an American party-food favorite and restaurant menu staple. Tortilla chips are the natural accompaniment, but you can also serve it with veggies like jicama, bell peppers, and radishes.

¼ cup finely chopped red onion

¼ teaspoon kosher salt

2 ripe avocados, peeled and chopped (about 1½ cups)

½ cup chopped plum tomato (1 large)

1 tablespoon fresh lime juice

1. Place onion, salt, and avocado in a medium bowl; mash with back of a wooden spoon. Stir in tomato. Add lime juice, stirring until avocado just begins to lose its shape but is still very chunky. Serves 6 (serving size: ¼ cup)

CALORIES 112; FAT 9.9g (sat 1.4g, mono 6.6g, poly 1.4g); PROTEIN 1.5g; CARB 9.6g; FIBER 4.7g; CHOL 10mg; IRON 0.4mg; SODIUM 104mg; CALC 11mg

Best-ever guacamole

When I served as a judge for the Best Guacamole Contest at the California Avocado Festival in Carpinteria, California, I tasted 29 different guacamoles. Needless to say, I learned a few things about what makes a guac rock or flop. These are a couple of the most important tips I learned about how to make great guacamole:

1. Rich, nutty Haas avocados are key—the riper the avocado, the more buttery the texture. You'll know they're ripe when they give just a little to gentle finger-tip pressure.

2. If you think everything tastes better with bacon, know that "everything" doesn't include guacamole.

3. Sprinkle generously with salt and add a hefty squeeze of lime juice for seasoning and some acidity.

4. Add a little bit of sweet onion, very finely chopped—or better yet, grind it into the guacamole in a molcajete (a mortar and pestle hewn from volcanic rock)—to add a nice hint of spice and depth of flavor.

5. Add tomato; it brightens the flavor and adds sweetness and color.

6. Don't overthink it! Like most dishes, guacamole is best with excellent ingredients that are treated simply.

ARTICHOKE-SPINACH DIP

HANDS-ON TIME: 30 MINUTES ★ TOTAL TIME: 60 MINUTES

Order this warm, creamy, and cheesy dish in most American chain restaurants and you could be looking at nearly a day's worth of calories! Not so here; my version has fewer than 150 per serving. Assemble the dish up to two days ahead and bake just before serving. Serve with tortilla chips, pita chips, or sliced baguette.

8 ounces part-skim mozza-rella cheese, shredded (about 2 cups), divided

½ cup fat-free sour cream

¼ cup (1 ounce) grated fresh Parmesan cheese, divided

¼ teaspoon freshly ground black pepper

3 garlic cloves, crushed

1 (14-ounce) can artichoke hearts, drained and chopped

1 (8-ounce) block ⅓-less-fat cream cheese, softened

1 (8-ounce) block fat-free cream cheese, softened

½ (10-ounce) package frozen chopped spinach, thawed, drained, and squeezed dry

Baked pita or tortilla chips (optional)

Mel's Burger Bar, New York, NY

1. Preheat oven to 350°.
2. Combine 1½ cups mozzarella, sour cream, 2 tablespoons Parmesan, and next 6 ingredients (through spinach) in a large bowl; stir until well blended.
3. Spoon mixture into a 1½-quart glass or ceramic baking dish. Sprinkle with ½ cup mozzarella and 2 tablespoons Parmesan.
4. Bake at 350° for 30 minutes or until bubbly and golden brown. Serve with pita or tortilla chips, if desired. Serves 22 (serving size: ¼ cup)

CALORIES 148; FAT 5g (sat 2.9g, mono 1.5g, poly 0.5g); PROTEIN 7.7g; CARB 18.3g; FIBER 1.5g; CHOL 17mg; IRON 0.6mg; SODIUM 318mg; CALC 164mg

LIGHTEN UP

A better-for-you dip

My version omits the butter and cream and substitutes a few practical low-fat, low-calorie choices to slash the calories in this popular dip by 75%.

TEXAS CAVIAR

HANDS-ON TIME: 15 MINUTES ★ TOTAL TIME: 15 MINUTES

Although this dish originally hails from Texas, I first sampled these jazzed-up black-eyed peas at Paco's Tacos and Tequila restaurant in Charlotte, North Carolina. Texas caviar makes a perfect side for barbecue but is equally delicious as a starter salad or a dip for tortilla chips.

2 tablespoons red wine vinegar

2 tablespoons canola or grapeseed oil

½ teaspoon kosher salt

½ teaspoon ground cumin

¼ teaspoon freshly ground black pepper

1 small garlic clove, minced

1 cup fresh corn kernels (about 2 ears)

⅔ cup chopped, drained, rinsed, bottled roasted red bell peppers (about 2 peppers)

½ cup finely chopped green onions

¼ cup chopped pickled jalapeño peppers

2 tablespoons chopped fresh cilantro

1 (15.8-ounce) can black-eyed peas, rinsed and drained

1. Combine first 6 ingredients (through garlic) in a large bowl, stirring with a whisk. Add corn and remaining ingredients; toss well. Chill until ready to serve. Serves 12 (serving size: ¼ cup)

CALORIES 70; FAT 2.3g (sat 0.3g, mono 1.6g, poly 0.4g); PROTEIN 2.5g; CARB 20g; FIBER 2g; CHOL 0mg; IRON 0mg; SODIUM 215mg; CALC 14mg

FIVE-LAYER DIP

HANDS-ON TIME: 10 MINUTES ★ TOTAL TIME: 60 MINUTES

This popular party dip gets a face-lift with a few simple changes. I keep fat and calories to a minimum by swapping whole-kernel corn for the customary layer of ground beef.

6 (8-inch) flour tortillas
Cooking spray
½ teaspoon paprika
2 teaspoons fresh lime juice
½ teaspoon ground cumin
1 (16-ounce) can organic refried beans (such as Amy's or Eden Organic)
1 cup organic bottled salsa (such as Muir Glen)
⅔ cup frozen whole-kernel corn, thawed
¼ cup chopped green onions
2 tablespoons chopped black olives
3 ounces preshredded 4-cheese Mexican blend cheese (about ¾ cup)
¾ cup (6 ounces) light sour cream
2 tablespoons chopped fresh cilantro

1. Preheat oven to 350°.
2. Cut each tortilla into 8 wedges, and arrange wedges in single layers on 2 baking sheets. Lightly spray wedges with cooking spray; sprinkle with paprika. Bake at 350° for 15 minutes or until lightly browned and crisp. Cool.
3. Combine juice, cumin, and beans in a medium bowl, stirring until well combined. Spread mixture evenly into an 11 x 7–inch glass or ceramic baking dish coated with cooking spray. Spread salsa evenly over beans. Combine corn, onions, and olives; spoon corn mixture evenly over salsa. Sprinkle cheese over corn mixture. Bake at 350° for 20 minutes or until bubbly. Let stand 10 minutes. Top with sour cream; sprinkle with cilantro. Serve with tortilla chips. Serves 12 (serving size: ½ cup dip and 4 tortilla wedges)

CALORIES 162; FAT 5.6g (sat 2.4g, mono 1.9g, poly 0.4g); PROTEIN 6.8g; CARB 23.2g; FIBER 2.8g; CHOL 13mg; IRON 1.3mg; SODIUM 331mg; CALC 143mg

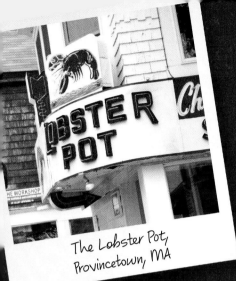

The Lobster Pot,
Provincetown, MA

MAIN COURSE

Entrées &
One-Dish Meals

Mojave Desert Chili Cook-Off,
Mesquite, NV

There's really nothing more soul-satisfying than good ol' American comfort food. It just makes us feel good.

*i*t doesn't ask much of you, except that you eat it while it's hot, and in return, it just makes you feel loved. But what *I* don't always love are the fat and calories that come with it. For these recipes, I chose those foods I dream about, and my family craves, and I got to work. The challenge was keeping every last bit of crispy, crunchy, creamy, cheesy comfort while cutting the calories. My secret? I added stealth veggies to classic dishes, thickened sauces with a roux instead of heavy cream, and modified the portion sizes just a tad. If you've been lucky enough to inherit your grandmother's china, pull it out for these; plate sizes back then were 50% smaller so you'll never notice the difference.

Cioppino, p. 179

Big spoonful of gumbo
scooped from a 40-gallon vat

Pasta Puttanesca, p. 172

Smothered Pork
Chops, p. 127

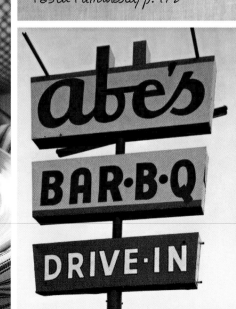
abe's
BAR·B·Q
DRIVE·IN

Me tossing pizza dough
at the World Pizza Games,
Las Vegas, NV

SMOTHERED PORK CHOPS

HANDS-ON TIME: 38 MINUTES ★ TOTAL TIME: 53 MINUTES

This rich sauce gets its velvety consistency from a flour roux, chicken stock, and a touch of half-and-half.

2.25 ounces all-purpose flour (about ½ cup)

1½ teaspoons freshly ground black pepper

¾ cup panko (Japanese bread-crumbs)

1 cup half-and-half, divided

1 large egg

4 (4-ounce) boneless center-cut loin pork chops (about ½ inch thick)

½ teaspoon kosher salt

2 tablespoons canola oil

1 tablespoon butter

½ cup finely chopped onion

1 (8-ounce) package cremini mushrooms, sliced

1 garlic clove, minced

⅓ cup dry white wine

½ teaspoon all-purpose flour

1 teaspoon water

1 cup unsalted chicken stock

2 tablespoons chopped fresh flat-leaf parsley

1 tablespoon chopped fresh chives

Durham, NC

1. Combine ½ cup flour and pepper in a shallow bowl or dish. Place panko in a second shallow bowl or dish. Combine ½ cup half-and-half and egg in a third shallow bowl or dish; stir with a whisk.
2. Sprinkle both sides of pork chops with salt. Dredge 1 pork chop in flour mixture. Dip in egg mixture; dredge in breadcrumb mixture. Repeat procedure with remaining pork chops, flour mixture, egg mixture, and breadcrumb mixture. Cover and chill 15 minutes.
3. Heat 1 tablespoon oil in a large nonstick skillet over medium-high heat until hot. Add chops to pan; cook 2 minutes or until lightly browned. Remove chops from pan; add remaining 1 table-spoon oil to pan. Turn chops over; return to pan. Cook 2 minutes or until lightly browned. Remove from pan; keep warm.
4. Heat butter in pan over medium-high heat. Add onion; sauté 1 minute. Add mushrooms; sauté 3 minutes. Add garlic; sauté 1 minute. Add wine to pan; cook until liquid almost evaporates, scraping pan to loosen browned bits. Combine ½ teaspoon flour and 1 teaspoon water in a small bowl; stir with a whisk. Add to cooking liquid in pan. Bring to a boil; cook 1 minute, stirring constantly. Add stock; bring to a boil. Cook until reduced to 1¼ cups (about 6 minutes). Stir in ½ cup half-and-half. Cook 3 minutes or until thick, stirring constantly. Remove from heat; stir in parsley and chives. Serve sauce with pork chops. Serves 4 (serving size: 1 pork chop and about ⅓ cup sauce)

CALORIES 399; FAT 20.5g (sat 5.5g, mono 8.5g, poly 5g); PROTEIN 28.8g; CARB 22.1g; FIBER 1.9g; CHOL 122mg; IRON 1.8mg; SODIUM 402mg; CALC 84mg

SLOW-ROASTED PULLED PORK

HANDS-ON TIME: 10 MINUTES ★ TOTAL TIME: 4 HOURS 53 MINUTES

This recipe was inspired by one created by Lee and Jack Manfred, a father-son cooking team from Vienna, VA. They're both avid cooks, sports fans, and Notre Dame alumni; this is their legendary dish at tailgates. It's the best pulled pork I've ever eaten—tender meat with flavorful, crispy edges.

Lee and Jack Manfred
pulling their signature pork

1 tablespoon kosher salt
1 tablespoon chili powder
1 tablespoon paprika
1 tablespoon brown sugar
1½ teaspoons garlic powder
1½ teaspoons onion powder
1½ teaspoons ground cumin
1½ teaspoons ground red pepper
1½ teaspoons Hungarian hot paprika
1 (4¾-pound) pork shoulder (Boston butt), trimmed

1. Preheat oven to 300°.
2. Combine first 9 ingredients (through hot paprika). Rub seasoning mixture on all sides of pork. Place pork in a shallow roasting pan.
3. Bake at 300° for 4 hours and 15 minutes or until a thermometer inserted in center registers 190° and pork is very tender.
4. Remove from oven. Cover with foil, and let stand 20 minutes. Remove pork from bone; shred with 2 forks. Serves 13 (serving size: 3 ounces)

CALORIES 243; FAT 15.6g (sat 5.8g, mono 7g, poly 1.9g); PROTEIN 22.1g; CARB 2.1g; FIBER 0.5g; CHOL 85mg; IRON 1.8mg; SODIUM 514mg; CALC 29mg

A pilgrimage to barbecue mecca

for over 30 years, champion grill masters from across America have gathered in Memphis, Tennessee, for the World Championship Barbecue Cooking Contest, the edible portion of a city-wide party known as Memphis in May. On a one-mile stretch along the Mississippi River, more than 250 teams of barbecue kings and queens set up their tents—some with two stories, others with dance floors, and all with hefty charcoal- or wood-fired grills—and begin the three-day cooking event that offers some of the very best in brisket, rib, and whole-hog barbecue.

Despite the constant playfulness and good-natured barbecue banter being tossed around by the participants, each one of the contestants is very serious about technique. The fires are built on Friday and, by the time the sun dips below the horizon, most contestants have placed their pig on the grill. The cooks nurse their meat all night long—adding a rub of spice here, a mop of sauce there, a careful nudge to the meat, a stoke to the fire—and continue until judging the next day.

Secrets of the grill masters? Some use fruitwood for smoking; others use hickory. Whole hogs often get injections of fruit juice or moonshine while they cook or their bellies are loaded with aromatic ingredients like oranges to infuse the pork with flavor. Pork shoulders benefit from a careful blending of "sweet and heat" while on the grill: They're caressed with apricot vinegar or apple juice, and secretive spice rubs provide just the right balance of heat. And for ribs, it's all about proper cooking, so that you get just a mouthful of meat you can tear with your teeth; proper barbecue doesn't actually fall off the bone.

> **More than 250 teams of barbecue kings and queens compete annually at "Memphis in May."**

BARBECUE PORK RIBS

HANDS-ON TIME: 20 MINUTES ★ TOTAL TIME: 3 HOURS

Pork loin back ribs are meaty and lean, so they cook quickly. To ensure they get a nice char and have smoky flavor, start them on a grill with wood chips, but then wrap them in foil and finish in the oven. This ensures even cooking and allows the ribs to make their own pan sauce, which you'll want to spoon over the top when you serve them.

1 cup hickory wood chips

2 cups water

1½ tablespoons Hungarian sweet paprika

1½ tablespoons ground cumin

1 tablespoon dark brown sugar

1½ teaspoons Spanish smoked paprika

1¼ teaspoons ground red pepper

½ teaspoon celery seeds

2 tablespoons canola oil

2 tablespoons cider vinegar

8 garlic cloves, minced

1 (3-pound) rack pork loin back ribs, trimmed

1½ teaspoons kosher salt

Cooking spray

1. Soak wood chips in water 1 hour. Drain well.

2. Preheat grill to medium-high heat using both burners. After preheating, turn the left burner off (leave the right burner on). Place wood chips on heat element on right side. Place a disposable aluminum foil pan on heat element on left (unheated) side. Pour 2 cups water in pan.

3. Combine sweet paprika and next 5 ingredients (through celery seeds) in a small bowl. Stir in oil, vinegar, and garlic to form a paste. Rinse and pat ribs dry. If desired, remove thin membrane from back of ribs by slicing into it with a knife and then pulling it off. (This will make ribs more tender.) Sprinkle both sides of ribs with salt; rub with spice paste. Coat grill rack with cooking spray; place on grill. Place ribs, meaty sides down, on grill rack over direct heat; cover and grill 10 minutes. Turn ribs over, and move them over indirect heat, covering left burner. Cover and grill 20 minutes.

4. Preheat oven to 250°.

5. Remove ribs from grill; wrap with heavy-duty foil. Place foil-wrapped ribs on a baking sheet; bake at 250° for 2 hours or until meat begins to pull away from the bone. Let ribs stand 10 minutes before slicing. Serve with drippings. Serves 7 (serving size: 2 ribs)

CALORIES 317; FAT 19.5g (sat 6.5g, mono 8.9g, poly 3.8g); PROTEIN 23.7g; CARB 3.3g; FIBER 0g; CHOL 24mg; IRON 1.4mg; SODIUM 521mg; CALC 53mg

DANDELION-STUFFED PORK LOIN

HANDS-ON TIME: 37 MINUTES ★ TOTAL TIME: 1 HOUR 22 MINUTES

This is a special-occasion entrée that doesn't take too much time to make. The original version of this recipe won the blue ribbon at the Great Dandelion Cook-Off in Dover, Ohio, and was developed by Sherry Schie.

Pork:

2 tablespoons olive oil

½ cup chopped onion

8 garlic cloves, minced

3 (7-ounce) bunches dandelion greens, trimmed (6 cups)

½ cup muscadine wine or other sweet white wine

½ cup pitted dates, chopped

¼ cup raisins, soaked in 1 cup water

1 cup panko (Japanese breadcrumbs)

1½ tablespoons chopped fresh rosemary

¾ teaspoon kosher salt

1 (3½-pound) boneless pork loin roast, trimmed

⅓ pound thinly sliced pancetta

Cooking spray

Sauce:

1 cup fat-free, lower-sodium chicken broth

¼ cup muscadine wine or other sweet white wine

¼ cup chardonnay or other dry white wine

2 tablespoons cornstarch

1 tablespoon water

2 teaspoons butter

1. Preheat oven to 450°.

2. To prepare pork, heat a large skillet over medium heat. Add oil to pan; swirl to coat. Add onion and garlic; sauté 3 minutes. Add greens and next 3 ingredients (through raisins); cover and cook 4 minutes or until greens wilt, stirring occasionally. Uncover, and cook 3 minutes or until liquid evaporates.

3. Place greens mixture in a food processor; pulse 3 times or until chopped. Transfer mixture to a bowl. Add breadcrumbs, rosemary, and salt, tossing to combine.

4. Cut horizontally through center of pork, cutting to, but not through, other side using a sharp knife; open flat as you would a book. Place pork between 2 sheets of plastic wrap; pound to an even thickness using a meat mallet or small heavy skillet. Layer pancetta over pork. Spread dandelion stuffing over pork, leaving a ½-inch margin around outside edges. Roll up pork, jelly-roll fashion, starting with short side. Secure at 2-inch intervals with twine.

5. Place pork in a shallow pan coated with cooking spray. Bake at 450° for 15 minutes. Reduce oven temperature to 325°; bake 30 minutes or until a thermometer inserted in center registers 145°. Transfer pork to a platter, reserving drippings in pan. Cover pork with foil, and let stand 15 minutes.

6. To prepare sauce, stir broth, ¼ cup muscadine wine, and white wine into pan drippings, scraping pan to loosen browned bits. Pour wine mixture into a small saucepan.

7. Combine cornstarch and 1 tablespoon water in a small bowl. Add cornstarch mixture to broth mixture; bring to a boil. Cook 1 minute, stirring constantly. Remove from heat; stir in butter.

8. Cut pork into 14 slices. Serve with sauce. Serves 14 (serving size: 3 ounces pork and 1½ tablespoons sauce)

CALORIES 242; FAT 6.7g (sat 2.1g, mono 3.1g, poly 1g); PROTEIN 26.3g; CARB 16.2g; FIBER 1.7g; CHOL 78mg; IRON 2mg; SODIUM 273mg; CALC 60mg

A real dandy cook-off

The 25 contestants who enter the Great Dandelion Cook-Off in Dover, Ohio, gather their dandelions from backyards, fields, and roadsides, then use them in ways that reveal something about the thrifty and enterprising aspects of their Midwestern upbringing.

With the blossoms, the contestants make honey, jelly, infused olive oil, and wine. With the stems and roots, they make soups and stews. And the bigger green leaves might be found replacing spinach or other popular greens in a calzone or in a stuffing for pork loin.

The competition is more about sharing ideas than winning, and the whole event has the air of a community picnic. When local cooking teacher Sherry Schie (pictured above) took home the blue ribbon for her Dandelion-Stuffed Pork Tenderloin, she tearfully responded, "I cook because I want to make people happy!" To me, the best home cooking comes from the heart.

A Lone Star favorite

I've heard it said that there are three food groups in Texas: barbecue, Tex-Mex, and chicken-fried steak. Ranking among the very few contenders for state dish of Texas, chicken-fried steak is a slab of tenderized top-round beef that's battered and fried in a pan much like chicken (hence the name), then served up with a healthy dollop of cream gravy.

The dish was originally conceived by German immigrants who, having no veal for their schnitzel, chose the only beef they had on hand to fry on the griddle (and it wasn't porterhouse or filet!).

CHICKEN-FRIED STEAK
WITH MILK GRAVY

HANDS-ON TIME: 40 MINUTES ★ TOTAL TIME: 40 MINUTES

The secret to this steak's crispy crust is crumbled saltine crackers. To achieve a crispy outside and a tender inside, firmly push the cracker crumbs into the cube steak to fill crevices and to keep the steak from shrinking as it cooks.

Steak:

2.25 ounces all-purpose flour (about ½ cup)

½ teaspoon cayenne pepper

¼ teaspoon salt

¼ teaspoon baking powder

¼ teaspoon freshly ground black pepper

8 saltine crackers, crushed

⅓ cup 1% low-fat buttermilk

2 large egg whites

¼ cup canola oil

4 (3-ounce) cube steaks

Gravy:

2 cups 1% low-fat milk

2 tablespoons all-purpose flour

½ teaspoon salt

¼ teaspoon freshly ground black pepper

1. Lightly spoon flour into a dry measuring cup; level with a knife. Combine flour and next 5 ingredients (through crackers) in a shallow bowl. Combine buttermilk and egg whites in another shallow bowl, stirring with a whisk.

2. Heat canola oil in a cast-iron or other nonstick skillet over medium-high heat until oil shimmers.

3. Coat cube steaks with cracker mixture; dip in buttermilk mixture, then coat again in cracker mixture, pressing into steaks. Use all the cracker mixture.

4. Cook steaks until brown and crispy, about 3 minutes on each side. Remove steaks from pan, and place on a rack over a baking sheet.

5. To prepare gravy, place milk in a medium bowl. Whisk 2 tablespoons flour, ½ teaspoon salt, and ¼ teaspoon black pepper into milk. Pour mixture into pan, and cook over medium-high heat, stirring constantly and scraping pan to loosen browned bits, about 5 minutes or until gravy is thick. Serve gravy over steaks. Serves 4 (serving size: 1 steak and about ½ cup gravy)

CALORIES 417; FAT 21.4 (sat 4g, mono 11.5g, poly 4.6g); PROTEIN 28.6g; CARB 26.3g; FIBER 0.8g; CHOL 55mg; IRON 3.1mg; SODIUM 606mg; CALC 200mg

MEATBALLS AND SPAGHETTI

HANDS-ON TIME: 25 MINUTES ★ TOTAL TIME: 1 HOUR 40 MINUTES

It takes a tender hand to make a light meatball. The key is in the rolling; you want to leave air pockets in the meatballs, so shape the balls gently in your hand, making sure not to squash them.

1 tablespoon olive oil

2 cups minced onion

¼ cup water

4 cups lower-sodium marinara sauce

½ cup chopped fresh basil

¼ cup (1 ounce) grated fresh Parmesan cheese

1 teaspoon dried oregano

¼ teaspoon salt

¼ teaspoon crushed red pepper

1 garlic clove, minced

1 large egg, lightly beaten

¾ pound ground sirloin

¾ pound ground pork

1 (1.5-ounce) slice firm white bread, crumbled

8 ounces uncooked spaghetti

Grated fresh Parmesan cheese (optional)

An entry from Carmine's restaurant at the Meatball Madness contest in New York City, NY

1. Heat a large skillet over medium heat. Add oil to pan; swirl to coat. Stir in onion; cover and cook 10 minutes. Uncover; stir, and reduce heat to medium. Cook 15 minutes or until onion is tender, stirring frequently. Add ¼ cup water, stirring to loosen browned bits; cook 10 minutes, stirring frequently. Remove from heat; cool 10 minutes.

2. Place marinara sauce in a Dutch oven. Bring to a simmer over low heat.

3. Combine onion mixture, basil, and next 6 ingredients (through egg) in a large bowl. Add ground sirloin, ground pork, and crumbled bread; stir gently to combine. Shape meat mixture into 18 (2-inch) balls. Place meatballs in sauce. Bring to a boil; cover, reduce heat, and simmer 30 minutes or until meatballs are done.

4. While meatballs simmer, cook pasta according to package directions, omitting salt and fat; drain.

5. Serve meatballs and sauce over pasta. Sprinkle with Parmesan cheese, if desired. Serves 6 (serving size: ⅔ cup pasta, 3 meatballs, and ⅔ cup sauce)

CALORIES 537; FAT 24.3g (sat 8.3g, mono 10.3g, poly 4.1g); PROTEIN 31.4g; CARB 46.7g; FIBER 3.8g; CHOL 113mg; IRON 5.7mg; SODIUM 406mg; CALC 147mg

CHICKEN PARMESAN

HANDS-ON TIME: 35 MINUTES ★ TOTAL TIME: 1 HOUR 10 MINUTES

This is my stepdaughter's favorite dish. To make the cooking process easy, purchase pre-pounded cutlets or ask your butcher to pound them for you.

1 teaspoon dried oregano

2 garlic cloves, minced

1 (25-ounce) jar lower-sodium marinara sauce

2.25 ounces all-purpose flour (about ½ cup)

1 cup panko (Japanese breadcrumbs)

½ cup (2 ounces) grated fresh Parmesan cheese, divided

2 tablespoons water

1 large egg, beaten

6 chicken cutlets or chicken breasts pounded to ⅓-inch thickness (about 1½ pounds)

5 tablespoons olive oil

Cooking spray

6 ounces part-skim mozzarella cheese, shredded (about 1½ cups)

2 tablespoons sliced fresh basil

1. Preheat oven to 375°.

2. Combine first 3 ingredients. Place flour in a shallow bowl or dish. Place breadcrumbs and ¼ cup cheese in a second shallow bowl or dish. Combine 2 tablespoons water and egg in a third bowl; stir with a whisk.

3. Working with 1 cutlet at a time, dredge cutlets in flour; dip in egg mixture, and dredge in breadcrumb mixture.

4. Heat a large nonstick skillet over medium-high heat. Add 2½ tablespoons oil to pan; swirl to coat. Cook half of cutlets 3 minutes on each side or until golden brown. Remove cutlets from pan; keep warm. Repeat procedure with remaining oil and cutlets.

5. Pour ⅔ cup pasta sauce mixture into bottom of a 3-quart casserole coated with cooking spray. Arrange chicken cutlets in a single layer over sauce mixture; cover with remaining sauce mixture. Top with mozzarella cheese and ¼ cup Parmesan cheese.

6. Cover and bake at 375° for 20 minutes. Uncover and bake an additional 15 minutes or until cheese melts and top is brown and bubbly around edges. Sprinkle with basil. Serves 6 (serving size: 1 chicken cutlet and ½ cup sauce)

CALORIES 428; FAT 22.3g (sat 5.7g, mono 11.4g, poly 4.4g); PROTEIN 38.7g; CARB 16g; FIBER 1.5g; CHOL 128mg; IRON 2.5mg; SODIUM 597mg; CALC 391mg

MEAT LOAF

HANDS-ON TIME: 15 MINUTES
TOTAL TIME: 1 HOUR 25 MINUTES

Whether you enjoy it hot out of the oven or on a cold sandwich, meat loaf is a time-tested American classic. Here, it gains nutrition with the addition of baby spinach and excitement with a sweet-and-spicy glaze.

Meat Loaf:

1 (5-ounce) package fresh baby spinach
2 tablespoons water
1 pound ground sirloin
½ pound ground veal
½ pound ground pork
1½ cups finely chopped onion
2 tablespoons Worcestershire sauce
1½ teaspoons dry mustard
1 teaspoon kosher salt
½ teaspoon dried thyme
½ teaspoon freshly ground black pepper
1 large egg
1 large egg white
½ cup uncooked old-fashioned rolled oats
Cooking spray

Glaze:

¼ cup ketchup
2 tablespoons brown sugar
2 tablespoons cider vinegar

1. Preheat oven to 450°.
2. To prepare meat loaf, heat a large sauté pan over medium heat; add spinach and 2 tablespoons water to pan. Cover and steam 2 minutes or until spinach wilts. Remove pan from heat; cool 5 minutes.
3. Combine ground sirloin, veal, pork, and next 8 ingredients (through egg white) in a large bowl; gently mix just until combined. Add spinach and oats; gently mix until blended.
4. In a 9 x 13–inch glass or ceramic baking dish coated with cooking spray, shape mixture into a 9 x 5–inch loaf.
5. To prepare glaze, combine ketchup, brown sugar, and cider vinegar, stirring with a whisk until blended. Brush glaze over meat loaf. Bake at 450° for 15 minutes. Reduce oven temperature to 350°. Bake an additional 45 minutes or until done; let stand 10 minutes before slicing. Serves 8 (serving size: 1 slice meat loaf)

CALORIES 218; FAT 6.8g (sat 2.5g, mono 2.6g, poly 0.8g); PROTEIN 25.3g; CARB 14.7g; FIBER 1.9g; CHOL 93mg; IRON 2.7mg; SODIUM 498mg; CALC 42mg

CHICKEN MARBELLA

HANDS-ON TIME: 18 MINUTES ★ TOTAL TIME: 9 HOURS 3 MINUTES

Various adaptations of this popular recipe from the Silver Palate Cookbook have been a go-to dinner party favorite for decades. It's a simple and delicious one-dish recipe for the busy host, and tastes best when prepared a day or two ahead.

⅔ cup pitted dried plums
½ cup packed brown sugar
½ cup dry white wine
⅓ cup pitted green olives
¼ cup capers
¼ cup red wine vinegar
¼ cup olive oil
2 tablespoons chopped fresh oregano
6 garlic cloves, chopped
3 bay leaves
2 bone-in chicken breast halves, skinned
2 bone-in chicken thighs, skinned
2 chicken drumsticks, skinned
2 tablespoons chopped fresh parsley

1. Combine dried plums and next 9 ingredients (through bay leaves) in a large zip-top plastic bag. Add chicken; seal and marinate in refrigerator 8 hours, turning bag occasionally.
2. Preheat oven to 350°.
3. Remove chicken from bag, reserving marinade.
4. Arrange chicken in a single layer in a 13 x 9–inch glass or ceramic baking dish; pour reserved marinade evenly over chicken.
5. Bake for 350° for 45 minutes or until chicken is done, basting about every 10 minutes with baking liquid.
6. Place chicken, dried plums, olives, and capers on a platter, reserving pan drippings. Discard bay leaves. Sprinkle chicken with parsley, and serve with reserved pan drippings. Serves 4 (serving size: 1 breast half or 1 thigh plus 1 drumstick and about ¼ cup plum mixture)

CALORIES 417; FAT 15g (sat 2.9g, mono 8.6g, poly 2.4g); PROTEIN 37.8g; CARB 28.4g; FIBER 1.6g; CHOL 149mg; IRON 1.6mg; SODIUM 564mg; CALC 58mg

Best. Chicken. Ever.

When Julee Rosso and Sheila Lukins decided to write the *Silver Palate Cookbook* in the early 1980s, their Upper East Side gourmet take-out shop was already a huge success. Chicken Marbella was the first main-dish course offered at their restaurant, and after the recipe was printed in the cookbook, it became a staple of Manhattan dinner parties.

The dish is marinated for at least eight hours, which keeps the meat moist, and the combination of prunes, olives, and capers is unexpected and delicious. It reheats beautifully, so it's a favorite dish to make ahead of time.

Everyone I know falls in love with this sweet and savory New York classic: One mom I know serves it without fail every Friday night, and my husband just can't get enough.

CHICKEN DIVAN

HANDS-ON TIME: 30 MINUTES ★ TOTAL TIME: 1 HOUR 20 MINUTES

In the early part of the 20th century, chicken divan was the signature dish of the elegant Divan Parisien in New York's Chatham Hotel. Years later, the Campbell Soup Company redeveloped the recipe for the back of the can of condensed cream of chicken soup. My version skips the can, which reduces the sodium.

2 tablespoons butter

1 cup finely chopped onion

1 (8-ounce) container cremini mushrooms, sliced

½ cup dry white wine

2 tablespoons all-purpose flour

1¼ cups unsalted chicken stock

¾ cup 2% reduced-fat milk

1 teaspoon kosher salt

¼ teaspoon freshly ground black pepper

1.3 ounces sharp cheddar cheese, shredded (about ⅓ cup)

¼ cup canola mayonnaise

1 tablespoon fresh lemon juice

4 cups broccoli florets (about 2 large crowns), steamed

1 pound skinless, boneless chicken breast, cooked and cut into 1-inch chunks

Cooking spray

3 tablespoons grated fresh Parmesan cheese

½ cup panko (Japanese bread-crumbs)

THE DIVAN PARISIEN RESTAURANT

1. Preheat oven to 350°.

2. Melt butter in a large skillet over medium-high heat. Add onion to pan; sauté 2 minutes. Add mushrooms; sauté 5 minutes. Add wine. Bring to a boil; boil, uncovered, 3 minutes or until liquid almost evaporates.

3. Sprinkle flour over mushrooms. Cook, stirring constantly, 1 minute. Stir in stock and next 3 ingredients (through pepper). Bring to a boil; reduce heat, and simmer, uncovered, 7 minutes or until mixture thickens, stirring occasionally. Remove from heat, and let stand 3 minutes.

4. Stir in cheddar cheese, mayonnaise, and lemon juice. Stir in broccoli and chicken. Spoon mixture into a 13 x 9–inch glass or ceramic baking dish coated with cooking spray.

5. Sprinkle 1 tablespoon Parmesan cheese over top of casserole. Sprinkle panko over cheese; coat panko with cooking spray. Sprinkle 2 tablespoons Parmesan cheese over panko.

6. Bake, uncovered, at 350° for 20 to 22 minutes or until bubbly and browned. Let stand 10 minutes before serving. Serves 6 (serving size: ⅙ of casserole)

CALORIES 271; FAT 12.5g (sat 5.2g, mono 4.2g, poly 1.6g); PROTEIN 24.5g; CARB 14.2g; FIBER 2.4g; CHOL 71mg; IRON 1.2mg; SODIUM 667mg; CALC 162mg

CHICKEN TIKKA MASALA

HANDS-ON TIME: 10 MINUTES ★ TOTAL TIME: 2 HOURS 50 MINUTES

Chicken tikka masala is probably the most popular dish in Indian restaurants in America. My version was inspired by New York-based Indian chef Suvir Saran's take on the original.

Devi, Suvir Saran's restaurant,
New York City, NY

2 medium onions, cut into wedges

5 garlic cloves

2 teaspoons ground cumin, divided

1½ teaspoons ground red pepper, divided

1 (2-inch) piece peeled fresh ginger, sliced

½ cup plain fat-free Greek yogurt

1 tablespoon fresh lemon juice

6 skinless, boneless chicken thighs (1¾ pounds)

¾ teaspoon kosher salt, divided

Cooking spray

3 tablespoons canola oil

1 (2-inch) cinnamon stick

1 teaspoon ground coriander

½ teaspoon ground turmeric

1½ cups crushed tomatoes

¾ cup half-and-half

¼ cup milk

2 tablespoons cilantro leaves

1. Preheat oven to 375°. Place onion and garlic in a food processor; process until a smooth paste forms. Spoon half of paste into a small bowl; cover and chill. Add 1 teaspoon cumin, 1 teaspoon red pepper, and ginger to remaining paste in food processor; process until smooth. Stir in yogurt and lemon juice.

2. Combine chicken and yogurt mixture in a large zip-top plastic bag; seal and marinate in refrigerator 2 hours.

3. Remove chicken from bag; discard marinade. Sprinkle ½ teaspoon salt evenly over both sides of chicken. Place chicken on a rack coated with cooking spray; place rack in a foil-lined pan. Bake at 375° for 16 minutes or until done, turning after 8 minutes. Let stand 10 minutes; cut chicken into bite-sized pieces.

4. Heat a large nonstick skillet over medium-low heat. Add oil to pan; swirl to coat. Add cinnamon stick; cook 1 minute or until fragrant, stirring frequently. Stir in 1 teaspoon cumin, ½ teaspoon red pepper, ¼ teaspoon salt, coriander, and turmeric; cook 1 minute, stirring constantly. Reduce heat to low; stir in reserved onion-garlic paste. Cook 12 minutes or until lightly browned, stirring occasionally. Stir in tomatoes; bring to a simmer over medium heat, and cook 8 minutes, stirring occasionally. Stir in half-and-half and milk; bring to a simmer. Stir in chicken; simmer 2 minutes or until heated. Sprinkle with cilantro. Serves 4 (serving size: about 1 cup)

CALORIES 333; FAT 16.8g (sat 4.2g, mono 6.9g, poly 3.3g); PROTEIN 30.5g; CARB 15.8g; FIBER 3.5g; CHOL 137mg; IRON 4.8mg; SODIUM 470mg; CALC 119mg

AMERICA LOVES: FIRE
Local eats that bring the heat

NORTHWEST
Wood-Plank Smoked Salmon

Salmon was a staple ingredient of the Pacific Northwest's Native American population. Fillets were tied to planks of alder or cedar, then smoked over open fires or in smokehouses to preserve the fish. Today, this is done using store-bought wood boards near beach bonfires or in modern grills.

WEST
Pizza on the Grill

On the West Coast, barbecuing is a year-round activity. Pizza is a natural choice; the dough is a delicious canvas for all types of fresh vegetables, cheese, and other ingredients, and grilling pizza adds lots of natural flavor while keeping it light.

SOUTHWEST
Texas Brisket

Good old-fashioned slow-smoked beef brisket is practically a religion in the Lone Star State. Brisket, a tough and stringy piece of meat, can become meltingly tender when slow-cooked over a smoky, water-logged hardwood fire. Each Texan has a secret recipe, but most begin with a spicy rub, lengthy marinade, and low fire in a covered grill.

NORTHEAST
Lobster Bake

Along the rugged coastline of Maine, lobster bakes have been a tradition for centuries. Usually, a fire is built right on the beach. Lobsters (and often clams, potatoes, and corn, too) are placed on a large griddle kept aloft from the flames by a framework of large stones or bricks.

MIDWEST
Kansas City Burnt Ends

The fatty, pointed end of a beef brisket may seem like low-grade meat to some, but for the Kansas City barbecue crowd, it's a choice cut. The end is trimmed away (either before or after the brisket is cooked), seasoned again, and returned to the grill until dark brown and tender; it is usually served with plenty of barbecue sauce.

EAST
Steamed Crabs

When Native Americans first introduced European settlers to choice spots for harvesting the region's blue crabs, the early colonists quickly set about building seaside fires on which to place pots for steaming. In the 1940s, Old Bay Seasoning was added for flavor; spiced, steamed crabs remain an Eastern seaboard favorite today.

SOUTH
Pig Pickin'

Unless you're from the South, you may not have heard of a pig pickin'. A whole hog is cooked over a pit of glowing coals until the skin is crisp and glossy and the meat meltingly tender. The meat is picked right from the carcass to feed a crowd.

SOUTHEAST
Frogmore Stew

When this lowcountry stew originated in the Frogmore community of St. Helena Island off the South Carolina coast, it was a chunky seafood mixture cooked slowly over a beachside bonfire in a massive cast-iron pot. The mixture of shrimp, corn, potatoes, and kielbasa is still a casual-cooking favorite.

MAINE LOBSTER BAKE

HANDS-ON TIME: 32 MINUTES ★ TOTAL TIME: 32 MINUTES

An authentic lobster bake is a memorable and festive event. This recipe was inspired by my friend and food photographer Ted Axelrod. He steams lobsters, clams, corn, and potatoes in a large pot covered with seaweed. My version uses a simple stovetop cooking method.

1 pound steamer clams, scrubbed

2 tablespoons freshly ground black pepper

8 small red bliss potatoes (about ¾ pound)

2 ears shucked corn, cut in half

4 (1-pound) whole live Maine lobsters

¼ cup unsalted butter

2 tablespoons fresh lemon juice

1. Rinse clams under cold running water; place in a large bowl. Cover with cold water; add black pepper. Let stand 30 minutes; drain and rinse. (This helps clean the clams of any grit.)

2. Add water to a large stockpot to a depth of 2 inches; bring to a boil. Add potatoes and corn; steam, covered, 5 minutes. Add lobsters headfirst, and add clams; steam, covered, 8 to 10 minutes. Discard any unopened clam shells.

3. Combine butter and lemon juice in a small saucepan; cook over medium-low heat until butter melts.

4. Divide lobster, clams, corn, and potatoes among 4 large plates. Ladle broth from bottom of stockpot into a bowl for dipping clams. Serve with melted lemon-butter. Serves 4 (serving size: 1 lobster, ¼ of clams, 1 piece of corn, 2 potatoes, and 4 teaspoons lemon-butter)

CALORIES 455; FAT 15g (sat 7.2g, mono 4.7g, poly 2.8g); PROTEIN 45.6g; CARB 34.1g; FIBER 3.4g; CHOL 283mg; IRON 8.8mg; SODIUM 633mg; CALC 230mg

My friend Ted at the stove

CATFISH CLASSIQUE

HANDS-ON TIME: 37 MINUTES ★ TOTAL TIME: 37 MINUTES

In the Deep South, cooks in local catfish houses typically coat the fillets in a mixture of cornmeal and flour, then deep-fry to a golden brown.

4.5 ounces all-purpose flour (about 1 cup)

1¼ cups plain yellow cornmeal

2 tablespoons flour

1 teaspoon freshly ground black pepper

1 cup nonfat buttermilk

1 large egg, lightly beaten

5 cups peanut or canola oil

4 (4-ounce) farm-raised catfish fillets

¾ teaspoon kosher salt, divided

2 applewood-smoked bacon slices

1 tablespoon butter

18 medium shrimp, peeled and deveined (about 1 pound)

½ cup finely chopped onion

1 teaspoon minced fresh garlic

1 cup 2% reduced-fat milk

¾ cup fat-free, lower-sodium chicken broth

¼ cup sliced green onions

1. Preheat oven to 250°. Place 1 cup flour in a shallow dish or bowl. Combine cornmeal, 2 tablespoons flour, and pepper in a second shallow dish, stirring well with a whisk. Combine buttermilk and egg in a third shallow bowl or dish, stirring well with a whisk.

2. Heat oil to 385° in a Dutch oven. Sprinkle both sides of fillets with ½ teaspoon salt. Dredge 2 fillets in flour. Dip in buttermilk mixture, and dredge in cornmeal mixture. Fry breaded fillets for 5 minutes or until golden brown and fish flakes easily when tested with a fork. Place fried fillets on a wire rack in a jelly-roll pan, and keep warm in a 250° oven. Repeat procedure with remaining fillets, flour, buttermilk mixture, and cornmeal mixture.

3. Cook bacon in a large nonstick skillet over medium heat until crisp. Remove bacon from pan; crumble. Add butter to drippings in pan. Add shrimp; sauté 3 to 5 minutes or until done. Remove shrimp from pan; keep warm. Add onion to pan; sauté 3 minutes or until tender. Add garlic; sauté 30 seconds. Sprinkle with 2 tablespoons flour; cook 1 minute, stirring constantly. Stir in milk, broth, and ¼ teaspoon salt; bring to a simmer. Cook 3 minutes or until slightly thick, stirring frequently.

4. Place 1 catfish fillet on each of 6 plates; top each serving with about ⅓ cup sauce, 3 shrimp, 2 teaspoons green onions, and crumbled bacon. Serve immediately. Serves 6 (serving size: 1 topped fillet)

CALORIES 398; FAT 22.4g (sat 5.9g, mono 8.9g, poly 5g); PROTEIN 29g; CARB 18.9g; FIBER 1g; CHOL 125mg; IRON 1.2mg; SODIUM 611mg; CALC 107mg

OVEN-FRIED FISH STICKS
WITH TARTAR SAUCE

HANDS-ON TIME: 20 MINUTES ★ TOTAL TIME: 50 MINUTES

Fish sticks have been a staple since the 1950s. The premade, frozen variety offers a simple, inexpensive way to get dinner on the table, but this homemade version, which uses fresh cod, is superior in flavor, texture, and nutrition. They're definitely worth the time it takes to make them.

Fish Sticks:

4.5 ounces all-purpose flour (about 1 cup)

1½ cups panko (Japanese breadcrumbs)

3 tablespoons water

1 large egg, lightly beaten

1¼ pounds cod fillets (½ inch thick)

Cooking spray

½ teaspoon kosher salt

Tartar Sauce:

⅓ cup light mayonnaise

2 tablespoons chopped kosher dill pickles

1 tablespoon finely chopped red onion

1 tablespoon chopped fresh parsley

1 tablespoon capers, rinsed, drained, and chopped

1 tablespoon fresh lemon juice

1. Preheat oven to 375°.
2. To prepare fish sticks, place flour in a shallow dish or bowl. Place breadcrumbs in a second shallow dish or bowl. Combine 3 tablespoons water and egg in a third shallow dish or bowl, stirring with a whisk.
3. Cut fish into 20 (4 x ½–inch) strips. Dredge fish in flour, shaking off excess. Dip fish in egg mixture, and dredge in breadcrumbs. Place on a baking sheet coated with cooking spray. Coat fish with cooking spray.
4. Bake at 375° for 30 minutes or until crisp. Sprinkle fish sticks with salt.
5. To prepare tartar sauce, combine all sauce ingredients in a small bowl. Serve tartar sauce with fish. Serves 4 (serving size: 5 fish sticks and 3 tablespoons tartar sauce)

CALORIES 279; FAT 8.6g (sat 1.4g, mono 3.4g, poly 2.8g); PROTEIN 29g; CARB 19.3g; FIBER 0.8g; CHOL 91mg; IRON 1.5mg; SODIUM 592mg; CALC 34mg

TUNA CASSEROLE

HANDS-ON TIME: 30 MINUTES ★ TOTAL TIME: 50 MINUTES

This American classic is a great cold-weather family meal. My version takes out some of the fat and sodium but keeps the flavor and satisfaction. Petite peas add a touch of sweetness to this rich dish.

8 ounces uncooked elbow macaroni

2 tablespoons canola oil

2 tablespoons unsalted butter

⅓ cup finely chopped red onion

1.1 ounces all-purpose flour (about ¼ cup)

2½ cups 2% reduced-fat milk

4 ounces reduced-fat cheddar cheese, shredded (about 1 cup)

½ teaspoon kosher salt

¼ teaspoon freshly ground black pepper

1 cup frozen petite green peas

2 (5-ounce) cans solid white tuna in water, drained

Cooking spray

½ cup panko (Japanese breadcrumbs)

¼ cup (1 ounce) grated fresh Parmesan cheese

1. Preheat oven to 375°. Cook pasta according to package directions, omitting salt and fat; drain.
2. Heat oil and butter in a Dutch oven over medium-high heat until butter melts. Add onion; sauté 3 minutes. Reduce heat to medium. Sprinkle flour over onion mixture, stirring until blended; cook, stirring constantly, 2 minutes. Gradually stir in milk. Bring to a simmer; stir in cheddar cheese, salt, and pepper. Cook 1 minute or just until cheese melts. Stir in peas and tuna.
3. Add pasta, tossing to coat. Pour pasta mixture into an 11 x 7–inch glass or ceramic baking dish coated with cooking spray. Sprinkle with panko and Parmesan cheese.
4. Bake at 375° for 20 minutes or until bubbly and golden. Serves 8 (serving size: ⅛ of casserole)

CALORIES 332; FAT 13.2g (sat 5.5g, mono 4.5g, poly 2.6g); PROTEIN 21.6g; CARB 33.2g; FIBER 2.1g; CHOL 41mg; IRON 1.4mg; SODIUM 511mg; CALC 354mg

CHILES RELLENOS

HANDS-ON TIME: 44 MINUTES ★ TOTAL TIME: 60 MINUTES

Unlike traditional stuffed chiles, these peppers are cooked on the stovetop with a small amount of oil and then baked instead of deep-fried. The result is a crispy exterior that rivals that of the fried version, but with significantly less fat and calories.

Cooking spray
1¼ cups coarsely chopped onion
2 cups chopped tomatoes
½ cup low-sodium salsa verde
¼ teaspoon salt
¼ cup cilantro leaves
4 poblano chiles
4 ounces reduced-fat Monterey Jack cheese, shredded (about 1 cup)
2 tablespoons goat cheese

3 large egg whites
3 large egg yolks, beaten
1.1 ounces all-purpose flour (about ¼ cup)
¼ teaspoon freshly ground black pepper
3 tablespoons cornmeal
¼ cup canola oil
Chopped tomatoes, chopped green bell pepper, cilantro leaves, goat cheese (optional)

1. Preheat broiler. Heat a large skillet over medium-high heat. Coat pan with cooking spray. Add onion; sauté 4 minutes or until tender. Stir in tomatoes, salsa verde, and salt; cook 15 minutes or until thick, stirring frequently. Place tomato mixture in a food processor; add cilantro. Process mixture until smooth.
2. Place poblanos on a foil-lined baking sheet; broil 3 inches from heat 8 minutes or until blackened and charred, turning after 6 minutes. Place in a paper bag; fold to close tightly. Let stand 15 minutes. Peel and discard skins. Cut a lengthwise slit in each chile; discard seeds, leaving stems intact. Spoon ¼ cup Monterey Jack cheese and 1½ teaspoons goat cheese in cavity of each chile.
3. Preheat oven to 350°. Place egg whites in a bowl; beat with a mixer at high speed until stiff peaks form. Fold egg yolks into egg whites. Combine flour and black pepper in a shallow dish. Place cornmeal in a second shallow dish. Dredge poblanos in flour mixture, and dip into egg mixture. Dredge in cornmeal.
4. Heat a large skillet over medium-high heat; reduce heat to medium. Add oil to pan; swirl to coat. Add coated poblanos to oil; cook 6 minutes or until crisp, turning to cook on all sides. Place chiles on a baking sheet, and bake at 350° for 8 minutes or until cheese melts. Top with additional tomatoes, bell pepper, cilantro, and goat cheese, if desired. Serve with tomato sauce. Serves 4 (serving size: 1 chile and about ⅓ cup sauce)

CALORIES 297; FAT 14.8g (sat 5.8g, mono 4.1g, poly 1.8g); PROTEIN 16.1g; CARB 25.6g; FIBER 2.7g; CHOL 159mg; IRON 1.9mg; SODIUM 562mg; CALC 254mg

ENTRÉES & ONE-DISH MEALS | 155

VEGETARIAN ENCHILADAS

HANDS-ON TIME: 45 MINUTES ★ TOTAL TIME: 60 MINUTES

Ranchero sauce gives this dish authentic Tex-Mex flavor. You can make the sauce ahead, then simply assemble the enchiladas just before baking.

Me at the Arizona Taco Festival in Scottsdale, AZ

2 dried ancho chiles, stemmed and seeded

2 cups water

2 teaspoons olive oil

1 cup chopped yellow onion

5 garlic cloves, sliced

¼ teaspoon kosher salt

2 cups organic vegetable broth

2 tablespoons chopped fresh oregano

2 tablespoons unsalted tomato paste

½ teaspoon ground cumin

1 tablespoon fresh lime juice

⅛ teaspoon ground red pepper

1 (15-ounce) can black beans, rinsed and drained

8 ounces preshredded reduced-fat 4-cheese Mexican-blend cheese (about 2 cups), divided

3 thinly sliced green onions, divided

Cooking spray

12 (6-inch) corn tortillas

6 tablespoons light sour cream

1. Preheat oven to 400°. Combine chiles and 2 cups water in a saucepan; bring to a boil, reduce heat, and simmer 5 minutes. Remove from heat; let stand 5 minutes. Drain chiles in a colander over a bowl, reserving 1 cup cooking liquid.

2. Heat a medium saucepan over high heat. Add oil to pan; swirl to coat. Add onion; sauté 1 minute. Reduce heat to medium; add garlic and salt. Cook 5 minutes or until golden, stirring occasionally. Add broth and next 3 ingredients (through cumin); cook 8 minutes or until thick, stirring occasionally.

3. Pour onion mixture into a blender; add chiles and reserved liquid. Remove center piece of blender lid (to allow steam to escape); secure lid on blender. Place a clean towel over opening in lid (to avoid splatters). Blend until smooth; stir in lime juice and red pepper.

4. Combine beans, 1 cup cheese, and half the green onions in a bowl. Spread ½ cup ranchero sauce in bottom of a 13 x 9–inch glass or ceramic baking dish coated with cooking spray. Warm tortillas according to package directions. Spoon 3 tablespoons bean mixture down center of each tortilla; roll up. Place, seam sides down, in prepared dish. Pour remaining ranchero sauce over filled tortillas. Top with 1 cup cheese. Bake at 400° for 15 minutes or until lightly browned. Sprinkle with green onions; serve with sour cream. Serves 6 (serving size: 2 enchiladas and 1 tablespoon sour cream)

CALORIES 302; FAT 12.9g (sat 5.3g, mono 3.9g, poly 1.3g); PROTEIN 17.3g; CARB 36.1g; FIBER 6.4g; CHOL 32mg; IRON 1.7mg; SODIUM 574mg; CALC 426mg

HOISIN-GLAZED SALMON BURGERS

HANDS-ON TIME: 20 MINUTES ★ TOTAL TIME: 55 MINUTES

Quick-pickled cukes give these burgers some crunch. Use cilantro leaves on the burgers instead of lettuce for herby freshness.

⅓ cup water

¼ cup cider vinegar

1 teaspoon sugar

½ teaspoon minced garlic

½ teaspoon minced peeled fresh ginger

¼ teaspoon crushed red pepper

8 thin English cucumber vertical slices

½ cup panko (Japanese breadcrumbs)

⅓ cup thinly sliced green onions

2 tablespoons chopped fresh cilantro

1 tablespoon lower-sodium soy sauce

1½ teaspoons grated peeled fresh ginger

1 teaspoon grated lime rind

1 (1-pound) skinless wild fresh or frozen Alaskan salmon fillet, finely chopped

1 large egg white

1½ teaspoons dark sesame oil

1 tablespoon hoisin sauce

4 (1½-ounce) hamburger buns with sesame seeds, toasted

1. Combine first 6 ingredients (through red pepper) in a small saucepan; bring to a boil. Remove from heat; add cucumber. Let stand 30 minutes. Drain.

2. Combine panko and next 7 ingredients (through egg white) in a bowl, and stir well. Divide mixture into 4 equal portions, gently shaping each into a ½-inch-thick patty. Press a nickel-sized indentation in the center of each patty.

3. Heat a large cast-iron skillet over medium-high heat. Add sesame oil to pan; swirl to coat. Add patties; cook patties 3 minutes on each side or until desired degree of doneness. Brush tops of patties evenly with hoisin; cook 30 seconds.

4. Place 1 patty on bottom half of each bun; top each patty with 2 cucumber slices and top half of bun. Serves 4 (serving size: 1 burger)

CALORIES 324; FAT 8.6g (sat 1.5g, mono 2.3g, poly 3.1g); PROTEIN 29.4g; CARB 30.1g; FIBER 1.7g; CHOL 59mg; IRON 2.6mg; SODIUM 473mg; CALC 89mg

BRISKET BURGERS

HANDS-ON TIME: 20 MINUTES ★ TOTAL TIME: 50 MINUTES

For a truly perfect burger, grind your own beef or ask your butcher to do it for you. Ground beef from the supermarket is often made from trim and scraps, which can mean inconsistent flavor.

1 (1-pound) flat-cut beef brisket, trimmed and cut into 1-inch pieces
2 tablespoons olive oil
¼ teaspoon kosher salt
⅛ teaspoon freshly ground black pepper
Cooking spray
4 (½-ounce) slices cheddar cheese
4 (1½-ounce) hamburger buns or water rolls, toasted
8 teaspoons canola mayonnaise
4 green leaf lettuce leaves
4 (⅛-inch-thick) slices tomato

1. To prepare grinder, place feed shaft, blade, and ¼-inch die plate in freezer 30 minutes or until well chilled. Assemble grinder just before grinding. Arrange meat in a single layer on jelly-roll pan. Freeze 15 minutes.
2. Combine meat and oil in a large bowl, and toss to combine. Pass meat through meat grinder completely. Immediately pass meat through grinder a second time. Divide mixture into 4 equal portions, gently shaping each into a ½-inch-thick patty. Press a nickel-sized indentation in center of each patty. Cover and chill until ready to grill.
3. Preheat grill to medium-high heat. Sprinkle patties with salt and pepper. Place on grill rack coated with cooking spray; grill 2 minutes or until grill marks appear. Carefully turn patties; grill 3 minutes. Top each patty with 1 cheese slice; grill 1 minute or until cheese melts and beef reaches desired degree of doneness. Place 1 patty on bottom half of each bun; top each serving with 2 teaspoons mayonnaise 1 lettuce leaf, 1 tomato slice, and top half of bun. Serves 4 (serving size: 1 burger)

CALORIES 407; FAT 23.6g (sat 5.8g, mono 11.6g, poly 4g); PROTEIN 25.3g; CARB 21g; FIBER 2g; CHOL 53mg; IRON 2mg; SODIUM 549mg; CALC 126mg

SPICY SAUSAGE AND MUSHROOM PIZZA

HANDS-ON TIME: 13 MINUTES ★ TOTAL TIME: 40 MINUTES

Hot sausage gives this classic pizza a welcome spicy kick. Choosing turkey rather than traditional pork sausage keeps down the calories and fat.

1 pound refrigerated fresh pizza dough

Cooking spray

4 ounces hot turkey Italian sausage

1 cup thinly sliced onion

1 (8-ounce) package presliced mushrooms

1 cup diced red or green bell pepper

1 tablespoon yellow cornmeal

½ cup lower-sodium marinara sauce

2 ounces part-skim mozzarella cheese, shredded (about ½ cup)

¼ cup (1 ounce) grated fresh Parmigiano-Reggiano cheese

1. Preheat oven to 450°.

2. Place dough in a bowl coated with cooking spray; let dough stand, covered, 15 minutes.

3. Heat a large nonstick skillet over medium-high heat. Remove casings from sausage. Add sausage to pan; cook 3 minutes, stirring to crumble. Add onion and mushrooms; sauté 4 minutes. Add bell pepper; sauté 2 minutes.

4. Sprinkle a baking sheet with cornmeal; roll dough into a 12-inch circle on prepared baking sheet. Spread sauce over dough, leaving a ½-inch border. Top with sausage mixture. Sprinkle cheeses over sausage mixture. Bake at 450° on bottom oven rack for 17 minutes or until crust is golden. Serves 6 (serving size: 1 slice)

CALORIES 311; FAT 7.3g (sat 1.9g, mono 2.8g, poly 1.5g); PROTEIN 15.6g; CARB 51.8g; FIBER 2.4g; CHOL 21mg; IRON 3.1mg; SODIUM 751mg; CALC 134mg

A fun sign at Home Slice Pizza, Austin, TX

PIZZA THAT DELIVERS

Each slice has only—get this—200 calories!

CHICKEN PESTO

 West

BASE: 3 tablespoons prepared pesto
TOPPINGS: ½ cup shredded roasted chicken breast + ½ cup sliced red bell pepper + ¼ cup grated fresh Parmigiano-Reggiano cheese. SERVES 8 (serving size: 1 slice) CALORIES 204; FAT 5.2g (sat 1.1g); SODIUM 420mg

ROASTED BEET & GOAT CHEESE

Northwest

BASE: 1 tablespoon olive oil
TOPPINGS: 6 ounces sliced roasted beets + 3 tablespoons toasted walnut halves + 3 tablespoons crumbled goat cheese + 2 tablespoons chopped flat-leaf parsley. SERVES 8 (serving size: 1 slice) CALORIES 202; FAT 5.6g (sat 0.8g); SODIUM 393mg

HAWAIIAN PEPPERONI

West

BASE: ½ cup lower-sodium marinara sauce
TOPPINGS: 3 ounces turkey pepperoni slices + ¾ cup pineapple chunks (fresh or canned) + ⅓ cup shredded part-skim mozzarella cheese. SERVES 8 (serving size: 1 slice) CALORIES 200; FAT 3.8g (sat 0.9g); SODIUM 589mg

PEPPERED PROSCIUTTO & PARMESAN

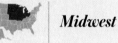 *Midwest*

BASE: 1 tablespoon olive oil
TOPPINGS: 3 ounces sliced prosciutto + ⅓ cup shaved Parmigiano-Reggiano cheese + 4 cups fresh baby arugula + cracked black pepper. SERVES 8 (serving size: 1 slice) CALORIES 203; FAT 5.5g (sat 1.3g); SODIUM 561mg

SMOKED SALMON & DILL

 *Northeast*

BASE: 1 tablespoon fresh lemon juice + ½ cup ⅓-less-fat cream cheese
TOPPINGS: 4 ounces sliced smoked salmon + ⅓ cup thinly sliced red onion + 1 tablespoon chopped fresh dill. SERVES 8 (serving size: 1 slice) CALORIES 203; FAT 5.1g (sat 1.9g); SODIUM 529mg

CHICKEN & CHEDDAR

South

BASE: ½ cup ready-made barbecue sauce
TOPPINGS: ½ cup sliced roasted chicken breast + ½ cup shredded cheddar cheese + ½ cup sliced red onion + ½ cup chopped fresh cilantro. SERVES 8 (serving size: 1 slice) CALORIES 202; FAT 4.2g (sat 1.6g); SODIUM 504mg

MARGHERITA

 East

BASE: ½ cup lower-sodium marinara sauce
TOPPINGS: 1 cup thinly sliced fresh mozzarella cheese + ⅓ cup small fresh basil leaves. SERVES 8 (serving size: 1 slice) CALORIES 194; FAT 4.9g (sat 1.9g); SODIUM 369mg

PEACH & GORGONZOLA CHICKEN

Southeast

BASE: 1 teaspoon extra-virgin olive oil
TOPPINGS: ⅓ cup shredded part-skim mozzarella cheese + ½ cup shredded cooked chicken breast + 3 tablespoons crumbled Gorgonzola cheese + 1 thinly sliced unpeeled peach + 2 tablespoons balsamic glaze. SERVES 8 (serving size: 1 slice) CALORIES 205; FAT 4.1g (sat 1.2g); SODIUM 423mg

Pizza tip To create any of these delicious pizzas at home, roll a 1-pound ball of fresh dough into a 14-inch base. Add the ingredients, and then bake according to package directions. Cut into 8 slices each.

MUSHROOM AND SPINACH LASAGNA

HANDS-ON TIME: 40 MINUTES ★ TOTAL TIME: 1 HOUR 40 MINUTES

I have yet to meet an American who doesn't love lasagna. Unfortunately, the original is often served with a side of, "But I shouldn't...." This recipe will change all that.

2 tablespoons olive oil
1 (9-ounce) red onion, sliced
1 pound portobello mushroom caps, sliced
4 garlic cloves, minced
3 (6-ounce) packages fresh baby spinach
½ cup water
2 large eggs, lightly beaten
⅓ cup chopped fresh basil
1 tablespoon dried oregano
¼ teaspoon freshly ground black pepper
¼ cup skim milk
1 (15-ounce) container part-skim ricotta cheese
2 (24.5-ounce) jars lower-sodium pasta sauce
Cooking spray
16 no-boil lasagna noodles
8 ounces part-skim mozzarella cheese, shredded (about 2 cups)
¼ cup (1 ounce) grated fresh Parmesan cheese

1. Preheat oven to 375°.
2. Heat a large skillet over medium-high heat. Add oil to pan; swirl to coat. Add onion; sauté 2 minutes. Add mushrooms; sauté 6 minutes. Add garlic; sauté 30 seconds. Transfer mushroom mixture to a bowl.
3. Return pan to heat; add half of spinach and ¼ cup water. Cook 2 minutes or until spinach wilts, turning with tongs. Add cooked spinach to mushroom mixture. Repeat procedure with remaining half of spinach and remaining ¼ cup water. Stir vegetable mixture until blended.
4. Combine eggs and next 3 ingredients (through pepper) in a bowl, stirring with a whisk. Stir in milk and ricotta cheese.
5. Pour 1 cup pasta sauce into bottom of a 13 x 9–inch glass or ceramic baking dish coated with cooking spray. Arrange 4 lasagna noodles over sauce. Top with one-third of ricotta mixture, one-third of vegetable mixture, and ⅓ cup mozzarella cheese. Repeat layers twice with sauce, noodles, ricotta mixture, vegetable mixture, and mozzarella cheese. Spread 1 cup sauce over mozzarella. Arrange 4 noodles over sauce. Top with 1 cup sauce, 1 cup mozzarella cheese, and Parmesan cheese.
6. Cover with a sheet of foil coated with cooking spray, coated side down. Bake at 375° for 45 minutes. Remove from oven, and let stand 15 minutes. Serves 8 (serving size: ⅛ of lasagna)

CALORIES 462; FAT 16.6g (sat 6.9g, mono 7.3g, poly 2g); PROTEIN 26.5g; CARB 54.2g; FIBER 7.1g; CHOL 84mg; IRON 6.2mg; SODIUM 568mg; CALC 524mg

CHICKEN RIGGIES

HANDS-ON TIME: 54 MINUTES ★ TOTAL TIME: 54 MINUTES

This spicy, creamy pasta dish is a regional specialty from the Utica-Rome area of New York state, where my mom grew up.

2 red bell peppers

2 tablespoons olive oil, divided

1 pound skinless, boneless chicken breast or chicken tenders, cut into 1-inch pieces

1½ cups diced onion (about 1 large)

1 cup thinly sliced seeded Anaheim chile (1 large chile)

¼ cup finely diced seeded bottled pickled hot cherry pepper (2 peppers)

1 (8-ounce) container cremini mushrooms, sliced

4 garlic cloves, minced

¼ cup dry sherry

1 (28-ounce) can unsalted peeled whole plum tomatoes, undrained and chopped

1 teaspoon kosher salt

½ teaspoon freshly ground black pepper

1 pound uncooked rigatoni

12 pimiento-stuffed olives, sliced (optional)

½ cup whipping cream

½ cup (2 ounces) grated fresh Parmesan cheese

Downtown Utica in upstate NY

1. Preheat broiler.

2. Cut bell peppers in half lengthwise; discard seeds and membranes. Place pepper halves, skin sides up, on a foil-lined baking sheet; flatten with hand. Broil 15 minutes or until blackened. Place in a heavy-duty zip-top plastic bag; seal bag. Let stand 10 minutes. Peel and cut into strips.

3. Heat a 6-quart Dutch oven over medium-high heat. Add 1 tablespoon olive oil to pan; swirl to coat. Add chicken to pan; cook 6 minutes, turning to brown on all sides. Remove chicken from pan. Add 1 tablespoon olive oil to pan. Add onion and next 4 ingredients (through garlic). Cook over medium heat 4 minutes or until vegetables are tender, stirring occasionally.

4. Add sherry to pan; cook until liquid evaporates, scraping pan to loosen browned bits. Stir in tomatoes, salt, and pepper. Bring to a boil; reduce heat and simmer, uncovered, 20 minutes, stirring occasionally. While sauce simmers, cook pasta according to package directions, omitting salt and fat; drain.

5. Add roasted bell pepper, chicken, and, if desired, olives to tomato mixture. Bring to a simmer. Stir in cream; cook 2 minutes or just until thoroughly heated, stirring occasionally. Add pasta, tossing well. Sprinkle with Parmesan cheese. Serves 8 (serving size: 1½ cups)

CALORIES 485; FAT 14.2g (sat 6.1g, mono 4.8g, poly 0.8g); PROTEIN 26.4g; CARB 57.7g; FIBER 5.3g; CHOL 63mg; IRON 2.9mg; SODIUM 765mg; CALC 203mg

Our family dinner

This was the kind of dish that my mom would defrost for dinner after she got home from work. Between her job, my dad's job, and our afternoon activities…it's a wonder there weren't more microwaved meals in our house. But dinner was always served around 6 p.m. Dishes like these remind me of the fun times that my brother, parents, and I had eating together when I was growing up. It's a tradition that I plan to continue with my own children.

So, when you're going to have a busy week ahead, this is a great dish to prepare on the weekend, keep in the freezer, and have ready for when you need to prepare a family meal in a hurry.

STUFFED SHELLS

HANDS-ON TIME: 18 MINUTES ★ TOTAL TIME: 1 HOUR 13 MINUTES

What an American classic! Stuffed shells are a bit more involved than a simple pasta dish, but at the same time, a lot less fussy than homemade lasagna. This vegetarian version is packed with flavorful vegetables like zucchini, mushrooms, and spinach. Even though they're lighter, these shells will fill you up.

1 (12-ounce) package jumbo pasta shells

2 teaspoons olive oil

2 medium zucchini, halved lengthwise and cut into ¼-inch-thick slices (3 cups)

1 (8-ounce) package mushrooms, cut into ¼-inch-thick slices

2 garlic cloves, minced

1 (5-ounce) package fresh baby spinach

½ teaspoon kosher salt

¼ cup chopped fresh basil

2 tablespoons dried parsley

1½ teaspoons dried oregano

½ teaspoon crushed red pepper

1 (15-ounce) container part-skim ricotta cheese

6 ounces part-skim mozzarella cheese, shredded (about 1½ cups), divided

1 (24.5-ounce) jar lower-sodium marinara sauce, divided

Cooking spray

½ cup (2 ounces) grated fresh Parmesan cheese

1. Preheat oven to 350°.

2. Cook pasta according to package directions, omitting salt and fat; drain.

3. While pasta cooks, heat a large nonstick skillet over medium-high heat. Add oil to pan; swirl to coat. Add zucchini and mushrooms; sauté 6 minutes or until vegetables are tender and beginning to brown. Add garlic; sauté 1 minute. Add spinach and salt; cover, and cook 1 minute or until spinach wilts. Remove pan from heat; cool 10 minutes.

4. Combine basil, next 4 ingredients (through ricotta cheese), and ½ cup mozzarella cheese in a large bowl; stir in vegetable mixture.

5. Spread 1 cup marinara sauce over bottom of a 13 x 9–inch glass or ceramic baking dish coated with cooking spray. Stuff cheese mixture evenly into shells. Place shells on top of sauce in dish. Pour remaining sauce over shells. Top with 1 cup mozzarella cheese and Parmesan cheese. Cover with a sheet of foil coated with cooking spray, coated side down.

6. Bake at 350° for 40 minutes or until sauce is bubbly and cheese melts. Let stand 15 minutes before serving. Serves 9 (serving size: 4 stuffed shells and ⅓ cup sauce)

CALORIES 384; FAT 14g (sat 7.2g, mono 4.5g, poly 2g); PROTEIN 24.1g; CARB 40.1g; FIBER 3.3g; CHOL 43mg; IRON 3.2mg; SODIUM 603mg; CALC 549mg

PASTA WITH VODKA CREAM SAUCE

HANDS-ON TIME: 15 MINUTES ★ TOTAL TIME: 30 MINUTES

Nothing coats pasta quite like whipping cream. This dish uses canned tomatoes and broth for convenience, and fresh basil is stirred in at the end for a boost of flavor. For a nonalcoholic version, replace the vodka with additional chicken broth.

½ pound uncooked penne pasta

1 tablespoon olive oil

½ cup finely chopped onion

1 teaspoon salt, divided

¼ teaspoon crushed red pepper

1 garlic clove, minced

½ cup vodka

¼ cup fat-free, lower-sodium chicken broth

1 (14.5-ounce) can unsalted diced tomatoes, undrained

¼ cup whipping cream

3 tablespoons thinly sliced fresh basil

1. Cook pasta according to package directions, omitting salt and fat. Drain and keep warm.

2. Heat a large nonstick skillet over medium-high heat. Add oil to pan; swirl to coat. Add onion to pan; sauté 4 minutes or until tender. Add ¼ teaspoon salt, red pepper, and garlic; sauté 1 minute. Add vodka; bring to a boil. Reduce heat, and simmer 3 minutes or until liquid is reduced by about half. Stir in ½ teaspoon salt, broth, and tomatoes; bring to a boil. Reduce heat, and simmer 8 minutes. Place tomato mixture in a blender. Remove center piece of blender lid (to allow steam to escape); secure blender lid on blender. Place a clean towel over opening in blender lid (to avoid splatters). Process until smooth. Return tomato mixture to pan; stir in cream. Cook 2 minutes over medium heat, stirring constantly. Remove from heat. Stir in cooked pasta, ¼ teaspoon salt, and basil. Serve immediately. Serves 4 (serving size: 1 cup)

CALORIES 354; FAT 9.9g (sat 3.9g, mono 4.1g, poly 0.6g); PROTEIN 8.5g; CARB 48.6g; FIBER 3.1g; CHOL 20mg; IRON 1.2mg; SODIUM 662mg; CALC 36mg

FETTUCCINE ALFREDO

HANDS-ON TIME: 21 MINUTES ★ TOTAL TIME: 30 MINUTES

Restaurateur Alfredo Di Lelio is credited with creating this pasta classic, a favorite of American tourists who visited his restaurant in Rome in the early part of the 20th century. The original dish was made with butter, Parmesan cheese, and fettuccine.

1 tablespoon butter
2 garlic cloves, minced
1 tablespoon all-purpose flour
1⅓ cups 1% low-fat milk
5 ounces fresh Parmigiano-Reggiano cheese, shredded (about 1¼ cups), divided
2 tablespoons ⅓-less-fat cream cheese

½ teaspoon salt
4 cups hot cooked fettuccine (8 ounces uncooked pasta)
2 teaspoons chopped fresh flat-leaf parsley
Cracked black pepper (optional)

1. Melt butter in a medium saucepan over medium heat. Add garlic; cook 1 minute, stirring frequently. Stir in flour. Gradually add milk, stirring with a whisk. Cook 6 minutes or until mixture thickens, stirring constantly. Add 1 cup Parmigiano-Reggiano cheese, cream cheese, and salt, stirring with a whisk until cheeses melt. Toss sauce with hot pasta. Sprinkle with ¼ cup Parmigiano-Reggiano cheese and chopped parsley. Garnish with black pepper, if desired. Serve immediately. Serves 4 (serving size: 1 cup)

CALORIES 399; FAT 13.5g (sat 8g, mono 3.4g, poly 1.1g); PROTEIN 21.3g; CARB 48.9g; FIBER 2g; CHOL 34mg; IRON 2.1mg; SODIUM 822mg; CALC 451mg

PASTA PUTTANESCA

HANDS-ON TIME: 23 MINUTES ★ TOTAL TIME: 33 MINUTES

The right amount of salt and spice makes this Italian pasta dish feel decadent, while fresh Parmesan, basil, and arugula keep it light. The canned tomatoes make it a quick dish, easy to pull together during the week. To make the cheese shavings, gently drag a vegetable peeler against the side of a Parmesan cheese wedge.

8 ounces uncooked spaghetti
3 tablespoons olive oil
1 teaspoon anchovy paste
¼ teaspoon crushed red pepper
5 garlic cloves, minced
2 (14.5-ounce) cans un-salted diced tomatoes, undrained
½ cup pitted kalamata olives, chopped
1 tablespoon drained capers, rinsed and chopped
1 cup baby arugula leaves
½ cup baby basil leaves
1 ounce fresh Parmesan cheese, shaved (about ¼ cup)

1. Cook pasta according to package directions, omitting salt and fat; drain.
2. Heat a large skillet over medium heat. Add oil to pan; swirl to coat. Add anchovy paste, red pepper, and garlic; sauté 2 minutes. Stir in tomatoes. Bring to a boil; reduce heat, and simmer, uncovered, 5 minutes, stirring often.
3. Stir in olives and capers; simmer 2 minutes. Stir in pasta. Remove from heat, and stir in arugula and basil. Sprinkle with cheese. Serves 4 (serving size: 1¾ cups)

CALORIES 402; FAT 15.7g (sat 2.7g, mono 8.6g, poly 3.9g); PROTEIN 12.9g; CARB 54.7g; FIBER 5.3g; CHOL 10mg; IRON 3.2mg; SODIUM 611mg; CALC 191mg

Jambalaya: Cajun versus Creole

*i*n New Orleans and the surrounding regions, Creole cooks make a "red" jambalaya that starts with meat and the "trinity" of onion, celery, and bell pepper. Seafood and tomatoes are then added, followed by equal portions of rice and stock. In the Louisiana bayous, where tomatoes were likely once very hard to come by, the jambalaya of Cajun origin begins with smoked meat browned in a cast-iron pot, providing this variation with its distinctive flavor and earthy hue. The "trinity," stock, and seasonings are then cooked together, the meat returned to the pot, and the rice added in last.

> **There are as many variations of jambalaya as there are cooks who make it.**

Like most dishes of early American origin, jambalaya was born of necessity, a delicious and inexpensive means of using whatever ingredients were likely on hand. Each cook and culture contributed their own unique variations: Tomato was likely the addition of Spanish cooks, a practical substitution for the orange saffron they commonly included in paella, and the French doubtless contributed spices brought from the

Caribbean. Rural Cajun cooks concentrated on the meats of the low-lying swamps, appropriately adding a variety of bayou game.

Jambalaya continues to be a multi-faceted mixture, with as many variations as there are cooks who make it. These days it's often enjoyed as a one-pot party food, and remains a heartily delicious and inexpensive way to serve a crowd.

JAMBALAYA

HANDS-ON TIME: 60 MINUTES ★ TOTAL TIME: 60 MINUTES

Slightly spicy andouille sausage, shrimp, rice, and the cooking "trinity" of the Bayou—onion, celery, and bell pepper—give this regional dish its distinctive flavor. If you want to keep it mild, omit the additional ground red pepper from the rice mixture.

1½ teaspoons canola oil

6 ounces andouille sausage, chopped

1 cup chopped onion

1 cup chopped green bell pepper

½ cup chopped celery

5 garlic cloves, minced

2 cups cooked whole-grain rice

½ teaspoon ground red pepper

2½ cups chicken broth

½ teaspoon salt

1 (14.5-ounce) can unsalted diced tomatoes, undrained

12 ounces large shrimp, peeled and deveined

3 tablespoons sliced green onions

1. Heat a large skillet over medium-high heat. Add oil to pan; swirl to coat. Add sausage; sauté 4 minutes or until browned. Reduce heat to medium. Add onion, bell pepper, and celery; cook 8 minutes, stirring occasionally. Add garlic; cook 1 minute, stirring constantly.

2. Stir in rice and red pepper; cook 1 minute, stirring frequently. Stir in broth, salt, and tomatoes; bring to a boil. Cover, reduce heat, and simmer 10 minutes or until liquid is nearly absorbed. Add shrimp, nestling them into rice mixture. Cover and simmer 5 minutes or until shrimp are almost done. Uncover; cook 3 to 5 minutes or until shrimp are done. Remove from heat; sprinkle with green onions. Serves 6 (serving size: about 1 cup)

CALORIES 386; FAT 7.7g (sat 2.1g, mono 2.8g, poly 2.4g); PROTEIN 21.4g; CARB 57.1g; FIBER 5.6g; CHOL 88mg; IRON 2.3mg; SODIUM 374mg; CALC 90mg

NEW ORLEANS GUMBO

HANDS-ON TIME: 60 MINUTES ★ TOTAL TIME: 1 HOUR 43 MINUTES

The key to an outstanding Cajun gumbo is a deep, dark roux. To get it just right, use a flat-bottomed wooden spoon to get into all the corners of the pot, and be attentive. Cook, stirring continuously, especially during the last 15 minutes. Reduce the heat as needed if you're concerned the roux is cooking too fast. There's no rescuing a burnt roux—best to toss it and start over.

6 boneless chicken thighs (about 1¼ pounds), skinned

1½ tablespoons Cajun seasoning

Cooking spray

½ cup canola oil

2.25 ounces all-purpose flour (about ½ cup)

1½ cups chopped onion

1 cup chopped green bell pepper

2 celery stalks, chopped

4 ounces andouille sausage, thinly sliced

½ teaspoon kosher salt

2 bay leaves

1 (14.5-ounce) can unsalted diced tomatoes, undrained

5 cups fat-free, lower-sodium chicken broth

2 garlic cloves, minced

1 tablespoon Worcestershire sauce

5 cups cooked brown rice

¼ cup chopped green onions

Hot pepper sauce (optional)

1. Preheat oven to 400°.

2. Rub chicken thighs with Cajun seasoning. Place on a baking sheet coated with cooking spray. Bake at 400° for 25 minutes or until a thermometer registers 165°. Cool chicken; shred.

3. Place oil in a Dutch oven. Weigh or lightly spoon flour into a dry measuring cup; level with a knife. Add flour to pan, stirring constantly with a whisk. Cook over medium heat 35 to 40 minutes or until very brown, stirring constantly with a flat-bottomed wooden spoon. Add onion, bell pepper, and celery to pan; sauté 5 minutes or until vegetables are tender. Add sausage and next 3 ingredients (through tomatoes); cook 2 minutes. Gradually add broth, stirring constantly with a whisk. Bring to a boil. Cover, reduce heat, and simmer 30 minutes.

4. Add chicken; cook 5 minutes. Add garlic; cook 5 minutes. Remove from heat; add Worcestershire sauce. Discard bay leaves. Serve over rice; sprinkle with green onions. Serve with hot pepper sauce, if desired. Serves 10 (serving size: 1 cup gumbo and ½ cup rice)

CALORIES 353; FAT 16.4g (sat 2.5g, mono 4.5g, poly 9.2g); PROTEIN 18.7g; CARB 32.2g; FIBER 2.9g; CHOL 63mg; IRON 1.8mg; SODIUM 577mg; CALC 34mg

It's all in the sauce

McIlhenny Company has produced Tabasco brand hot sauce on Avery Island since 1868 and remains family owned and operated to this day.

Tabasco is the invention of patriarch Edmund McIlhenny. He found the diet of the Reconstruction South after the Civil War to be bland and monotonous, so he added zing with a hot sauce crafted from a blend of chile peppers that he grew himself. The sauce was so popular with family and friends that McIlhenny quit his day job as a banker to devote all his time to his new enterprise. The rest, as they say, is history.

Tiny jars of the super-concentrated hot sauce are as much a staple on the tables of Southern barbecue joints, crab shacks, and even fancy restaurants as ketchup and mustard. You'll find many different types of hot sauce on the market today, but none as popular country-wide as Tabasco.

The fisherman's feast

The Italians really had an impact on early San Francisco cooking. They captured the early deli scene with their cured meats and freshly made pasta and dominated down on the wharves.

Local legend says that in the 1930s, Italian fishermen along the wharf were asked to contribute the remnants of their catch to seaside eateries' pots that were already bubbling away with tomatoes and wine. The soup was called cioppino; some think this is an Italian-American derivative of "chip in," but it's more likely a variation of *ciuppin*, a Ligurian word meaning "little soup." Nothing is little about this hearty fisherman's stew, however, which usually contains a combination of clams, mussels, prawns, shrimp, and chunks of flaky fish in a zesty, wine-spiked tomato broth.

CIOPPINO

HANDS-ON TIME: 34 MINUTES ★ TOTAL TIME: 34 MINUTES

This dish has been a local favorite for more than 80 years. Today, no trip to the City by the Bay is complete without it. Serve with crusty bread—ideally, San Francisco's sourdough.

2 tablespoons olive oil

3½ cups thinly sliced fennel bulb (about 1 medium bulb)

1½ cups thinly sliced shallots (4 large)

5 thyme sprigs

2 garlic cloves, minced

1 cup white wine

1 teaspoon dried oregano

¼ teaspoon crushed red pepper

2 (14.5-ounce) cans unsalted diced tomatoes, undrained

1 (8-ounce) bottle clam juice

1 pound cod (1½ inches thick), cut into 8 (2-inch) chunks

1 pound littleneck clams in shells

1 pound mussels, scrubbed and debearded

16 jumbo shrimp, peeled and deveined (about 1 pound)

½ cup chopped fresh parsley

1. Heat oil in a large Dutch oven over medium-high heat. Add fennel and next 3 ingredients (through garlic); sauté 5 minutes or until fennel is tender. Add wine; cook, uncovered, 2 minutes. Stir in oregano, red pepper, and tomatoes. Bring to a boil; cover, reduce heat, and simmer 10 minutes. Add clam juice; return to a simmer.

2. Add fish; cover and cook 3 minutes. Add clams and mussels; cover and cook 5 minutes or until shellfish open, adding shrimp in last 3 minutes of cooking time. Discard any unopened shells. Remove from heat. Discard thyme sprigs, and ladle seafood evenly into 8 shallow bowls. Ladle broth evenly over seafood. Sprinkle evenly with parsley. Serves 8 (serving size: 1 piece of fish, 2 clams, 5 mussels, 2 shrimp, about ½ cup broth, and 1 tablespoon parsley)

CALORIES 287; FAT 6.3g (sat 1g, mono 1.5g, poly 3.5g); PROTEIN 35.2g; CARB 18.2g; FIBER 3.2g; CHOL 130mg; IRON 5.2mg; SODIUM 716mg; CALC 136mg

BACON-CORN CHOWDER
WITH SHRIMP

HANDS-ON TIME: 34 MINUTES ★ TOTAL TIME: 38 MINUTES

The trick to this light yet rich-tasting soup is blending part of the corn mixture in a blender. This technique creates a thick, creamy texture and eliminates the need for butter and heavy cream. This soup can also serve six as a first course instead of an entrée.

6 center-cut bacon slices, chopped

1 cup prechopped onion

½ cup prechopped celery

1 teaspoon chopped fresh thyme

1 garlic clove, minced

4 cups fresh or frozen corn kernels, thawed

2 cups fat-free, lower-sodium chicken broth

¾ pound medium shrimp, peeled and deveined

⅓ cup half-and-half

¼ teaspoon freshly ground black pepper

⅛ teaspoon salt

1. Heat a large Dutch oven over medium-high heat. Add bacon to pan; sauté 4 minutes or until bacon begins to brown. Remove ⅓ of chopped bacon. Drain on paper towels; reserve for garnishing soup. Add onion and next 3 ingredients (through minced garlic) to pan, and sauté 2 minutes. Add corn, and cook 2 minutes, stirring occasionally. Add broth; bring to a boil, and cook 4 minutes.

2. Place 2 cups corn mixture in a blender. Remove center piece of blender lid (to allow steam to escape), and secure lid on blender. Place a clean towel over opening in blender lid (to avoid splatters). Blend until smooth. Return pureed corn mixture to pan. Stir in shrimp; cook 2 minutes or until shrimp are done. Stir in half-and-half, pepper, and salt. Sprinkle reserved bacon over soup. Serves 4 (serving size: about 1⅔ cups)

CALORIES 294; FAT 7g (sat 2.7g, mono 1.3g, poly 1.2g); PROTEIN 26.8g; CARB 34.8g; FIBER 4.3g; CHOL 144mg; IRON 3.1mg; SODIUM 547mg; CALC 94mg

Soup made simple

One of my favorite parts of being a *Cooking Light* contributing editor is when I join my colleagues in the Birmingham, Alabama–based Test Kitchen to shoot video recipes that appear on cookinglight.com.

On one very ambitious shoot, we attempted to produce 25 recipes in two days. Now that's a lot of cooking and chopping and yammering for me. But at *Cooking Light*, we're nothing if not ambitious.

This recipe for corn chowder was my hands-down favorite from that shoot. It's a simple chowder that can be made in 40 minutes, but it tastes like it's been cooking all day. It makes an easy and delicious light dinner, and is low-cal enough that you can enjoy it with crusty bread and a glass of wine. Now that's my favorite way to keep it light!

BROCCOLI-CHEDDAR SOUP

HANDS-ON TIME: 38 MINUTES ★ TOTAL TIME: 38 MINUTES

Hearty and satisfying, this soup gets its rich creaminess from potatoes.

4 cups cubed peeled baking potato

½ teaspoon salt, divided

3 tablespoons unsalted butter

1 cup chopped onion

⅓ cup chopped carrot

1 garlic clove, minced

5 cups chopped fresh broccoli florets, divided

3 cups fat-free, lower-sodium chicken broth

2 cups plus 2 tablespoons water, divided

2 cups 1% low-fat milk

4 ounces reduced-fat sharp cheddar cheese, shredded (about 1 cup)

1. Place potato and ¼ teaspoon salt in a large saucepan; cover with water. Bring to a boil. Reduce heat, and simmer 10 minutes or until tender; drain.

2. While potatoes cook, melt butter in a large Dutch oven over medium heat. Sauté onion, carrot, and garlic 5 minutes or until tender. Add 4 cups broccoli, broth, 2 cups water, and ¼ teaspoon salt; bring to a simmer, and cook 10 minutes or until broccoli is tender. Stir in potatoes.

3. Combine 1 cup broccoli and 2 tablespoons water in a microwave-safe bowl. Cover with plastic wrap; vent. Microwave at HIGH 1 minute or until bright green. Drain.

4. Process mixture in Dutch oven with a hand-held immersion blender until smooth or place half of broccoli mixture in a blender. Remove center piece of blender lid (to allow steam to escape); secure blender lid on blender. Place a clean towel over opening in blender lid (to avoid splatters). Blend until smooth. Pour into a large bowl. Repeat procedure with remaining broccoli mixture. Return puréed mixture to Dutch oven.

5. Add milk and cheese; cook over low heat 2 minutes, stirring until cheese melts and soup is smooth. Stir in steamed broccoli. Ladle soup into individual bowls. Serves 6 (serving size: 1 cup soup)

CALORIES 256; FAT 10g (sat 6.4g, mono 1.7g, poly 1.4g); PROTEIN 14.6g; CARB 28.9g; FIBER 3.6g; CHOL 32mg; IRON 1.5mg; SODIUM 447mg; CALC 275mg

LENTIL SOUP

HANDS-ON TIME: 20 MINUTES ★ TOTAL TIME: 60 MINUTES

This one-hour soup is surprisingly simple to make, considering how much satisfying flavor it delivers. Lentils, a nutritional powerhouse full of fiber, make a hearty winter soup when combined with a little bit of sausage and a lot of vegetables.

1 (3¾-ounce) link hot Italian pork sausage
1 tablespoon olive oil
1½ cups chopped red onion
1 cup sliced celery
2 carrots, peeled, halved lengthwise, and sliced
2 garlic cloves, minced
7 cups water
4 cups fat-free, lower-sodium chicken broth
1 cup lower-sodium tomato sauce

1 teaspoon kosher salt
1 teaspoon freshly ground black pepper
5 (4-inch-long) thyme sprigs
2 bay leaves
1 (16-ounce) package dried lentils
1 (6-ounce) package fresh baby spinach
Shaved fresh Parmesan cheese (optional)

1. Remove casing from sausage. Heat a 4-quart saucepan over medium-high heat. Add oil to pan; swirl to coat. Add sausage to pan, and cook until browned; stir to crumble. Add onion, celery, and carrot; sauté 4 minutes or until tender. Add garlic; sauté 30 seconds.
2. Stir in 7 cups water and next 6 ingredients (through bay leaves). Bring to a boil; stir in lentils. Return to a boil; reduce heat, and simmer, uncovered, 40 minutes or until lentils are tender.
3. Stir in spinach; cover and cook 2 minutes or just until spinach wilts. Remove and discard thyme sprigs and bay leaves. Ladle soup into bowls, and, if desired, sprinkle evenly with cheese. Serves 10 (serving size: 1¼ cups)

CALORIES 248; FAT 5.4g (sat 1.1g, mono 2.3g, poly 1.6g); PROTEIN 17.2g; CARB 33.9g; FIBER 8.6g; CHOL 8mg; IRON 3.8mg; SODIUM 381mg; CALC 57mg

SPLIT PEA SOUP WITH HAM

HANDS-ON TIME: 30 MINUTES ★ TOTAL TIME: 1 HOUR 15 MINUTES

Although a favorite across the nation, this dish was introduced to the U.S. by early English settlers. I've omitted the salty ham hock, but added smoked paprika for extra smoky flavor.

1 pound green split peas

1 leek

2 bacon slices, cut cross-wise into ¼-inch slices

1 cup chopped onion

1 cup sliced celery

1 cup chopped carrot

1 tablespoon canola oil

7 cups water

1 cup lower-sodium chicken broth

1 teaspoon dried thyme

½ teaspoon dried tarragon

½ teaspoon freshly ground black pepper

¼ teaspoon kosher salt

1 bay leaf

4 ounces ham, cut into ½-inch cubes

½ teaspoon Spanish smoked paprika

1. Sort and wash split peas; drain.

2. Remove roots, outer leaves, and tops from leeks, leaving ½ inch of dark leaves. Slice leek in half lengthwise; cut each half crosswise into thin slices. Rinse thoroughly with cold water.

3. Cook bacon in a large heavy saucepan over medium-high heat until pieces begin to crisp. Add onion, celery, carrot, oil, and leek; reduce heat to medium, and cook 10 minutes, stirring occasionally. Add split peas, and cook 1 minute, stirring constantly. Add 7 cups water and next 6 ingredients (through bay leaf); bring to a boil over medium-high heat. Partially cover, reduce heat to medium-low, and simmer 45 minutes or until split peas are tender.

4. Discard bay leaf. Stir in ham and smoked paprika; simmer 2 minutes or until ham is thoroughly heated. Serves 7 (serving size: 1 cup)

CALORIES 339; FAT 8g (sat 2.1g, mono 3.8g, poly 1.5g); PROTEIN 22.8g; CARB 45g; FIBER 17.9g; CHOL 21mg; IRON 3.5mg; SODIUM 267mg; CALC 62mg

CHILI

HANDS-ON TIME: 45 MINUTES ★ TOTAL TIME: 3 HOURS 30 MINUTES

Sometimes you just don't mess with a classic. This Texas-style chili recipe was inspired by Mark Haught, who won the 2011 Mojave Desert Chili Cook-Off. If you like, you can add beans (or my favorite secret ingredient, refried beans) to stretch the dish— but try it first as it's meant to be.

Chili:

4 tablespoons chili powder

2 tablespoons New Mexico chili powder

1 tablespoon ancho chili powder

3 tablespoons olive oil, divided

4 pounds trimmed tri-tip beef (or sirloin), cut into ¼-inch cubes

1 medium-sized red onion, minced

4 garlic cloves, minced

3 serrano chiles, minced, with seeds

½ pound hot breakfast sausage

3 tablespoons ground cumin

1 teaspoon ground cayenne

1 teaspoon onion powder

1 teaspoon garlic powder

1 cup lower-sodium tomato sauce

1 cup dark beer

1 teaspoon kosher salt

Finishing Spice Mixture:

1 teaspoon ground cumin

½ teaspoon garlic powder

½ teaspoon onion powder

½ teaspoon chili powder

½ teaspoon ancho chili powder

Remaining Ingredients:

8 cups cooked rice

Fat-free Greek yogurt, pickled jalapeños, lime wedges, cilantro leaves (optional)

1. Add first three chili powders (through ancho chili powder) to a medium skillet. Toast over medium heat until fragrant, stirring constantly, about 2 to 3 minutes. Remove powders from pan, and reserve.

2. Heat 2 tablespoons olive oil in a 6-quart pot. Add beef to pan, and cook, in batches, until browned on each side. Remove and reserve. Add 1 tablespoon olive oil and onion; cook until beginning to soften, about 3 minutes. Add garlic and serrano chiles, and cook until fragrant, 1 to 2 minutes. Add breakfast sausage, breaking up with a spoon, and cook until brown, about 3 minutes.

3. Return beef to pan, and stir in toasted spices. Cover with 6 to 8 cups warm water. Allow chili to come to a gentle simmer; cover, and simmer slowly 1½ hours.

4. In a small skillet, toast cumin, cayenne, onion powder, and garlic powder over medium-low heat until fragrant, stirring constantly, about 1 to 2 minutes. Add spices to pan; stir in tomato sauce, beer, and salt.

5. Return chili to a slow simmer and cook, uncovered, 1 hour, stirring occasionally.

6. Add all ingredients for finishing spice mixture to a small skillet. Toast over medium-low heat until fragrant, stirring constantly, about 1 to 2 minutes. Add to chili, and cook 30 minutes. Serve warm, over rice, garnished as desired. Serves 16 (serving size: ¾ cup chili and ½ cup rice)

CALORIES 340; FAT 11.9g (sat 3.6g, mono 2.5g, poly 5.5g); PROTEIN 28.2g; CARB 26.4g; FIBER 1.1g; CHOL 79mg; IRON 3.3mg; SODIUM 436mg; CALC 52mg

Western-style chili

Chili is a religion to some, and debates about chili ingredients can get about as hot as a ghost pepper (the world's hottest pepper). Southwesterners and Texans like their chili with onions, peppers, and plenty of heat. Beans are a no-no, as are tomatoes. Californians, however, are known for putting the whole dang vegetable garden in their chili—and sometimes don't even include meat!

At the Mojave Desert Chili Cook-Off in Mesquite, Nevada, the base recipe is for true Western-style chili: hand-chopped meat, spices, and sauce (no ground beef and certainly no beans). Each contestant varies the recipe with a preferred technique and a unique spice blend. It's the equivalent of wearing a uniform to elementary school but letting your personality shine through in your choice of footwear.

A few of the tips I picked up: Add prunes for extra glossiness (but remove them before serving); add spices throughout the chili cooking time (early and often, with a special spice blend used right before serving); grind red chili flakes in your coffee grinder just before adding them to the mix; don't add the cumin until halfway through cooking (or it can turn bitter); and keep the heat slow and low.

A most unusual food festival

Some might not think roadkill a worthwhile subject for a food festival, but the motto of the unique festival held in the one-stoplight Appalachian town of Marlinton, West Virginia, is, "You kill it. We grill it." They take their critter-cooking craft quite seriously.

Though all competing dishes are checked for gravel prior to judging, I did get the sense that the competition featured roadkill in concept only—that the dishes could contain roadkill, but the meat was typically killed in a different manner.

No matter how it's brought to the cook, all wild meat is fair game at the festival. I sampled tree rat-atouille (squirrel), wild boar nachos, possum burgoo, and bear-ron-ta-saur-us meat loaf, in addition to dishes featuring deer, alligator, porcupine, and more.

Possum was my favorite of these meats, boasting a deep, rich taste. Squirrel was bland, nutty, and somewhat mushy. Bear is quite interesting—the fat tastes a bit like sushi, whereas the meat itself can be bitter.

No matter what my personal preferences, I admire the ingenuity of these rural, resourceful cooks. As the locals say, there's no reason to throw away free meat.

> **Believe it or not, West Virginians take their critter-cooking craft quite seriously.**

POSSUM BURGOO

KENTUCKY BURGOO

HANDS-ON TIME: 30 MINUTES ★ TOTAL TIME: 1 HOUR 30 MINUTES

This versatile Southern dish has many different interpretations. Here I use a combination of smoked bacon, Italian pork sausage, beef chuck steak, and flavorful chicken thighs to add heady flavor. I cook the rice in with the stew, so the entire dish is permeated with rich, robust flavor.

2 smoked bacon slices, chopped

6 ounces bulk sweet Italian pork sausage

8 ounces chuck roast, cut into 1-inch pieces

¾ cup chopped onion

½ cup chopped carrot

¼ cup chopped celery

2 chicken thighs, skinned and cut into bite-sized pieces

1 teaspoon kosher salt

½ teaspoon freshly ground black pepper

5 garlic cloves, minced

½ cup dry white wine

3 cups unsalted chicken cooking stock

3 cups water

1 cup uncooked brown rice

8 ounces small red potatoes, quartered

1½ cups (1-inch) fresh green bean pieces

1 cup fresh or frozen corn kernels, thawed

Hot sauce (optional)

1. Cook bacon in a Dutch oven over medium heat 3 minutes, stirring frequently. Add sausage; cook 4 minutes or until browned, stirring to crumble. Add beef; cook 3 minutes or until browned, stirring occasionally.

2. Add onion, carrot, and celery to pan; cook 5 minutes, stirring occasionally. Add chicken, salt, and pepper to pan; cook 4 minutes, stirring occasionally. Add garlic; cook 1 minute, stirring constantly. Stir in wine; bring to a boil. Cook until liquid almost evaporates (about 3 minutes). Stir in stock, 3 cups water, and rice; bring to a boil. Reduce heat to medium-low, cover, and simmer gently about 30 minutes. Stir in potatoes; cover and simmer gently about 20 minutes, stirring occasionally. Stir in green beans and corn; simmer gently for 8 minutes or until done, skimming as necessary. Sprinkle with hot sauce, if desired. Serves 6 (serving size: about 1¾ cups)

CALORIES 353; FAT 8.7 (sat 2.9g, mono 3.2g, poly 2.3g); PROTEIN 26.1g; CARB 41.6g; FIBER 3.7g; CHOL 53mg; IRON 2.8mg; SODIUM 680mg; CALC 62mg

BEEF AND MUSHROOM STEW

HANDS-ON TIME: 15 MINUTES ★ TOTAL TIME: 2 HOURS 45 MINUTES

There are just a few minutes of browning required before the oven does all the work for this dish. So easy!

1.1 ounces all-purpose flour (about ¼ cup)

½ teaspoon kosher salt

¼ teaspoon freshly ground black pepper

2½ pounds beef stew meat

3 tablespoons canola oil

1½ cups (½-inch) sliced carrot (4 carrots)

1 cup (½-inch) diagonally sliced celery (4 stalks)

1 cup spicy vegetable juice

1 cup fat-free, lower-sodium chicken broth

½ teaspoon dried thyme

3 red bliss potatoes, cut into 1-inch chunks

2 onions, each cut into 8 wedges

1 (8-ounce) package cremini mushrooms, halved

1. Preheat oven to 300°.
2. Combine flour, salt, and pepper in a large heavy-duty zip-top plastic bag. Add half of beef; seal bag, and shake until beef is evenly coated. Remove beef from bag, shaking off excess flour mixture, and place on large plate. Repeat procedure with remaining beef and flour mixture.
3. Heat a Dutch oven over medium heat. Add 1½ tablespoons oil to pan; swirl to coat. Add half of beef; cook 3 minutes, turning to brown on all sides. Remove beef from pan. Repeat procedure with remaining oil and beef, leaving beef in pan.
4. Return first half of beef to pan. Add carrot and remaining ingredients, scraping pan to loosen browned bits.
5. Cover and bake at 300° for 2 hours and 30 minutes or until beef and vegetables are tender. Serves 8 (serving size: about ¾ cup)

CALORIES 386; FAT 11.6g (sat 2.8g, mono 5.9g, poly 1.9g); PROTEIN 31g; CARB 39g; FIBER 4.2g; CHOL 77mg; IRON 4.3mg; SODIUM 280mg; CALC 60mg

MINNESOTA WILD RICE SOUP

HANDS-ON TIME: 35 MINUTES ★ TOTAL TIME: 1 HOUR 30 MINUTES

Here's a hearty winter favorite from the upper Midwest. Wild rice—the official state grain of Minnesota—"pops" when you cook it, adding creaminess to the soup.

2 leeks (about 1 pound)

1 tablespoon unsalted butter

2 celery stalks, finely chopped (about ¾ cup)

10 ounces sliced button or cremini mushrooms

7 cups fat-free, lower-sodium chicken broth, divided

¾ cup uncooked wild rice

1 teaspoon kosher salt

½ teaspoon dried thyme

½ teaspoon freshly ground black pepper

2.25 ounces all-purpose flour (about ½ cup)

2 cups chopped cooked chicken breast (about 1 pound)

1 cup half-and-half

3 tablespoons dry white wine

1 tablespoon Dijon mustard

1. Remove roots, outer leaves, and tops from leeks. Cut leeks in half lengthwise. Rinse thoroughly with cold water, and cut each half into ¼-inch slices.

2. Melt butter in a Dutch oven over medium heat. Add leeks, celery, and mushrooms; sauté 10 minutes or until tender. Stir in 6 cups broth. Add rice and next 3 ingredients (through pepper); bring to a boil. Cover, reduce heat, and simmer 45 to 55 minutes or until rice has "popped."

3. Weigh or lightly spoon flour into a dry measuring cup; level with a knife. Combine flour and 1 cup broth, stirring with a whisk until smooth. Add broth mixture to soup. Cook over medium heat 2 minutes or until slightly thick, stirring constantly. Reduce heat to low; add chicken, half-and-half, wine, and mustard. Cook 2 minutes or just until thoroughly heated (do not boil). Serves 8 (serving size: about 1¼ cups)

CALORIES 350; FAT 9.6g (sat 5.1g, mono 3.2g, poly 1.2g); PROTEIN 29.5g; CARB 34.2g; FIBER 2.7g; CHOL 70mg; IRON 2.3mg; SODIUM 598mg; CALC 86mg

The wild rice that isn't

Wild rice may look like rice but it's the seed of a marsh grass that has grown along the shallow lakes and slow-moving streams of what is now northern Minnesota for thousands of years. The Sioux and Ojibwe Native Americans were the first to harvest and cook with the wild grain, which is the only cereal grain native to North America. It is now commonly cultivated in the same region where it once grew wild.

Wild rice has a crunchy texture and earthy flavor. It is a versatile ingredient that's delicious in stuffings, casseroles, and salads.

Signature specialty

During the Great Depression, the French Canadians brought chicken and dumplings to the American South and Midwest. While the exact location of where it first became popular in the U.S. is disputed, it's generally accepted that there are two regionally distinct dumpling styles—the Midwestern biscuit-like option and the Southern pasta-like version. Regardless of which region truly gave this dish its claim to fame, both versions are still considered to be a signature comfort food specialty in each area.

My recipe was inspired by the Midwestern version of the dish, in which chicken is cooked in water with seasonings then topped with small balls of biscuit dough. The result—fluffy dumplings with a tender, biscuit-like texture topping a savory mixture that's reminiscent of chicken soup.

CHICKEN AND DUMPLINGS

HANDS-ON TIME: 47 MINUTES ★ TOTAL TIME: 11 HOURS 21 MINUTES

How do you make a thick, homemade chicken soup even better? Add dumplings! This lightened-up version is rich and satisfying enough to be a meal.

Stock:

1 (4-pound) whole chicken

10 cups water

4 cups unsalted chicken stock

1 tablespoon black peppercorns

3 celery stalks, coarsely chopped (about 6 ounces)

2 carrots, cut into 1-inch pieces (about 5 ounces)

2 bay leaves

1 onion, peeled and cut into wedges (about 10 ounces)

½ bunch fresh flat-leaf parsley (about 2 ounces)

Dumplings:

3 tablespoons butter, divided

1 cup chopped onion

¼ cup sliced celery

1 carrot, halved lengthwise and sliced

1 tablespoon all-purpose flour

1 teaspoon kosher salt, divided

½ teaspoon freshly ground black pepper

4.5 ounces all-purpose flour (about 1 cup)

1 teaspoon baking soda

6 tablespoons nonfat buttermilk

Remaining Ingredients:

1 tablespoon chopped fresh thyme

3 tablespoons chopped fresh flat-leaf parsley

1. To prepare stock, remove giblets and neck from chicken; trim excess fat. Place chicken, 10 cups water, and next 7 ingredients (through parsley bunch) in an 8-quart stock pot. Bring to a boil; reduce heat, and simmer, uncovered, 1 hour, skimming foam from surface as necessary. Remove from heat; let stand 20 minutes.

2. Remove skin from chicken; remove chicken from bones, discarding skin and bones. Shred chicken with 2 forks into bite-sized pieces. Strain broth through a sieve into a large bowl; discard solids. Cool broth and chicken to room temperature. Cover and chill broth and chicken 8 to 24 hours. Skim solidified fat from surface; discard. Reserve 8 cups broth and chicken. Refrigerate remaining broth in an airtight container for up to 1 week, or freeze for up to 3 months for another use.

3. To prepare dumplings, melt 1 tablespoon butter in a Dutch oven over medium heat. Add onion, celery, and carrot to pan; cook 8 minutes, stirring occasionally. Stir in 1 tablespoon flour, ¾ teaspoon salt, and pepper; cook, stirring constantly, 1 minute. Stir in 8 cups reserved stock. Bring to a boil; reduce heat and simmer 15 minutes, stirring occasionally.

4. Weigh or lightly spoon 4.5 ounces flour (about 1 cup) into a dry measuring cup; level with a knife. Combine flour, baking soda, and ¼ teaspoon salt, stirring with a whisk. Cut in 2 tablespoons butter with a pastry blender or 2 knives until mixture resembles coarse meal. Add buttermilk, stirring until moist.

5. Drop dough in 24 (about 1-teaspoon) portions into broth mixture. Cover and cook 8 minutes. Gently stir in reserved shredded chicken and thyme. Simmer very low 6 minutes or until thoroughly heated and dumplings are done. Remove from heat, and ladle into shallow bowls. Sprinkle evenly with chopped parsley. Serves 8 (serving size: 1¼ cups chicken mixture, 3 dumplings, and 1 teaspoon parsley)

CALORIES 258; FAT 7.4g (sat 3.5g, mono 2g, poly 1g); PROTEIN 26.2g; CARB 20.7g; FIBER 2.2g; CHOL 77mg; IRON 2.5mg; SODIUM 629mg; CALC 69mg

CHICKEN— MATZOH BALL SOUP

HANDS-ON TIME: 60 MINUTES ★ TOTAL TIME: 5 HOURS 5 MINUTES

For a shortcut version of this dish, use unsalted chicken stock instead of making your own.

Stock:

3 pounds chicken wings

2 large carrots, peeled and coarsely chopped

2 celery stalks, coarsely chopped

1 medium onion, cut into wedges

3 quarts cold water

1 tablespoon whole black peppercorns

1 bunch fresh flat-leaf parsley

1 bay leaf

Soup:

¼ cup club soda

1 tablespoon canola oil

2 large eggs

⅔ cup matzoh meal

1 tablespoon chopped fresh dill

1 teaspoon kosher salt, divided

½ teaspoon freshly ground black pepper, divided

3 chicken leg quarters, skinned

1 cup diagonally sliced carrot

1 cup sliced celery

1 cup vertically sliced onion

2 tablespoons chopped fresh flat-leaf parsley

1 tablespoon chopped fresh chives

1. To prepare stock, preheat oven to 425°. Spread chicken wings and next 3 ingredients (through onion wedges) in a single layer on a large baking sheet; bake at 425° for 40 minutes or until golden. Scrape chicken wing mixture and pan drippings into a large Dutch oven. Add 3 quarts cold water and next 3 ingredients (through bay leaf); bring to a boil over medium heat. Reduce heat to low, and simmer very gently 2½ hours, skimming surface as necessary. Strain mixture through a fine-mesh sieve lined with a double layer of cheesecloth over a bowl; discard solids. Wipe pan with paper towels. Return stock to pan; bring to a boil. Cook until reduced to 6 cups.

2. To prepare soup, combine club soda, oil, and eggs in a medium bowl, stirring well. Stir in matzoh meal, dill, ¼ teaspoon salt, and ¼ teaspoon pepper; chill 30 minutes. Shape dough into 24 (½-inch) balls.

3. Combine reduced stock and chicken leg quarters in a large Dutch oven over medium-high heat; bring to a simmer. Reduce heat, and cook 30 minutes or until chicken is done, skimming surface as necessary. Remove chicken from pan; cool slightly. Shred chicken with 2 forks; discard bones. Add matzoh balls, sliced carrot, and sliced celery to stock in pan; bring to a simmer. Cook 20 minutes. Stir in vertically sliced onion; cook 5 minutes or until matzoh balls are thoroughly cooked. Remove from heat; stir in shredded chicken, ¾ teaspoon salt, ¼ teaspoon pepper, 2 tablespoons chopped parsley, and chives. Serves 6 (serving size: about 1¼ cups soup and 4 matzoh balls)

CALORIES 240; FAT 8.7g (sat 1.9g, mono 3.7g, poly 2g); PROTEIN 20g; CARB 21g; FIBER 2.6g; CHOL 132mg; IRON 1.7mg; SODIUM 447mg; CALC 52mg

The hidden matzoh

Matzoh is a type of unleavened bread that has a special role at the Passover Seder, which is a holiday meal enjoyed by Jewish people in the spring. Observant Jews do not eat bread or any leavened food for the week-long holiday and enjoy matzoh instead.

During the Seder, the matzoh is used in symbolic ways, representing many traditions. But when I was a child, my favorite tradition was the time during the meal when an adult hid a piece of matzoh somewhere in the house. Technically speaking, the meal does not end until a child at the table finds the hidden matzoh (called an *afikomen*), returns it to the person running the Seder, and then this found piece of matzoh is shared for dessert.

Though matzoh will never win a prize for best dessert, something about the festivities surrounding the hunt makes the cracker taste that much sweeter.

Salad on a stick at the
Iowa State Fair

ON THE
SIDE

Casseroles & Veggies

French
Fries

Mel's Burger Bar,
New York, NY

Everyone always talks about the main dish, but a really good side dish—or two, or three— can steal the show.

*t*hink about it. What would Thanksgiving be without sweet potato casserole? Who wants meat without the potatoes? I love offering a variety of side dishes, and I always try to choose dishes that complement each other as well as the main dish. I also try to balance a heavier main dish with a lighter side, and vice versa.

Casseroles can be especially complicated to lighten up because so often they're made with lots of cream and cheese, and because right-sizing portions is difficult with a large deep dish. I share my secrets —some stolen from the *Cooking Light* Test Kitchen!—for keeping the calories low enough so that a second helping won't do much damage. Feel free to dig in.

Brussels Sprouts
with Bacon p. 225

SWEET ONION CASSEROLE

HANDS-ON TIME: 26 MINUTES ★ TOTAL TIME: 61 MINUTES

This is THE way to enjoy sweet onions from Washington, California, or Georgia. Rice and cheese add heft and flavor to this casserole while letting the star veggie shine.

1 quart water

¾ cup uncooked long-grain rice

2 tablespoons canola oil

3¾ cups chopped sweet onion

1 tablespoon all-purpose flour

½ teaspoon kosher salt

1 cup fat-free milk

3 ounces Gruyère cheese, shredded (about ¾ cup)

Cooking spray

¼ cup (1 ounce) grated fresh Parmesan cheese

2 tablespoons chopped fresh parsley

1. Preheat oven to 350°.

2. Bring 1 quart water to a boil; stir in rice. Cook 5 minutes; drain.

3. Heat a large skillet over medium-high heat. Add oil to pan; swirl to coat. Add onion; cook 6 minutes or until tender, stirring occasionally. Sprinkle flour and salt over onion mixture, stirring until blended. Cook, stirring constantly, 1 minute.

4. Gradually add milk, stirring with a whisk until blended. Cook 3 minutes or until thick, stirring frequently. Add Gruyère cheese and rice, stirring until cheese melts. Pour onion mixture into an 11 x 7–inch glass or ceramic baking dish coated with cooking spray. Sprinkle with Parmesan cheese.

5. Bake, uncovered, at 350° for 35 minutes or until bubbly and brown. Sprinkle with parsley. Serves 8 (serving size: ⅛ of casserole)

CALORIES 199; FAT 8g (sat 2.9g, mono 3.7g, poly 1.3g); PROTEIN 7.8g; CARB 23.4g; FIBER 1.6g; CHOL 15mg; IRON 1.1mg; SODIUM 227mg; CALC 207mg

An onion a day...

A low sulfur content and high moisture make sweet onions extremely mild; in fact, some people enjoy eating sweet onions as they would an apple. They are often thinly sliced and served in salads or sandwiches. When cooked, their natural sweetness is intensified, delivering fantastic flavor to casseroles, soups, and skillet dishes.

Popular varieties are named for the regions in which they are grown—Walla Walla onions come from the Walla Walla Valley in Washington state, Vidalia onions from Vidalia, Georgia, and Imperial Sweet onions from the Imperial Valley in California. Each varies slightly in size, sweetness, and flavor.

Puttin' on the Ritz

Squash casserole originated as a back-of-box recipe for Ritz crackers, but was introduced to me by my sister-in-law Laurie Prohaska Fishman (that's us in the picture above). She often had it as a kid—her mother knew how to get fresh vegetables into her three daughters. She now prepares the same recipe for her own children. I'm generally a fan of back-of-box recipes, as they're tried-and-true dishes that people love to eat time and time again. This lighter version is guaranteed to be a success with your family—especially your kids.

SQUASH CASSEROLE

HANDS-ON TIME: 22 MINUTES ★ TOTAL TIME: 52 MINUTES

Moms often serve this dish to picky eaters who don't want to eat their vegetables. It works every time, thanks to the crumbled crackers and creamy cheese traditionally found in this dish. My version is lighter—but your kids will never know the difference.

2 tablespoons canola oil

1½ cups sliced onion

6 cups sliced yellow squash (about 1½ pounds)

¼ teaspoon freshly ground black pepper

3 ounces ⅓-less-fat cream cheese (about ⅓ cup), softened

¼ cup fat-free milk

2 large eggs

3 ounces reduced-fat cheddar cheese, shredded (about ¾ cup)

27 reduced-fat round buttery crackers, crushed

Cooking spray

1. Preheat oven to 375°.

2. Heat a large skillet over medium-high heat. Add oil to pan; swirl to coat. Add onion; cook 2 minutes. Add squash and pepper; sauté 10 to 12 minutes or until squash is golden brown. Remove from heat.

3. Combine cream cheese and milk in a large bowl, stirring with a whisk until smooth. Add eggs, stirring with a whisk. Stir in squash mixture, cheese, and half the crushed crackers. Spoon squash mixture into a 2-quart casserole dish coated with cooking spray.

4. Top with remaining crushed crackers. Bake at 375° for 30 minutes. Serves 10 (serving size: about ¾ cup)

CALORIES 145; FAT 8g (sat 2.7g, mono 3g, poly 1.5g); PROTEIN 6.2g; CARB 11.8g; FIBER 1.1g; CHOL 48mg; IRON 0.8mg; SODIUM 190mg; CALC 108mg

SWEET POTATO CASSEROLE
WITH MARSHMALLOW TOPPING

HANDS-ON TIME: 10 MINUTES ★ TOTAL TIME: 1 HOUR 30 MINUTES

Based on sweet potato pie, a favorite in the South, this famous Thanksgiving side dish has a rich history. The marshmallows were added by Janet McKenzie Hill, the founder of the Boston Cooking-School Magazine, in 1917, when the marshmallow evolved from a specialty confection into an everyday treat.

4¼ pounds sweet potatoes
2 tablespoons butter
½ teaspoon kosher salt
½ teaspoon ground ginger
½ teaspoon ground
   cinnamon

Cooking spray
3 cups miniature
   marshmallows

1. Preheat oven to 425°.
2. Place sweet potatoes in a shallow baking pan lined with foil. Bake at 425° for 1 hour or until tender. Reduce oven temperature to 350°.
3. Peel sweet potatoes; place in a large bowl. Add butter and next 3 ingredients (through cinnamon); mash with a potato masher until pureed. Spoon potato mixture into a 2-quart glass or ceramic baking dish coated with cooking spray.
4. Bake at 350° for 10 minutes. Top with marshmallows; bake an additional 10 minutes or until marshmallows are lightly browned. Serves 12 (serving size: ½ cup)

CALORIES 196; FAT 2.1g (sat 1.3g, mono 0.6g, poly 0.1g); PROTEIN 2.8g; CARB 42.6g; FIBER 4.9g; CHOL 5mg; IRON 1mg; SODIUM 195mg; CALC 50mg

CORN PUDDING

HANDS-ON TIME: 25 MINUTES ★ TOTAL TIME: 1 HOUR 10 MINUTES

Corn pudding is a specialty of the rural South. This recipe, which uses 5 cups of kernels, is great when you have a bumper crop of corn. Frozen, thawed kernels can be substituted when corn is out of season.

1 tablespoon butter
5 cups fresh corn kernels (8 ears)
½ cup chopped green onions
1½ cups fat-free milk
2 large eggs
1 cup part-skim ricotta cheese
½ cup yellow cornmeal
¼ cup chopped fresh basil

1 tablespoon sugar
1 teaspoon kosher salt
½ teaspoon freshly ground black pepper
6 ounces reduced-fat cheddar cheese shredded (1½ cups), divided
Cooking spray
Small fresh basil leaves (optional)

1. Preheat oven to 350°.
2. Melt butter in a large nonstick skillet over medium-high heat. Add corn and green onions; sauté 5 minutes. Remove from heat.
3. Combine milk and eggs in a large bowl, stirring with a whisk. Add ricotta cheese and next 5 ingredients (through pepper), stirring with a whisk. Stir in 1 cup cheddar cheese and corn mixture; pour into a 2½-quart glass or ceramic baking dish coated with cooking spray. Sprinkle with ½ cup cheddar cheese.
4. Bake at 350° for 45 minutes or until set. Garnish with basil, if desired. Serves 12 (serving size: ½₁₂ of casserole)

CALORIES 178; FAT 7.2g (sat 3.5g, mono 2.1g, poly 1.4g); PROTEIN 10g; CARB 21.2g; FIBER 1.6g; CHOL 53mg; IRON 0.7mg; SODIUM 349mg; CALC 285mg

FUNERAL POTATOES

HANDS-ON TIME: 10 MINUTES ★ TOTAL TIME: 60 MINUTES

This popular Utah comfort food is commonly brought to a post-funeral communal meal. The covered dish, or easy-to-reheat casserole, is a classic for potlucks and other large gatherings.

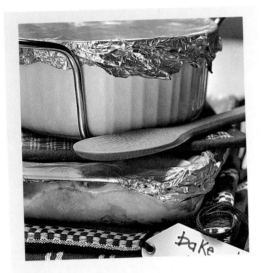

2 (10¾-ounce) cans condensed reduced-fat, reduced-sodium cream of chicken soup, undiluted

6 ounces reduced-fat cheddar cheese, shredded (about 1½ cups)

¾ cup reduced-fat sour cream

½ teaspoon salt

1 pound frozen Southern-style hash brown potatoes (about 5 cups)

5 cups fresh or frozen broccoli florets, thawed

1 cup chopped onion

Cooking spray

½ cup panko (Japanese breadcrumbs)

¼ cup (1 ounce) grated fresh Parmesan cheese

1. Preheat oven to 350°.

2. Combine chicken soup and next 3 ingredients (through salt) in a large bowl. Add hash browns, broccoli, and onion, stirring to coat.

3. Spoon hash brown mixture into a 13 x 9–inch glass or ceramic baking dish lightly coated with cooking spray. Top with bread-crumbs and Parmesan cheese. Bake at 350° for 50 minutes or until filling is bubbly and topping is browned. Serves 18 (serving size: ¾ cup)

CALORIES 103; FAT 4.5g (sat 2.5g, mono 1.1g, poly 0.5g); PROTEIN 5.5g; CARB 11g; FIBER 1.7g; CHOL 16mg; IRON 0.4mg; SODIUM 449mg; CALC 185mg

LIGHTEN UP

Keep it creamy & comforting

Rich cheese and sour cream keep this dish hearty and decadent. Some of the potatoes have been replaced with fiber-filled broccoli to bulk up the dish and reduce the calories. My secret for a crunchy topping that's lower in fat than potato chips? Breadcrumbs and a little Parmesan cheese.

NORTHWEST
Walla Walla Onion Casserole

Washington's Walla Walla onions enjoy only a short 10-week season beginning in mid-June, so local chefs look for many ways to use them when they come to market. Multiple variations of this casserole exist, but most highlight the Walla Walla's sweet flavor with a cheese-enhanced cream sauce and a crisp topping of buttered breadcrumbs or cracker crumbs.

AMERICA LOVES: CASSEROLES
The one dish that unites the nation

WEST
Cowboy Casserole

You'd have to be a fast-moving cowboy not to pack on a paunch after downing this Western favorite. A filling of ground beef, onions, peas, cheese, and cream of mushroom soup gets a crisp topping from neat rows of tater tots.

SOUTHWEST
King Ranch Casserole

If Texas had a state casserole, this would be it. This old-time Tex-Mex favorite melds cream sauce and shredded chicken with layers of cheese, bell peppers, onions, and tortillas. Although many Southerners would insist that it needs a cream-based soup for casserole authenticity, most Texans prefer a homemade roux-based sauce in this classic potluck and church-supper dish.

NORTHEAST
New Brunswick Lobster Casserole

This creamy casserole of cooked lobster, mushrooms, and shredded Swiss cheese is a Northeastern favorite during lobster season. Although named for New Brunswick, Canada, where lobster is the primary catch, the casserole is a favorite along the coastline of Maine and into other parts of New England.

MIDWEST
Spaghetti Casserole

Ever the thrifty and enterprising cooks, Midwesterners love this casserole—a repurposed spaghetti dinner. Traditional Bolognese-topped spaghetti is blended with a little bit of cream of mushroom soup to keep it moist, topped with cheese, and then baked in the oven.

EAST
Kugel

This time-honored noodle casserole was introduced into the New York region by Ashkenazi Jewish immigrants. The word *kugel* comes from the German word for "ball." It is traditionally a round, baked sweet or savory pudding or casserole made of noodles or potatoes (although many contemporary versions may include other grains and even vegetables).

SOUTH
Spoonbread

More akin to pudding than bread, this creamy Southern staple is best eaten with a spoon—hence its name. Spoonbread is usually made with cornmeal, milk, butter, flour, and eggs, and is said to have its origins in a Native American corn porridge called *suppone* or *suppawn*.

SOUTHEAST
Shrimp and Grits Dressing

This lowcountry favorite morphs a popular breakfast dish into a hearty dressing that's often served alongside turkey at Thanksgiving. Shrimp and grits casserole features fresh shrimp mixed with grits, butter, eggs, chicken broth, and Parmesan cheese.

FENNEL, SAUSAGE & CARAMELIZED-APPLE STUFFING

HANDS-ON TIME: 28 MINUTES ★ TOTAL TIME: 1 HOUR 28 MINUTES

This sophisticated stuffing truly satisfies. It combines the sweet licorice flavor of fennel, the tang of sourdough bread, the tartness of apple, and the rich spiciness of Italian sausage.

12 ounces sourdough bread, cut into ½-inch cubes

Cooking spray

9 ounces Italian sausage

5 teaspoons extra-virgin olive oil, divided

4 cups chopped onion

1¼ cups sliced fennel bulb

1¼ cups chopped carrot

2 tablespoons chopped fresh sage

½ teaspoon fennel seeds, crushed

5 garlic cloves, minced

½ teaspoon freshly ground black pepper, divided

3 cups chopped Golden Delicious apple

2 teaspoons sugar

1½ cups fat-free, lower-sodium chicken broth

2 large eggs

1. Preheat oven to 400°. Arrange bread cubes in a single layer on a baking sheet coated with cooking spray. Bake at 400° for 16 minutes or until golden, stirring after 8 minutes. Place in a large bowl.
2. Heat a skillet over medium-high heat. Remove casings from sausage. Coat pan with cooking spray. Add sausage; cook 8 minutes or until browned, stirring to crumble. Add sausage to bread.
3. Return pan to medium-high heat. Add 3 teaspoons oil to pan; swirl to coat. Add onion and next 5 ingredients (through garlic). Add ¼ teaspoon pepper; sauté 8 minutes or until vegetables are tender, stirring occasionally. Add vegetables to sausage mixture.
4. Return pan to medium-high heat. Add 2 teaspoons oil to pan; swirl to coat. Add apple and sugar; sauté 5 minutes or until apple caramelizes, stirring occasionally. Add to sausage mixture. Combine broth and eggs in a bowl, stirring with a whisk. Add broth mixture and ¼ teaspoon pepper to sausage mixture; toss.
5. Spoon sausage mixture into a 13 x 9–inch glass or ceramic baking dish coated with cooking spray. Cover with foil. Bake at 400° for 20 minutes. Uncover dish; bake at 400° for an additional 20 minutes or until browned and crisp. Serves 12 (serving size: about ⅔ cup)

CALORIES 180; FAT 5.4g (sat 1.3g, mono 2.5g, poly 0.7g); PROTEIN 8.4g; CARB 26.3g; FIBER 3g; CHOL 42mg; IRON 1.9mg; SODIUM 359mg; CALC 66mg

WILD RICE STUFFING
WITH DRIED CHERRIES & TOASTED PECANS

HANDS-ON TIME: 40 MINUTES ★ TOTAL TIME: 2 HOURS 5 MINUTES

The nutty, almost smoky flavor of wild rice pairs beautifully with sweet dried cherries. This dish works well with turkey and other poultry.

¼ cup butter, divided

2 cups thinly sliced leek (about 1 large)

1 tablespoon chopped fresh thyme

1 teaspoon kosher salt, divided

3 cups water

2 cups fat-free, lower-sodium chicken broth

1 cup uncooked wild rice

2 cups uncooked long-grain brown rice

½ cup finely chopped peeled turnip

⅓ cup finely chopped celery

⅓ cup finely chopped carrot

⅔ cup chopped pecans, toasted

½ cup chopped dried sweet cherries

2 green onions, thinly sliced

1. Heat 2 tablespoons butter in a large saucepan over medium heat; swirl to coat. Add leek, thyme, and ½ teaspoon salt; sauté 8 minutes, stirring occasionally. Add 3 cups water, broth, and wild rice; cover. Increase heat to high; bring to a boil. Reduce heat, and simmer 30 minutes. Stir in brown rice; cover and simmer 30 minutes. Remove from heat.

2. Preheat oven to 400°.

3. Heat 2 tablespoons butter over high heat in a large skillet; swirl to coat. Add turnip, celery, carrot, and ½ teaspoon salt; sauté 1 minute. Reduce heat to medium; cook 4 minutes, stirring occasionally. Remove from heat.

4. Combine rice mixture, turnip mixture, pecans, cherries, and onions in a large bowl. Spoon stuffing into a 13 x 9–inch glass or ceramic baking dish. Cover with foil; bake at 400° for 20 minutes or until liquid is absorbed. Let stand 5 minutes before serving. Serves 12 (serving size: 1 cup)

CALORIES 277; FAT 9.4g (sat 3g, mono 3.8g, poly 1.9g); PROTEIN 5.9g; CARB 43.1g; FIBER 3.9g; CHOL 10mg; IRON 1.5mg; SODIUM 268mg; CALC 40mg

America's sweet-tarts

My father was born in Michigan, where cherries are plentiful. He loves to tell sweet stories about his maternal grandparents who ran a kosher rooming house near the sulfur baths where people would come to take a soak for good health. Recently, my parents have been ordering dried sour cherries from the Great Lakes State, and they're a reminder of his childhood. I like to add them to morning oatmeal, but they're also terrific plumped and added to ice cream, and a small handful makes a quick and tasty dessert.

BAKED LOUISIANA DIRTY RICE AND BEANS

HANDS-ON TIME: 15 MINUTES ★ TOTAL TIME: 1 HOUR 30 MINUTES

This spicy casserole, an old Cajun favorite, traditionally features chicken livers and gizzards, but I've substituted juicy chicken thighs.

1 tablespoon olive oil

1 cup finely chopped green bell pepper

¾ cup finely chopped red onion

½ cup finely chopped celery

½ pound skinless, boneless chicken thighs, cut into ½-inch cubes

1 cup uncooked long-grain brown rice

2½ cups fat-free, lower-sodium chicken broth

½ cup thinly sliced green onions

2 teaspoons minced fresh thyme

1 teaspoon salt

½ teaspoon freshly ground black pepper

⅛ to ¼ teaspoon ground red pepper

2 garlic cloves, minced

1 (15-ounce) can red kidney beans, drained and rinsed

1. Preheat oven to 350°.

2. Heat a large Dutch oven over medium heat. Add oil to pan; swirl to coat. Add bell pepper, red onion, and celery to pan; cook 4 minutes or until vegetables are tender, stirring occasionally. Add chicken; cook 3 minutes or until lightly browned. Stir in rice; cook 30 seconds. Add broth and remaining ingredients; bring to a simmer. Cover and bake at 350° for 1 hour and 15 minutes or until liquid is absorbed and rice is tender. Serves 12 (serving size: about ½ cup)

CALORIES 125; FAT 3.1g (sat 0.7g, mono 1.5g, poly 0.7g); PROTEIN 6.8g; CARB 17.5g; FIBER 2.4g; CHOL 13mg; IRON 0.8mg; SODIUM 370mg; CALC 21mg

FRIED RICE

HANDS-ON TIME: 25 MINUTES ★ TOTAL TIME: 25 MINUTES

Enjoy a healthier version of this Chinese takeout favorite at home! To make it a meal, increase the portion size and top with a sunny-side-up egg.

2 tablespoons canola oil

½ cup thinly sliced green onions

1 tablespoon minced garlic

1 tablespoon minced peeled fresh ginger

1 large egg, beaten

3 cups cooked long-grain rice, chilled

½ cup frozen petite green peas

1 tablespoon lower-sodium soy sauce

1½ teaspoons dark sesame oil

2 ounces 33%-less-sodium ham, cut into ⅓-inch cubes

Chopped green onions (optional)

1. Heat a large nonstick skillet over medium heat. Add oil to pan; swirl to coat. Add ½ cup green onions; sauté 2 minutes. Add garlic and ginger; sauté 1 minute. Stir in egg. Cook, stirring constantly, 30 seconds or until set. Add rice and next 4 ingredients (through ham). Cook, stirring constantly, 5 minutes or until thoroughly heated. Remove from heat. Garnish with chopped green onions, if desired. Serves 8 (serving size: ½ cup)

CALORIES 149; FAT 6g (sat 0.8g, mono 3.1g, poly 1.6g); PROTEIN 4.5g; CARB 19g; FIBER 0.9g; CHOL 27mg; IRON 1.1mg; SODIUM 153mg; CALC 17mg

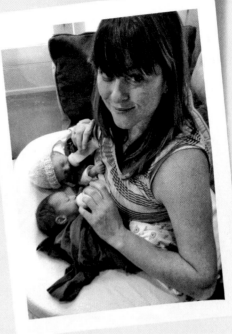

Healthy takeout

In the first few months after I gave birth to my twin boys, Abe and Zev, my eating and cooking patterns changed dramatically. While feeding two newborn babies, I found myself with a lot less time to cook, and turned to Chinese takeout instead—something I hadn't done in the past. In my desire to lose the baby weight, I found healthy options on the menu like steamed vegetables with garlic and ginger sauce, but I always had an abundance of leftover rice. This was one of my favorite dishes to make during that time—simple and tasty, with leftover rice and other ingredients I had in the house.

Prize-worthy mac and cheese

For the past few years, Aspen, Colorado, has hosted an immensely popular mac-and-cheese festival and cooking competition. Local chefs are invited to show off their tastiest versions of the dish to try and win the coveted golden noodle trophy. These chefs would know a thing or two about this comforting dish; mac and cheese is in especially hot demand among the après-ski crowd. And these chefs put their best foot forward.

At the festival, I asked local chefs to share tips for making the best mac and cheese. Some of their recommendations:

1. Use truffle oil. It has an intense earthiness that wakes up otherwise ordinary mac and cheese.

2. Make your own cheese sauce. Some chefs use milk steeped with onion and bay leaf to bump up the flavor.

3. Don't overcook the macaroni. Boil it just until al dente. It will cook more after it's mixed with the sauce and baked in the oven.

4. Use the macaroni cooking water in your sauce—the starch from the pasta is a perfect thickener.

5. Add beer. It contributes a little bite and bitterness to counteract the richness of the sauce.

TRUFFLED MAC AND CHEESE

HANDS-ON TIME: 20 MINUTES ★ TOTAL TIME: 44 MINUTES

This recipe is a lightened-up version of the double award-winning mac and cheese from Chef Tico Starr of Rustique Bistro in Aspen, Colorado. His secret ingredient is white truffle oil, which adds a rich, earthy flavor to the sauce.

2¼ cups 1% low-fat milk, divided

2 cups sliced onion (about 1 medium)

1 bay leaf

12 ounces uncooked elbow macaroni

2 tablespoons all-purpose flour

¾ teaspoon kosher salt

3 ounces fontina cheese, shredded (about ¾ cup)

2 ounces Comté or Gruyère cheese, shredded (about ½ cup)

1½ teaspoons white truffle oil

2 ounces French bread baguette, torn

2 tablespoons grated fresh Parmesan cheese

2 garlic cloves, crushed

1 tablespoon olive oil

1. Heat 1¾ cups milk, onion, and bay leaf in a large saucepan to 180° or until tiny bubbles form around edges (do not boil). Cover and remove from heat; let stand 15 minutes.

2. Cook pasta according to package directions; drain.

3. Strain milk mixture through a colander over a bowl; discard solids. Return milk to saucepan over medium heat. Combine remaining ½ cup milk and flour in a small bowl, stirring with a whisk until well blended. Gradually stir flour mixture and salt into warm milk, stirring constantly with a whisk. Bring mixture to a boil, stirring frequently; cook 1 minute, stirring constantly. Remove from heat; let stand 6 minutes or until mixture cools to 155°. Gradually add fontina and Comté cheeses, stirring until cheeses melt. Stir in pasta and truffle oil. Spoon mixture into a 2-quart broiler-safe glass or ceramic baking dish.

4. Preheat broiler. Place bread, Parmesan cheese, and garlic in a food processor; process until coarse crumbs form. Drizzle with olive oil; pulse until fine crumbs form. Sprinkle breadcrumb mixture over pasta. Place dish on middle rack in oven; broil 2 minutes or until golden brown. Serves 12 (serving size: about ½ cup)

CALORIES 209; FAT 6.6g (sat 3.1g, mono 2.6g, poly 0.6g); PROTEIN 9.5g; CARB 27.6g; FIBER 1.1g; CHOL 17mg; IRON 1.2mg; SODIUM 264mg; CALC 163mg

VERMONT BAKED BEANS

HANDS-ON TIME: 30 MINUTES ★ TOTAL TIME: 10 HOURS 42 MINUTES

In Boston, molasses and salt pork are the traditional additions to a pot of baked beans. The sauce for my baked beans isn't as thick and sweet as Boston's rendition, and the flavor of the maple syrup and bacon make it undeniably Vermont.

1 pound dried navy beans
4 bacon slices, chopped
½ cup chopped onion
¼ cup packed brown sugar
¼ cup maple syrup

1 tablespoon dry mustard
1 teaspoon kosher salt
¼ teaspoon freshly ground
    black pepper
6 cups water, divided

1. Sort and wash beans; place in a large Dutch oven. Cover with water to 2 inches above beans; cover and let stand 8 hours. Drain beans. Wipe pan dry with a paper towel.
2. Cook bacon in Dutch oven over medium-high heat 3 minutes, stirring frequently. Add onion; reduce heat to medium, and cook 4 minutes or until onion is tender, stirring occasionally.
3. Combine brown sugar and next 4 ingredients (through pepper) in a small bowl; stir well. Add 1 cup water; stir until well blended.
4. Add beans to pan, stirring to coat. Stir in brown sugar mixture. Add 5 cups water; bring to a boil. Reduce heat, and simmer 30 minutes, stirring occasionally.
5. Preheat oven to 300°. Bake beans for 2 hours or until beans are tender, stirring occasionally. Serves 10 (serving size: about ¾ cup)

CALORIES 203; FAT 1.5g (sat 0.4g, mono 0.3g, poly 0.5g); PROTEIN 9.7g; CARB 38.8g; FIBER 11.1g; CHOL 2mg; IRON 2.6mg; SODIUM 230mg; CALC 89mg

SOUTHERN FIELD PEAS

HANDS-ON TIME: 8 MINUTES ★ TOTAL TIME: 38 MINUTES

The Southerners in the Cooking Light Test Kitchen love this dish. It uses pink-eyed peas, which are a local favorite, but feel free to use black-eyed peas instead.

2 teaspoons olive oil
½ cup chopped onion
2 garlic cloves, minced
3 cups fresh pink-eyed peas
3 cups water

3 bacon slices
½ teaspoon salt
½ teaspoon freshly ground black pepper

1. Heat a large saucepan over medium-high heat. Add oil to pan; swirl to coat. Add onion and garlic; sauté 2 minutes. Add peas, 3 cups water, and bacon; bring to a boil. Reduce heat; simmer, partially covered, 30 minutes or until tender. Discard bacon. Stir in salt and pepper. Serves 6 (serving size: ½ cup)

CALORIES 167; FAT 5.3g (sat 1.6g, mono 2.8g, poly 0.6g); PROTEIN 4.1g; CARB 26.1g; FIBER 6.3g; CHOL 3mg; IRON 1.4mg; SODIUM 320mg; CALC 157mg

ROASTED CARROTS

HANDS-ON TIME: 8 MINUTES ★ TOTAL TIME: 43 MINUTES

This recipe was inspired by a dish I had at Nightwood restaurant in Chicago. Roasting carrots brings out their natural sweetness.

2 pounds small carrots, cut in half lengthwise
1½ tablespoons olive oil
½ teaspoon kosher salt
5 thyme sprigs
¼ cup loosely packed chopped fresh dill or parsley

1. Preheat oven to 400°.
2. Combine first 4 ingredients on a large baking sheet; toss to coat. Bake at 400° for 35 to 40 minutes or until tender, turning carrots after 20 minutes. Discard thyme sprigs.
3. Place carrots on a serving platter; garnish with dill or parsley. Serves 6 (serving size: about 5 carrot slices)

CALORIES 92; FAT 3.7g (sat 0.5g, mono 2.5g, poly 0.5g); PROTEIN 1.4g; CARB 14.6g; FIBER 4.3g; CHOL 0mg; IRON 0.5mg; SODIUM 264mg; CALC 52mg

BRUSSELS SPROUTS
WITH BACON

HANDS-ON TIME: 15 MINUTES ★ TOTAL TIME: 60 MINUTES

Roasting Brussels sprouts really brings out their nutty flavor, which goes so well with smoky bacon and sweet red onions.

2 pounds small Brussels sprouts, trimmed
1 red onion, peeled and cut into ⅓-inch wedges
2 tablespoons olive oil

½ teaspoon kosher salt
¼ teaspoon freshly ground black pepper
2 bacon slices, chopped

1. Preheat oven to 400°.
2. Place Brussels sprouts and red onion on a baking sheet. Drizzle olive oil over vegetables, and sprinkle with salt and pepper, tossing to coat. Sprinkle bacon over top of vegetables.
3. Bake at 400° for 45 minutes or until Brussels sprouts and onion are golden and tender and bacon is crisp, stirring every 20 minutes. Serves 6 (serving size: about 1 cup)

CALORIES 113; FAT 5g (sat 0.9g, mono 3.3g, poly 0.7g); PROTEIN 5.5g; CARB 13.9g; FIBER 5.5g; CHOL 2mg; IRON 1.9mg; SODIUM 224mg; CALC 62mg

ROASTED CAULIFLOWER
WITH MORNAY SAUCE

HANDS-ON TIME: 10 MINUTES ★ TOTAL TIME: 40 MINUTES

Roasting intensifies the delicate flavor of this vegetable, lending it a sweet, nutty flavor and creamy texture. The dry cooking technique far surpasses boiling, which can leave cauliflower soggy, bland, and depleted of nutrients.

1 (3-pound) head cauliflower, trimmed
Cooking spray
¼ teaspoon kosher salt
1 tablespoon all-purpose flour
¾ cup 2% reduced-fat milk
¼ teaspoon salt

1½ ounces Gruyère cheese, shredded (about ⅓ cup)
2 tablespoons sharp cheddar cheese, shredded (optional)
2 tablespoons coarsely chopped fresh flat-leaf parsley

1. Preheat oven to 425°.
2. Place cauliflower on a large cutting board, stalk end down; cut lengthwise into 6 planks (about 1 inch thick).
3. Place cauliflower on a large baking sheet coated with cooking spray. (You will have long cross sections as well as florets.) Spray cauliflower with cooking spray. Bake at 425° for 30 minutes or until cauliflower is tender and browned, turning after 15 minutes. Remove cauliflower to a serving platter. Sprinkle with salt.
4. Place flour in a small saucepan. Gradually add milk and salt, stirring constantly with a whisk until blended. Place over low heat; cook until thick (about 5 minutes), stirring constantly. Remove from heat; add cheeses, stirring with a whisk until cheese melts and sauce thickens. Keep warm.
5. Drizzle cheese sauce over cauliflower. Sprinkle with parsley. Serves 6 (serving size: 1 slice cauliflower and about 2 tablespoons sauce)

CALORIES 108; FAT 3g (sat 1.7g, mono 1.0g, poly 0.2g); PROTEIN 7.9g; CARB 14.1g; FIBER 4.7g; CHOL 10mg; IRON 1mg; SODIUM 268mg; CALC 156mg

Enticement for picky eaters

Although these roasted florets are fantastic on their own, no one (especially not kids) can resist them when dunked into a few spoonfuls of simple Mornay sauce.
My version uses low-fat milk and a reduced amount of cheese to lower the calories.

An historic side dish

According to early American food lore, the Algonquin people shared a version of this dish with the English settlers at the first Thanksgiving feast in Plymouth, Massachusetts. The name was derived from the Algonquin (Narragansett) word *msíckquatash*, which originally referred to boiled corn, although it now commonly applies to a mixture of corn and beans. Its use of inexpensive, plentiful ingredients made it a favorite throughout the Great Depression, when it was often served in casserole form with a light piecrust on top.

SUCCOTASH

HANDS-ON TIME: 20 MINUTES ★ TOTAL TIME: 20 MINUTES

Succotash is generally made with lima beans, but edamame add protein to this colorful side. Shelled edamame are now commonly available year-round in the frozen food section of most supermarkets.

1 applewood-smoked bacon slice
2 teaspoons butter
½ cup chopped onion
1½ cups fresh corn kernels
    (about 3 ears)
¾ cup frozen shelled edamame,
    thawed
⅓ cup unsalted chicken cooking stock
½ teaspoon kosher salt
¼ teaspoon freshly ground black
    pepper
1 cup grape tomatoes, halved
2 tablespoons chopped fresh basil

1. Cook bacon in a skillet over medium heat until crisp. Remove bacon from pan, reserving 2 teaspoons drippings in pan. Drain and crumble bacon.
2. Melt butter in bacon drippings. Add onion; cook 6 minutes or until tender, stirring occasionally. Add corn and next 4 ingredients (through pepper). Bring to a boil; reduce heat, and cook, uncovered, 4 minutes or until liquid evaporates, stirring occasionally. Remove from heat. Stir in bacon, tomatoes, and basil. Serves 6 (serving size: ½ cup)

CALORIES 85; FAT 3g (sat 1.1g, mono 0.8g, poly 0.7g); PROTEIN 4.7g; CARB 10.9g; FIBER 2.3g; CHOL 4.5mg; IRON 1mg; SODIUM 234mg; CALC 19mg

EAT YOUR VEGGIES

There's a healthy way to get your 5 a day wherever you are.

CREAMED CORN WITH BACON

Midwest

Cut kernels from 6 ears of corn; scrape milk and remaining pulp from cobs into a bowl. Place 1½ cups kernels, 2 cups 1% low-fat milk, 1 tablespoon cornstarch, 1 teaspoon sugar, ½ teaspoon salt, and ¼ teaspoon freshly ground black pepper in a food processor; process until smooth. Cook 4 bacon slices in a large nonstick skillet over medium heat. Remove bacon from pan, reserving 1 teaspoon drippings in pan; crumble bacon. Add 1 cup chopped leek to pan; cook 2 minutes, stirring constantly. Add pureed corn mixture, 1½ cups corn kernels, and corn milk mixture to pan. Bring to a boil, reduce heat, and simmer 3 minutes or until slightly thick. Stir in bacon just before serving. SERVES 6 (serving size ⅔ cup) CALORIES 151; FAT 4.6g (sat 1.7g); SODIUM 325mg

AVOCADO & ORANGE SALAD

West

Combine 1 tablespoon minced garlic, 1 teaspoon olive oil, ½ teaspoon black pepper, and ¼ teaspoon kosher salt in a bowl. Peel and section 1 orange; squeeze membranes to extract juice into bowl. Whisk mixture. Add orange sections, ½ cup grape tomatoes, ¼ cup sliced red onion, and 1 sliced peeled avocado to garlic mixture; toss gently. SERVES 4 (serving size: ½ cup) CALORIES 120; FAT 8.6g (sat 1.3g); SODIUM 126mg

JICAMA-CORN SALAD

Southwest

Heat 1 tablespoon olive oil in a large nonstick skillet over medium-high heat. Add ⅔ cup chopped jicama and 1 tablespoon minced jalapeño to pan; sauté 2 minutes, stirring frequently. Add 2 cups fresh corn kernels, 1¾ cups thinly sliced green onions, ⅔ cup chopped red bell pepper, ½ teaspoon ground cumin, and ¼ teaspoon salt; sauté 2 minutes, stirring frequently. SERVES 6 (serving size: 1 cup) CALORIES 151; FAT 6.1g (sat 0.5g); SODIUM 157mg

SOUR CREAM & ONION POTATO CHIPS

Northwest

Cut 1 large unpeeled baking potato into ⅛-inch-thick slices. Arrange one-third of potato slices on a large microwave-safe plate. Coat potatoes with cooking spray; sprinkle with ½ teaspoon ranch dressing mix. Microwave, uncovered, at HIGH 4 minutes. Turn potato slices over. Microwave at HIGH 3 to 4 minutes or until dried and beginning to brown. Remove from plate; cool on wire racks. Repeat procedure with remaining potato slices and dressing mix. SERVES 6 (serving size: about 10 chips) CALORIES 52; FAT 0.2g (sat 0g); SODIUM 71mg

BLACK BEANS

South

Heat 1½ tablespoons canola oil in a large Dutch oven over medium heat. Add 1 cup chopped onion and ¾ cup finely chopped red bell pepper to pan; cook 5 minutes or until tender, stirring occasionally. Stir in ½ teaspoon brown sugar, 1½ teaspoons minced garlic, ¼ teaspoon ground cumin, and ¼ teaspoon freshly ground black pepper; cook 1 minute, stirring constantly. Stir in 1 cup water and 2 (15-ounce) cans 50%-less-sodium black beans (undrained); bring to a boil. Partially cover, reduce heat, and simmer 30 minutes or until slightly thick, stirring frequently. Remove from heat, and stir in 1 teaspoon white wine vinegar. SERVES 6 (serving size ⅔ cup) CALORIES 128; FAT 3.6g (sat 0.3g); SODIUM 294mg

ROASTED ACORN SQUASH

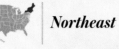

Northeast

Preheat oven to 400°. Cut 1 acorn squash in half lengthwise; discard seeds. Cut each half into 6 wedges. Melt 2 tablespoons butter in a large ovenproof skillet over medium heat. Add squash; cook 3 minutes or until browned on each side. Turn wedges; sprinkle with ¼ teaspoon salt. Place pan in oven; bake at 400° for 12 minutes or until tender. SERVES 4 (serving size: 3 wedges) CALORIES 94; FAT 5.9g (sat 3.7g); SODIUM 192mg

RED CABBAGE WITH SAUSAGE & APPLES

East

Heat 1 teaspoon canola oil in a large nonstick skillet over medium-high heat. Remove casings from 6 ounces turkey Italian sausage. Add sausage and 1 cup thinly sliced red onion to pan; cook 4 minutes or until sausage is browned, stirring to crumble. Add 6 cups thinly sliced red cabbage, 1½ cups finely chopped peeled Granny Smith apple, ⅔ cup apple juice, 2 tablespoons dark brown sugar, 2 tablespoons red wine vinegar, ¼ teaspoon salt, ¼ teaspoon dried thyme, ⅛ teaspoon black pepper, and 1 bay leaf; bring to a boil. Cover, reduce heat, and simmer 20 minutes or until cabbage is tender, stirring occasionally. Discard bay leaf. SERVES 6 (serving size: about ¾ cup) CALORIES 119; FAT 3.8g (sat 1g); SODIUM 255mg

GRILLED OKRA & TOMATOES

Southeast

Preheat grill to medium-high heat. Cut 2 small onions into 4 wedges each. Divide each onion wedge into 2 pieces. Thread 3 okra pods, 2 cherry tomatoes, and 2 onion pieces alternately onto each of 8 (12-inch) metal skewers. Combine 4 teaspoons olive oil, 1 teaspoon kosher salt, 1 teaspoon freshly ground black pepper, 1 teaspoon water, ½ teaspoon ground red pepper, and 2 minced garlic cloves in a bowl, stirring with a whisk. Brush olive oil mixture over skewers. Place on grill rack coated with cooking spray, and grill 3 minutes on each side or until tender. SERVES 8 (serving size: 1 skewer) CALORIES 44; FAT 2.4g (sat 0.3g); SODIUM 241mg

Vegetable tip Mix it up to keep your meals interesting. Try seasonal produce raw, grilled, roasted, or baked.

QUICK COLLARDS

HANDS-ON TIME: 10 MINUTES ★ TOTAL TIME: 10 MINUTES

Collard greens are a favorite in the American South, where the greens are traditionally boiled with ham hock. This modern technique relies instead on a speedy sauté, which cooks ribbons of greens in record time. The quick cooking preserves most of the greens' nutrients so they aren't lost to the "pot likker," the broth left at the bottom of the pot after the greens have been cooked.

2 bacon slices, chopped
5½ cups thinly sliced
    trimmed collard greens
    (about 7 leaves)

2 tablespoons water
¼ teaspoon kosher salt
Hot sauce (optional)

1. Cook bacon in a large skillet over medium-high heat 5 minutes or until crisp, stirring occasionally. Add collards, 2 tablespoons water, and salt; cook 3 minutes, turning with tongs until greens wilt. Serve with hot sauce, if desired. Serves 6 (serving size: about ½ cup)

CALORIES 17; FAT 0.6g (sat 0.2g, mono 0.2g, poly 0.1g); PROTEIN 1.5g; CARB 1.9g; FIBER 1.2g; CHOL 2mg; IRON 0.1mg; SODIUM 115mg; CALC 48mg

LOCAL ★ FLAVOR

American soul food

A "mess o' greens" remains a staple of Southern cuisine and American soul food. Because the cooked greens can resemble piles of folded money, a dish of greens, hog jowl, and black-eyed or field peas is traditionally eaten on New Year's Day to inspire wealth in the coming year.

BEANS & GREENS

HANDS-ON TIME: 15 MINUTES ★ TOTAL TIME: 24 MINUTES

This recipe takes its cue from Italian-American cooks, who know how to make fresh seasonal ingredients taste wonderful. For a hearty main dish, simply toss with whole wheat pasta.

2 tablespoons olive oil

¼ teaspoon crushed red pepper

2 garlic cloves, minced

1 (1-pound) bunch kale, trimmed

1 cup fat-free, lower-sodium chicken broth

¼ teaspoon kosher salt

1 (15-ounce) can cannellini beans, drained and rinsed

1 tablespoon red wine vinegar

Grated fresh pecorino Romano cheese (optional)

1. Heat a large Dutch oven over medium-high heat. Add oil to pan; swirl to coat. Add red pepper and garlic; sauté 30 seconds.

2. Add kale, turning with tongs to coat. Add broth; cover and cook 3 minutes. Add salt and beans; cook, uncovered, 5 minutes, stirring occasionally. Remove from heat, and stir in vinegar. Sprinkle with cheese, if desired. Serves 6 (serving size: 1 cup)

CALORIES 126; FAT 5g (sat 0.8g, mono 3.6g, poly 0.6g); PROTEIN 6.1g; CARB 15.4g; FIBER 3.7g; CHOL 1mg; IRON 2mg; SODIUM 260mg; CALC 126mg

CALABACITAS

HANDS-ON TIME: 25 MINUTES ★ TOTAL TIME: 25 MINUTES

This Southwestern summer squash mixture is a popular side dish throughout New Mexico and south Texas. Calabacitas means "little squash" in Spanish. Tuck it into tortillas for a vegetarian taco or add pork or chicken to make it a main.

2 tablespoons canola oil, divided

2 poblano chiles, seeded and cut into ¾-inch pieces

1 red onion, cut into ½-inch wedges

2 large garlic cloves, minced

1¼ pounds yellow squash (about 3 medium), halved lengthwise and thinly sliced

1 pound zucchini (2 medium), halved lengthwise and thinly sliced

1 cup fresh corn kernels (2 medium ears)

½ cup unsalted tomato sauce

¾ teaspoon salt

1 (4-ounce) can chopped green chiles, undrained

½ cup sliced green onion tops

½ cup chopped fresh cilantro

8 lime wedges

1. Heat a large nonstick skillet over medium-high heat. Add 1 tablespoon oil to pan; swirl to coat. Add poblano chiles and onion. Cook 5 minutes or until edges of vegetables are browned, stirring occasionally; add garlic last 1 minute of cook time. Remove vegetables from pan; keep warm.

2. Heat 1 tablespoon oil in pan. Add yellow squash and zucchini; cook 9 minutes or until edges are browned, stirring occasionally.

3. Stir in onion mixture, corn, and next 3 ingredients (through green chiles). Cook 3 minutes or until thoroughly heated, stirring frequently to deglaze pan. Remove from heat; stir in green onions. Sprinkle with cilantro, and serve with lime wedges. Serves 8 (serving size: about 1 cup squash mixture and 1 lime wedge)

CALORIES 104; FAT 4.6g (sat 0.5g, mono 2.3g, poly 1.4g); PROTEIN 3.3g; CARB 15.2g; FIBER 3.7g; CHOL 0mg; IRON 1.3mg; SODIUM 251mg; CALC 46mg

Seafood Sidecart

The Southwest's "little squash"

I was introduced to calabacitas on my first trip to Taos, New Mexico, in the late '90s. It was offered at every restaurant I visited, yet I'd never heard of it. It's a simple vegetable sauté anchored by three star ingredients: squash, corn, and onions. The rest is up to the preference of each chef—some add tomatoes while others include herbs. Since then it's become more popular; I've seen it in Mexican and Tex-Mex restaurants across America. It's even offered as a taco filling option at a food truck that parks at my local farmers' market right here in Montclair, New Jersey. Gotta love the way delicious food travels.

BUTTERNUT SQUASH AGRODOLCE

HANDS-ON TIME: 10 MINUTES ★ TOTAL TIME: 45 MINUTES

Roasted butternut squash is a classic fall dish. I've added a tangy sweet-and-sour vinaigrette made with honey and red wine vinegar and garnished it with vibrant basil and mint for a new take on this well-loved dish.

1 (2-pound) butternut squash, peeled and cut into ½-inch-thick wedges

2 tablespoons olive oil

1 teaspoon kosher salt, divided

¼ teaspoon freshly ground black pepper

3 tablespoons red wine vinegar

3 tablespoons honey

¼ cup chopped fresh basil

3 tablespoons chopped fresh mint

1. Preheat oven to 400°.

2. Place squash on a baking sheet. Drizzle with oil, and sprinkle with ½ teaspoon salt and pepper, tossing to coat. Bake at 400° for 35 minutes or until squash is tender and golden.

3. Combine vinegar, honey, and ½ teaspoon salt in a small bowl. Place cooked squash on a platter. Drizzle with honey mixture, and toss to coat. Sprinkle with basil and mint. Serves 6 (serving size: ⅙ of squash)

CALORIES 142; FAT 4.7g (sat 0.7g, mono 3.3g, poly 0.6g); PROTEIN 1.6g; CARB 26.6g; FIBER 3.2g; CHOL 0mg; IRON 1.3mg; SODIUM 327mg; CALC 79mg

STEWED OKRA & TOMATOES

HANDS-ON TIME: 15 MINUTES ★ TOTAL TIME: 45 MINUTES

Okra is a Southern classic that people tend to love or hate. Here, the acidity of the tomatoes helps thin the vegetable's viscous juices and preserves its crunchiness. Be sure to pick small pods, as they are more tender.

1 tablespoon canola oil
1½ cups vertically sliced sweet onion
½ teaspoon kosher salt
2 garlic cloves, chopped
1 pound okra, trimmed
1 (28-ounce) can whole tomatoes, undrained

3 thyme sprigs
1 tablespoon red wine vinegar
¼ teaspoon freshly ground black pepper
2 tablespoons chopped fresh parsley (optional)

1. Heat a large skillet over medium-high heat. Add oil to pan; swirl to coat. Add onion, salt, and garlic; sauté 3 minutes. Stir in okra.
2. Snip tomatoes in can until coarsely chopped using kitchen shears. Add tomatoes, their juice, and thyme to okra mixture. Bring to a boil; reduce heat, and simmer, uncovered, 35 minutes or until okra is tender, stirring occasionally.
3. Remove pan from heat; stir in vinegar and pepper. Sprinkle with parsley, if desired. Serves 6 (serving size: ⅔ cup)

CALORIES 85; FAT 3g (sat 0.2g, mono 1.5g, poly 0.8g); PROTEIN 3.1g; CARB 14.8g; FIBER 4.5g; CHOL 0mg; IRON 2mg; SODIUM 357mg; CALC 114mg

CLASSIC SLAW

HANDS-ON TIME: 10 MINUTES ★ TOTAL TIME: 1 HOUR 10 MINUTES

This is a simple slaw with a lot of attitude. It's the perfect complement to a pulled-pork sandwich and an ideal side dish to serve at a summer barbecue.

½ cup reduced-fat mayonnaise
¼ cup nonfat buttermilk
2 tablespoons finely chopped red onion or sweet onion
2 tablespoons cider vinegar
1 tablespoon chopped pickled jalapeño pepper

2 teaspoons sugar
½ teaspoon freshly ground black pepper
¼ teaspoon kosher salt
¼ teaspoon celery seeds
¾ cup grated carrot
1 pound green cabbage, thinly sliced (5 cups)

1. Combine first 9 ingredients (through celery seeds) in a large bowl, stirring with a whisk. Add carrot and cabbage; toss well to coat. Cover and chill at least 1 hour. Serves 11 (serving size: ½ cup)

CALORIES 38; FAT 1.5g (sat 0.4g, mono 0.3g, poly 0.7g); PROTEIN 0.8g; CARB 5.9g; FIBER 1.3g; CHOL 0mg; IRON 0.3mg; SODIUM 165mg; CALC 27mg

MASHED POTATOES

HANDS-ON TIME: 6 MINUTES ★ TOTAL TIME: 31 MINUTES

If you start with naturally creamy potatoes, like Yukon Golds, you won't need to add cream and sticks of butter to make delicious mashed potatoes. A gentle fresh chive garnish brightens these rich flavors.

4 Yukon Gold potatoes
   (2 pounds), unpeeled
   and cut into 2-inch
   cubes
3 tablespoons unsalted
   butter
½ teaspoon kosher salt

¼ teaspoon freshly ground
   black pepper
⅔ cup 2% reduced-fat milk
2 tablespoons chopped
   fresh chives (optional)

1. Place potato in a medium saucepan. Cover with water to 2 inches above potato. Bring to a boil; reduce heat, and simmer 25 minutes or until potato is tender. Drain and return to pan.

2. Add butter, salt, and pepper; mash with a potato masher until butter melts. Add milk, mashing until desired consistency. Garnish with chives, if desired. Serves 10 (serving size: about ½ cup)

CALORIES 115; FAT 4g (sat 2.4g, mono 1g, poly 0.1g); PROTEIN 2.8g; CARB 16.9g; FIBER 1.1g; CHOL 11mg; IRON 0.8mg; SODIUM 110mg; CALC 23mg

GARLIC-PARSLEY STEAK "FRIES"

HANDS-ON TIME: 7 MINUTES ★ TOTAL TIME: 57 MINUTES

These roasted potato wedges, blistered and brown from the heat of the oven, beautifully combine the rich flavors of potato and garlic.

2 tablespoons olive oil
1 large garlic clove, pressed
8 russet potatoes (about 3 pounds)
½ teaspoon kosher salt
Cooking spray
2 tablespoons chopped fresh parsley
Ketchup (optional)

1. Preheat oven to 425°.
2. Combine oil and garlic in a large bowl. Scrub potatoes; pat dry. Cut each potato lengthwise into 6 (1-inch-thick) wedges, and add to oil mixture. Toss wedges until thoroughly coated. Sprinkle wedges with salt; toss well. Place wedges on a large baking sheet coated with cooking spray.
3. Bake at 425° for 50 minutes or until wedges are tender and golden. Remove from pan; sprinkle with parsley. Serve with ketchup, if desired. Serves 6 (serving size: 8 wedges)

CALORIES 221; FAT 5g (sat 0.7g, mono 3.4g, poly 0.6g); PROTEIN 4.9g; CARB 41.3g; FIBER 3g; CHOL 0mg; IRON 2.1mg; SODIUM 172mg; CALC 32mg

LIGHTEN UP

Homemade fries

We all love French fries, but when you order them at restaurants and fast food joints, they are commonly fried not just once, but twice. Tossing hand-cut "fries" in oil and baking them in the oven drastically reduces both fat and calories.

GRILLED SWEET POTATO SALAD

HANDS-ON TIME: 11 MINUTES ★ TOTAL TIME: 31 MINUTES

Cooking the sweet potatoes on a grill retains vitamins that would be lost if they were boiled, and gives them a crisp, charred edge that contrasts with the sweet interior. Tossing them with the lemon-olive oil dressing brightens the flavor.

3 large sweet potatoes
   (2¼ pounds)
Cooking spray
6 green onions
2 tablespoons olive oil
2 tablespoons fresh lemon
   juice

½ teaspoon kosher salt
½ teaspoon ground cumin
¼ teaspoon ground red
   pepper

1. Preheat grill to medium heat.
2. Peel sweet potatoes, and cut diagonally into ½-inch-thick slices. Place sweet potato slices on grill rack coated with cooking spray; grill 18 minutes or until tender, turning once. Place onions on grill rack during last 2 minutes of cook time; cook onions 2 minutes or until browned and tender, turning once. Cut onions into 2-inch pieces.
3. Combine olive oil and next 4 ingredients (through red pepper) in a large bowl, stirring with a whisk. Add sweet potato and onions; toss well. Serves 6 (serving size: ¾ cup)

CALORIES 192; FAT 4.8g (sat 0.7g, mono 3.4g, poly 0.5g); PROTEIN 2.8g; CARB 35.4g; FIBER 5.4g; CHOL 0mg; IRON 1.2mg; SODIUM 256mg; CALC 59mg

The Varsity drive-in

In Atlanta, Georgia, you'll find the world's largest drive-in restaurant, The Varsity, which has been serving some of the best fast food fare since 1928. People from all over the world stop by for a bite, because there's no other experience like it. The Varsity has become a well-known Atlanta institution and has hosted famous people from the entertainment industry, sports industry, and the White House.

On a Georgia Tech game day, the restaurant—set on over 2 acres and accommodating over 600 cars—serves more than 30,000 people. On a daily basis, they serve 2 miles of hot dogs, a ton of onion rings, 2,500 pounds of potatoes, and 5,000 pies. To make their onion rings, they still use the original batter recipe from 1928.

ONION RINGS

HANDS-ON TIME: 40 MINUTES ★ TOTAL TIME: 50 MINUTES

Unlike deep-fried onion rings, these are cooked in a shallow pan with a smaller amount of oil. Be sure to check that the underside of each onion is nicely browned before you flip.

2 large onions, peeled (about 1½ pounds)

6 ounces all-purpose flour (about 1⅓ cups)

½ teaspoon salt

½ teaspoon paprika

½ teaspoon freshly ground black pepper

⅔ cup flat beer

2 large egg whites, lightly beaten

3 tablespoons oil

Cooking spray

Ketchup (optional)

1. Preheat oven to 400°.

2. Cut onion crosswise into ½-inch-thick slices, and separate into rings. Use 16 of the largest rings; reserve remaining onion for another use. Combine flour and next 3 ingredients (through pepper) in a medium bowl. Stir in beer and egg white (batter will be thick). Heat 1 tablespoon oil in a large nonstick skillet over medium-high heat. Dip 5 onion rings in batter, letting excess drip off. Add onion rings to pan; cook 2 minutes on each side or until golden. Place onion rings on a jelly-roll pan. Repeat procedure of dipping onion rings in batter and cooking in remaining oil twice, ending with 6 rings. Coat onion rings with cooking spray.

3. Bake at 400° for 10 minutes or until crisp. Serve rings with ketchup, if desired. Serves 4 (serving size: 4 onion rings)

CALORIES 152; FAT 8.9g (sat 0.6g, mono 5.6g, poly 2.5g); PROTEIN 2.6g; CARB 14.7g; FIBER 0.8g; CHOL 0mg; IRON 0.8mg; SODIUM 157mg; CALC 8mg

Magnolia Bakery,
New York, NY

BELOVED DESSERTS

Pies, Cakes, Cookies & More

Chatham Bakery and Cafe,
Chatham, MA

I'm going to come right out and say that dessert shouldn't be an everyday thing. Some things in life should be anticipated, and dessert is definitely one of them.

a lot of people feel that desserts should be indulgent—that cutting the fat and calories in a three-layer cake isn't worth the effort. And that's true, if you follow a lot of typical light recipes. You know, the ones that use applesauce in place of butter and artificial sweeteners in place of sugar. Yuck! But, these desserts in the following pages aren't typical. For starters, they've been triple-tested (and triple-tasted, too!) by the experts at *Cooking Light*, so you know they not only taste good but they have great texture. They're every bit as indulgent as their high-fat counterparts; they just won't blow your calorie budget.

Enjoying ice cream with a few locals

Pound Cake with Brown Butter Glaze, p. 270

Trifle, p. 263

Franklin Fountain in Philadelphia, PA

How 'bout these apples?

The small, upstate New York town of LaFayette is nestled in a hilly enclave at the center of Onondaga County's apple-growing region. For the past 40 years, the town has celebrated its rich harvest with an apple festival that welcomes tens of thousands.

The festival offers many activities which include operating an old cider press, an apple pie contest, and 5K and 15K runs through the orchards. There are numerous apple dishes, such as apple fritters, apple pie popcorn, and apple pizza in addition to live music and crafts. But the most spectacular thing about this event is that it's a fund-raiser for the town's schools and civic organizations. So those apples aren't just delicious—they also help to support the high school yearbook committee.

BLUE-RIBBON APPLE PIE

HANDS-ON TIME: 17 MINUTES ★ TOTAL TIME: 1 HOUR 17 MINUTES

This recipe was inspired by the version that won Pam Brunet a blue ribbon at the LaFayette Apple Festival in New York. She layers a flour-and-cinnamon-sugar mixture with apples to create a dense, rich layer of fruit. Pam credits this recipe to her mother-in-law, Grandma Brunet.

⅔ cup sugar

1 teaspoon ground cinnamon

2 tablespoons all-purpose flour

½ teaspoon kosher salt

1 (14.1-ounce) package
    refrigerated pie dough

Cooking spray

6 cups (¼-inch-thick) slices
    Empire apple (2 pounds)

1 large egg, beaten

1 tablespoon water

1. Preheat oven to 425°.

2. Combine sugar and cinnamon in a bowl, stirring with a whisk. Set aside 1 tablespoon cinnamon-sugar in a small bowl. Add flour and salt to remaining cinnamon-sugar, stirring with a whisk.

3. Fit one-half of dough into a 9-inch pie plate coated with cooking spray, allowing dough to extend ½ inch over edge of pie plate. Sprinkle 2½ tablespoons flour mixture in bottom of prepared crust. Layer one-third of apple slices over flour mixture. Repeat procedure twice; sprinkle remaining flour mixture over apples. Fit remaining half of dough over filling. Press edges of dough together. Fold edges under; flute. Cut several slits in top of dough to allow steam to escape.

4. Combine egg and 1 tablespoon water in a small bowl. Brush egg mixture over dough; sprinkle with reserved cinnamon-sugar. Bake at 425° for 30 minutes or until apples are tender and crust is golden. Remove from oven; cool completely on a wire rack. Serves 10 (serving size: 1 slice)

CALORIES 260; FAT 11g (sat 4.6g, mono 4.9g, poly 0.6g); PROTEIN 2.5g; CARB 41.1g; FIBER 1.4g; CHOL 23mg; IRON 0.2mg; SODIUM 311mg; CALC 9mg

KEY LIME PIE

HANDS-ON TIME: 60 MINUTES ★ TOTAL TIME: 3 HOURS 10 MINUTES

The small, pale green Key lime is prized for its almost herbal aroma and pronounced acidity. The compact fruits are tart, sharp, and memorably sour—some might say borderline bitter. It's a taste sensation that works particularly well in baking and in beverages.

1½ cups graham cracker crumbs (about 10 cookie sheets)

2 tablespoons butter, melted

4 large egg whites, divided

3½ tablespoons water, divided

Cooking spray

2 large eggs

2 large egg yolks

½ cup fresh Key lime juice or fresh lime juice (about 6 Key limes)

1 (14-ounce) can fat-free sweetened condensed milk

1 teaspoon grated Key lime or lime rind

½ cup sugar

1. Preheat oven to 350°.

2. Combine crumbs and melted butter in a bowl. Place 1 egg white in a small bowl; stir well with a whisk until foamy. Add 2 tablespoons foamy egg white to graham cracker mixture, tossing well with a fork to combine. Discard remaining foamy egg white. Add 1 tablespoon water to graham cracker mixture; toss gently to coat. Press into bottom and up sides of a 9-inch pie plate coated with cooking spray. (Moisten fingers, if needed, to bring mixture together.) Bake at 350° for 8 minutes. Cool completely on a wire rack.

3. Place 2 eggs and 2 egg yolks in a bowl; beat with a mixer at medium speed until well blended. Add juice and condensed milk, beating until thick; stir in rind. Spoon mixture into prepared crust. Bake at 350° for 20 minutes or until edges are set (center will not be firm but will set as it chills). Cool completely on a wire rack. Cover loosely, and chill at least 2 hours.

4. Place 3 egg whites in a bowl; beat with a mixer at medium speed until foamy using clean, dry beaters.

5. Combine sugar and 2½ tablespoons water in a small saucepan; bring to a boil. Cook, without stirring, until a candy thermometer registers 250°. Pour hot sugar syrup in a thin stream over egg whites, beating at high speed 2 minutes or until stiff peaks form. Spread meringue over chilled pie (completely cover pie with meringue).

6. Preheat broiler.

7. Broil pie 1 minute or until meringue is lightly browned. Serves 8 (serving size: 1 slice)

CALORIES 320; FAT 6.8g (sat 2.8g, mono 2.3g, poly 1.1g); PROTEIN 9g; CARB 55.5g; FIBER 0.5g; CHOL 118mg; IRON 1mg; SODIUM 214mg; CALC 146mg

PUMPKIN PIE
WITH VANILLA WHIPPED CREAM

HANDS-ON TIME: 10 MINUTES ★ TOTAL TIME: 2 HOURS 40 MINUTES

This is the pie you remember from many Thanksgivings, made better for you. Instead of using a can of regular evaporated milk, I swapped in a fat-free version.

1 cup plus 2 tablespoons sugar, divided

1 teaspoon ground cinnamon

½ teaspoon kosher salt

½ teaspoon ground ginger

¼ teaspoon ground cloves

2 large eggs

1 (15-ounce) can pumpkin

¾ cup evaporated fat-free milk

½ (14.1-ounce) package refrigerated pie dough

½ cup heavy whipping cream, chilled

½ teaspoon vanilla extract

1. Preheat oven to 425°.

2. Combine 1 cup sugar and next 4 ingredients (through cloves) in a large bowl; stir well with a whisk. Add eggs and pumpkin; stir well with a whisk. Gradually add evaporated milk, stirring with a whisk until blended.

3. Fit dough into a 9-inch pie plate. Fold edges under. Using kitchen shears, make ½-inch diagonal cuts at 45-degree angles around edge of crust. With fingertips, press every other tab toward center of pie. Pour pumpkin mixture into prepared crust.

4. Place pie plate on a baking sheet, and bake at 425° for 15 minutes. Reduce oven temperature to 350°; bake 45 minutes or until almost set. Shield edges of piecrust with foil, if necessary. (Do not insert a knife to test for doneness, as the slit will become larger and separate when the pie cools.) Cool on a wire rack 1½ hours.

5. Beat whipping cream with a mixer at high speed until foamy. Gradually add vanilla and 2 tablespoons sugar, beating until soft peaks form. Slice pie into 10 slices; top each serving with whipped cream. Serves 10 (serving size: 1 slice and about 2 tablespoons whipped cream)

CALORIES 255; FAT 10.7g (sat 5.4g, mono 4.2g, poly 0.6g); PROTEIN 3.9g; CARB 38.1g; FIBER 1.4g; CHOL 56mg; IRON 0.8mg; SODIUM 238mg; CALC 76mg

BELOVED DESSERTS

Pumpkin in a can

Of all the pumpkins grown in the United States, about 90% are grown within a 90-mile radius of Peoria, Illinois. The little town of Morton, near the heart of Peoria, lays claim to the title "Pumpkin Capital of the World" and is home to the processing plant for Libby's brand canned pumpkin. Libby's contracts with the area's farmers to grow the Dickinson variety of pumpkin on about 5,000 acres of land in Peoria. Dickinson pumpkins are tan and oblong, and about twice the size of most pie pumpkins with denser, thick orange flesh. They are a premium pumpkin variety especially well suited to canning.

The world's largest peach cobbler

every year in Peach County, Georgia, the small town of Fort Valley is home to the Georgia Peach Festival. Like many regional festivals, there's a parade, pancake breakfast, preserves, music, beauty queen contest, and even fireworks. But the festival in Fort Valley has one thing that no other peach festival in the nation can lay claim to: the world's largest peach cobbler.

It takes 150 pounds of sugar, 150 pounds of flour, 32 gallons of milk, 75 pounds of butter, and 75 gallons of local peaches to make a cobbler about the size of a one-car garage. They've even created a permanent brick oven on the grounds of the Fort Valley Courthouse where they bake it!

The recipe for the giant-sized cobbler is based on the time-honored "cuppa, cuppa, cuppa" method passed on to every Southerner with an oven and a pile of peaches. It's "a cuppa peaches, a cuppa sugar, a cuppa flour, and a sticka butter."

I had the good fortune to be able to help make this cobbler. Beginning at 3 a.m. on the serving day, the batter was mixed using rakes and boat paddles, then poured onto the hot, well-buttered griddle of the brick oven. It's covered with a lid made from the metal bottoms of school buses and baked. The world's largest peach cobbler takes 2 hours to prepare, 5 hours to cook, and 3 hours to cool.

> **Who knew?** It takes 150 pounds of sugar, 150 pounds of flour, 32 gallons of milk, 75 pounds of butter, and 75 gallons of local peaches to make a cobbler about the size of a one-car garage.

The aroma of baking fresh peach cobbler wafts over the festival all day long, inspiring a line that begins over an hour before the scheduled 2 p.m. serving time. More than 1,000 people are served up free bowls of the still-hot cobbler. Most will take home peaches of their own, ready to bake up their own cobblers so they don't have to wait another year to enjoy Georgia's quintessential peach dessert.

PEACH PIE

HANDS-ON TIME: 29 MINUTES ★ TOTAL TIME: 3 HOURS 44 MINUTES

Peach pie isn't that difficult to make in the summer, especially when you use a store-bought crust instead of one that's homemade. I make the process even quicker by adding my peaches with the skins on, rather than taking the time to remove them. I like the bright color the skin lends to the pie, and on a beautiful summer day, I'd rather skip the step that has me standing over a pot of steaming hot water blanching peaches to remove their skins.

½ cup granulated sugar
3 tablespoons cornstarch
½ teaspoon ground
    cinnamon
¼ teaspoon kosher salt
6 to 8 cups fresh peaches,
    pitted and sliced into
    eighths

1 (14.1-ounce) package
    refrigerated pie dough
Cooking spray
1 tablespoon milk
1 tablespoon turbinado
    sugar

1. Preheat oven to 425°.
2. Combine first 4 ingredients (through salt) in a large bowl, stirring with a whisk. Add peaches; toss gently to coat with sugar mixture.
3. Fit one-half of dough into a 9-inch pie plate coated with cooking spray. Cut remaining half of dough into 10 (¾-inch-wide) strips, reserving remaining dough for another use.
4. Spoon peach filling into prepared crust. Arrange dough strips in a lattice pattern on top of filling. Turn edges under; flute. Brush dough with milk, and sprinkle with turbinado sugar.
5. Bake at 425° for 30 minutes, shielding edges of piecrust with foil after 20 minutes. Reduce oven temperature to 375°. Bake an additional 15 minutes or until golden and bubbly. Cool on a wire rack at least 2 hours before cutting. Serves 8 (serving size: 1 slice)

CALORIES 292; FAT 10.8g (sat 4.4g, mono 4.5g, poly 0.1g); PROTEIN 1.3g; CARB 50.4g; FIBER 2.1g; CHOL 5mg; IRON 0.4mg; SODIUM 287mg; CALC 12mg

SHOOFLY PIE

HANDS-ON TIME: 16 MINUTES ★ TOTAL TIME: 2 HOURS 53 MINUTES

The name for this Pennsylvania Dutch treat likely came from the flies it attracts when it's pulled from the oven and left to cool on a breezy windowsill.

½ (14.1-ounce) package refrigerated pie dough
3.4 ounces all-purpose flour (about ¾ cup)
½ cup packed dark brown sugar
1 tablespoon unsalted butter, cut into pieces
¼ teaspoon salt
1 large egg
1 teaspoon vanilla extract
1 cup molasses
¾ teaspoon baking soda
¾ cup boiling water

1. Preheat oven to 350°.
2. Fit dough into a 9-inch pie plate. Fold edges under; flute.
3. Weigh or lightly spoon flour into dry measuring cups; level with a knife. Place flour and next 3 ingredients (through salt) in a food processor; process until a sandy texture. Remove and set aside ½ cup flour mixture from food processor, reserving remaining mixture in food processor bowl.
4. Combine egg and vanilla in a medium bowl, stirring with a whisk. Gradually add molasses, stirring with a whisk. Stir baking soda into ¾ cup boiling water. Add baking soda mixture to molasses mixture, whisking until blended. Stir in flour mixture from food processor bowl, stirring with a whisk until smooth. Pour mixture into prepared crust. Sprinkle with reserved ½ cup flour mixture.
5. Bake at 350° for 37 minutes or until slightly puffed and surface begins to crack. Cool completely on a wire rack. Serve at room temperature. Serves 10 (serving size: 1 slice)

CALORIES 270; FAT 6.5g (sat 2.9g, mono 2.5g, poly 0.6g); PROTEIN 1.7g; CARB 51.7g; FIBER 0.3g; CHOL 24mg; IRON 2.1mg; SODIUM 268mg; CALC 79mg

HOOSIER PIE

HANDS-ON TIME: 15 MINUTES
TOTAL TIME: 2 HOURS 30 MINUTES

This simple custard pie originated in the 1800s as a way to use ingredients typically on hand: butter, flour, and sugar or maple syrup. Similar to the Hoosier Pie is the Pennsylvania Chess Pie; both were created, it's believed, by Shaker and Amish cooks.

½ (14.1-ounce) package refrigerated pie dough
1 cup granulated sugar
5 tablespoons all-purpose flour
1 tablespoon cornstarch
¼ teaspoon salt
1 cup half-and-half
1 cup whole milk
2 large egg yolks
1 teaspoon vanilla extract
¼ to ½ teaspoon freshly grated nutmeg

1. Preheat oven to 375°.
2. Fit dough into a 9-inch pie plate. Fold edges under; flute.
3. In a large bowl, whisk together sugar, flour, cornstarch, and salt. Add half-and-half, and mix well.
4. Combine whole milk and egg yolks in a medium bowl, stirring with a whisk; add to sugar mixture, and whisk to combine well. Stir in vanilla.
5. Pour mixture into prepared crust and sprinkle nutmeg over top. Bake at 375° for 1 hour and 15 minutes, until filling is set and lightly browned. Cool completely before serving. Serves 10 (serving size: 1 slice)

CALORIES 239; FAT 10g (sat 4.5g, mono 1.8g, poly 3.2g); PROTEIN 3.2g; CARB 35.7g; FIBER 0.1g; CHOL 48mg; IRON 0.3mg; SODIUM 192mg; CALC 58mg

ROASTED BANANA PUDDING

HANDS-ON TIME: 26 MINUTES ★ TOTAL TIME: 2 HOURS 21 MINUTES

*The genius in this recipe is that the bananas are cooked two ways:
Some are partially roasted and sliced, so you get sweet bananas that keep their shape.
The rest are fully roasted, almost caramelized, so you get bananas with rich,
sweet flavor. For a fun presentation, scoop the pudding mixture into pretty ramekins.*

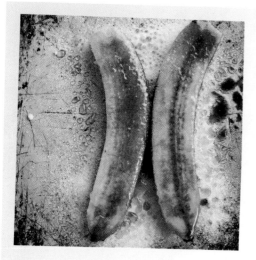

5 ripe unpeeled medium
    bananas (about
    2 pounds)
2 cups 2% reduced-fat milk
⅔ cup sugar, divided
2 tablespoons cornstarch
¼ teaspoon salt

2 large eggs
1 tablespoon butter
2 teaspoons vanilla extract
1 (12-ounce) container frozen
    fat-free whipped topping,
    thawed and divided
45 vanilla wafers, divided

1. Preheat oven to 350°.
2. Place bananas on a jelly-roll pan covered with parchment
paper. Bake at 350° for 20 minutes. Remove 3 bananas; cool
completely. Peel and cut into ½-inch-thick slices. Set aside. Bake
remaining 2 bananas at 350° for an additional 20 minutes. Carefully peel and place 2 bananas in a small bowl; mash with a fork
until smooth.
3. Combine milk and ⅓ cup sugar in a saucepan over medium-
high heat. Bring to a simmer (do not boil).
4. Combine ⅓ cup sugar and next 3 ingredients (through eggs) in
a medium bowl; stir well with a whisk. Gradually add hot milk
mixture to sugar mixture, stirring constantly with a whisk. Return
milk mixture to pan. Cook over medium heat until thick and
bubbly (about 3 minutes), stirring constantly. Remove from heat.
Add mashed bananas, butter, and vanilla, stirring until butter
melts. Place pan in a large ice-filled bowl for 15 minutes or until
mixture comes to room temperature, stirring occasionally. Fold
half of whipped topping into pudding.
5. Spread 1 cup pudding evenly over bottom of an 11 x 7–inch
glass or ceramic baking dish. Top with 20 vanilla wafers and half
of banana slices. Spoon half of remaining pudding over banana
slices. Repeat procedure with 20 wafers, banana slices, and
pudding. Spread remaining half of whipped topping evenly over
top. Crush 5 wafers; sprinkle over top. Refrigerate 1 hour or until
chilled. Serves 10 (serving size: about ⅔ cup)

CALORIES 295; FAT 5.6g (sat 2.1g, mono 1.7g, poly 0.2g); PROTEIN 3.9g; CARB 56.6g;
FIBER 2g; CHOL 46mg; IRON 1mg; SODIUM 165mg; CALC 73mg

VANILLA BEAN ICE CREAM
WITH FRESH STRAWBERRIES

HANDS-ON TIME: 26 MINUTES ★ TOTAL TIME: 5 HOURS 6 MINUTES

This recipe was inspired by my favorite ice cream book, Jeni's Splendid Ice Creams at Home, by Ohio-based ice cream maker Jeni Britton Bauer.

2 cups whole milk, divided
5 teaspoons cornstarch
1½ ounces ⅓-less-fat cream cheese, softened
¹⁄₁₆ teaspoon salt
1 cup half-and-half
⅔ cup sugar
¼ cup heavy cream
2 tablespoons light corn syrup
1 (4-inch) piece vanilla bean, split lengthwise
1 cup quartered strawberries
¼ cup sugar

1. Combine 2 tablespoons milk and cornstarch in a small bowl, stirring until smooth. Combine cream cheese and salt in a large bowl, stirring with a whisk.

2. Combine remaining milk, half-and-half, and next 3 ingredients (through corn syrup) in a medium saucepan. Scrape seeds from vanilla bean; stir seeds into milk mixture in pan, reserving bean for another use. Bring to a boil; boil 4 minutes, stirring occasionally.

3. Add cornstarch mixture; stir with a whisk. Cook, stirring constantly, 2 minutes or until slightly thick. Gradually add milk mixture to cream cheese mixture, stirring until smooth. Return milk mixture to saucepan. Place pan in a large ice-filled bowl until mixture cools to room temperature (about 10 minutes), stirring occasionally.

4. Pour mixture into the freezer can of an ice-cream freezer; freeze according to manufacturer's instructions.

5. While ice cream freezes, combine strawberries and ¼ cup sugar in a small saucepan. Bring to a boil over medium-high heat; cook 5 minutes or until fruit is soft and juice is syrupy. Place pan in a large ice-filled bowl until fruit is cold (about 10 minutes), stirring occasionally.

6. When ice cream is finished churning, transfer to a container suitable for the freezer, alternating spoonfuls of the ice cream with dollops of the fruit. Press a piece of parchment or wax paper directly on the surface of the ice cream, and freeze until firm, about 4 hours. Remove from freezer to soften before serving. Serves 8 (serving size: ½ cup)

CALORIES 233; FAT 9.4g (sat 5.8g, mono 2.6g, poly 0.4g); PROTEIN 3.5g; CARB 35.4g; FIBER 0.4g; CHOL 31mg; IRON 0.1mg; SODIUM 81mg; CALC 113mg

TRIFLE

HANDS-ON TIME: 25 MINUTES ★ TOTAL TIME: 2 HOURS

Trifle dishes are a popular wedding gift, but, sadly, many of them go unused. Pull yours out of storage and fill it, as intended, with pound cake, fruit, and whipped cream.

3 cups sliced strawberries
3 cups blueberries
3 cups fresh peach slices
½ cup sugar
2 tablespoons fresh lemon juice
2 tablespoons water
½ Pound Cake with Brown Butter Glaze (page 270), cut into ½-inch cubes (6¾ cups)
1 cup heavy cream, whipped

1. Combine first 6 ingredients (through water) in a large bowl, stirring gently. Let stand 5 minutes.
2. Layer one-third of cake cubes in bottom of a 3-quart trifle dish. Top with one-third of fruit mixture and one-third of whipped cream. Repeat layers twice, ending with remaining whipped cream. Cover and refrigerate 1½ hours. Serves 16 (serving size: ¾ cup)

CALORIES 261; FAT 12.1g (sat 5.8g, mono 4.3g, poly 1.3g); PROTEIN 2.6g; CARB 37.5g; FIBER 1.9g; CHOL 41mg; IRON 1.1mg; SODIUM 82mg; CALC 48mg

APPLE CRISP

HANDS-ON TIME: 13 MINUTES ★ TOTAL TIME: 1 HOUR 33 MINUTES

This is apple pie's less-fussy but just-as-tasty little sister.

Topping:

1.5 ounces all-purpose flour (about ⅓ cup)

⅓ cup granulated sugar

⅓ cup packed light brown sugar

¼ teaspoon kosher salt

⅓ cup uncooked old-fashioned rolled oats

6 tablespoons chilled unsalted butter, cut into small pieces

Filling:

¼ cup granulated sugar

2 tablespoons all-purpose flour

½ teaspoon ground cinnamon

¼ teaspoon kosher salt

8 cups peeled Fuji apple slices (about 3¼ pounds)

1 tablespoon fresh lemon juice

Cooking spray

Crow Farm, Cape Cod, MA

1. Preheat oven to 375°.

2. To prepare topping, weigh or lightly spoon 1.5 ounces flour into a dry measuring cup; level with a knife. Combine flour and next 3 ingredients (through salt) in a medium bowl, stirring with a whisk; stir in oats. Cut in butter with a pastry blender or 2 knives until crumbly. Cover and chill 20 minutes.

3. To prepare filling, combine ¼ cup sugar and next 3 ingredients (through salt) in a large bowl, stirring with a whisk. Add apple, and drizzle with lemon juice; toss well. Spoon apple mixture into an 8-inch square glass or ceramic baking dish coated with cooking spray. Sprinkle topping over filling.

4. Bake at 375° for 45 minutes or until apples are tender and topping is crisp. Let stand at least 15 minutes before serving. Serves 8 (serving size: ⅛ of crisp)

CALORIES 261; FAT 9.2g (sat 5.6g, mono 2.4g, poly 0.5g); PROTEIN 1.6g; CARB 45.8g; FIBER 2.1g; CHOL 23mg; IRON 0.7mg; SODIUM 124mg; CALC 19mg

CRANBERRY CRUNCH

HANDS-ON TIME: 15 MINUTES ★ TOTAL TIME: 1 HOUR 10 MINUTES

Cranberries, blueberries, and Concord grapes are the only berries native to America that are commercially grown. Cranberries were first used by Native Americans, who valued them as a food, fabric dye, and healing agent. American farmers now harvest over 40,000 acres of cranberries a year, meaning you can find them fresh over the fall and winter months. My family recipe high-lights their fresh natural flavor while adding a little oat-enhanced crunch for interest.

Topping:
2.25 ounces all-purpose flour (about ½ cup)
1 cup old-fashioned rolled oats
⅔ cup packed brown sugar
¼ cup unsalted butter, cut into small pieces

Filling:
1 (12-ounce) package fresh cranberries
¾ cup granulated sugar
¾ cup water
⅓ cup raisins
1 tablespoon cornstarch
1 teaspoon vanilla extract
Cooking spray
2½ cups reduced-fat vanilla bean ice cream

1. Preheat oven to 350°.
2. To prepare topping, weigh or lightly spoon flour into a dry measuring cup; level with a knife. Combine flour, oats, and brown sugar in a medium bowl. Cut in butter with a pastry blender or 2 knives until mixture resembles coarse meal. Cover and chill until ready to use.
3. To prepare filling, combine cranberries and next 4 ingredients (through cornstarch) in a medium saucepan. Bring to a boil over medium-high heat, stirring constantly. Reduce heat; simmer 5 to 8 minutes or until cranberries pop. Remove from heat. Stir in vanilla; pour mixture into an 8-inch square metal baking pan coated with cooking spray. Sprinkle topping over cranberry filling. Bake at 350° for 40 minutes or until bubbly and topping is browned. Cool at least 15 minutes in pan on a wire rack. Serve with ice cream. Serves 10 (serving size: ¹⁄₁₀ of cobbler and ¼ cup ice cream)

CALORIES 298; FAT 7g (sat 4g, mono 1.8g, poly 0.5g); PROTEIN 3.4g; CARB 56.8g; FIBER 2.4g; CHOL 22mg; IRON 0.9mg; SODIUM 28mg; CALC 48mg

Harvesting cranberries

Shortly before my husband Aaron and I got married, he invited me to Plymouth, Massachusetts, where his cousin Jeff Kapell and Jeff's wife Alex Pollard own a cranberry farm. They're part of the Ocean Spray cooperative, an agricultural organization that provides planting, growing, and harvesting support to their members. We arrived on the first day of the cranberry harvest, and by the time we got there, there were already a handful of people on the scene, ready to help out with the day's work.

Cranberries grow on low-lying vines close to the ground. When the cranberries are ready for harvest, the bogs are flooded with water, which lifts the berries to the surface. Then, an amphibious tractor trolls through the bog, gently knocking the berries from their vines and causing them to float to the water's surface. The berries are corralled with an enormous rubber "lasso" that farmers use to skim the water's surface.

The harvest at Jeff and Alex's cranberry bog began before sunrise and lasted well into early evening. Afterwards, we were rewarded for a job well done with—what else?—an enormous turkey dinner set on a hill overlooking the still-flooded bog. The meal ended with Cranberry Crunch, made fresh from our just-picked haul.

After a day of hard work, harvesters get to enjoy the day's ruby haul.

VANILLA CHEESECAKE
WITH CHERRY TOPPING

HANDS-ON TIME: 30 MINUTES ★ TOTAL TIME: 11 HOURS 15 MINUTES

You can make both the cheesecake and the topping up to three days ahead and store them separately in the refrigerator. Or chill the cooled cheesecake in the pan for two hours, then wrap in heavy-duty plastic wrap and freeze for up to two months. Thaw the cheesecake in the refrigerator.

Crust:

¾ cup graham cracker crumbs

¼ cup sugar

2 tablespoons butter, melted

2 teaspoons water

Cooking spray

Filling:

3 (8-ounce) blocks fat-free cream cheese, softened

2 (8-ounce) blocks ⅓-less-fat cream cheese, softened

1 cup sugar

3 tablespoons all-purpose flour

¼ teaspoon salt

1 (8-ounce) carton fat-free sour cream

4 large eggs

2 teaspoons vanilla extract

1 vanilla bean, split lengthwise

Topping:

⅔ cup tawny port or other sweet red wine

½ cup sugar

2 (10-ounce) bags frozen pitted dark sweet cherries

2 tablespoons fresh lemon juice

4 teaspoons cornstarch

4 teaspoons water

1. Preheat oven to 400°.

2. To prepare crust, combine first 3 ingredients (through butter), tossing with a fork. Add 2 teaspoons water; toss with a fork until moist and crumbly. Gently press mixture into bottom and 1½ inches up sides of a 9-inch springform pan coated with cooking spray. Bake at 400° for 5 minutes; cool on a wire rack.

3. Reduce oven temperature to 325°. To prepare filling, beat cheeses with a mixer at high speed until smooth. Combine 1 cup sugar, flour, and salt, stirring with a whisk. Add to cheese mixture; beat well. Add sour cream; beat well. Add eggs, 1 at a time, beating well after each addition. Stir in vanilla. Scrape seeds from vanilla bean; stir seeds into cheese mixture, reserving bean halves.

4. Pour cheese mixture into prepared pan; bake at 325° for 1 hour and 15 minutes or until cheesecake center barely moves when pan is touched. Remove cheesecake from oven; run a knife around outside edge. Cool to room temperature. Cover and chill at least 8 hours.

5. To prepare topping, combine port, ½ cup sugar, cherries, and reserved vanilla bean halves in a large saucepan; bring to a boil. Cook 5 minutes or until cherries are thawed and mixture is syrupy. Remove vanilla bean halves; discard.

6. Combine juice, cornstarch, and 4 teaspoons water, stirring with a whisk until well blended. Stir cornstarch mixture into cherry mixture; bring to a boil. Reduce heat; simmer 3 minutes or until mixture is slightly thick and shiny. Remove from heat; cool to room temperature. Cover and chill. Serve over cheesecake. Serves 16 (serving size: 1 cheesecake slice and about 2 tablespoons topping)

CALORIES 324; FAT 10.7g (sat 6.1g, mono 3.2g, poly 0.7g); PROTEIN 12.2g; CARB 42.8g; FIBER 1g; CHOL 83mg; IRON 0.8mg; SODIUM 458mg; CALC 134mg

Cheesecake on Broadway

Although cakes made from various cheeses were first crafted in Ancient Greece and Rome, the cheesecake we all know and love wasn't created until much later. Many New Yorkers claim to have created the original recipe, and by the early 1900s, every restaurant seemed to have its own version. But Arnold Reuben of the legendary Turf Restaurant on 49th and Broadway is officially credited with being the one to introduce what is now known as New York cheesecake to Manhattanites in 1929.

According to legend, he enjoyed a cake made of cream cheese at a dinner party and loved it so much that he developed his own recipe. His simple version—made of cream cheese, sugar, cream, and eggs—was introduced to the public on the menu of his iconic Broadway restaurant and is the variety still known as New York cheesecake.

POUND CAKE
WITH BROWN BUTTER GLAZE

HANDS-ON TIME: 38 MINUTES ★ TOTAL TIME: 1 HOUR 50 MINUTES

Heart-healthy canola oil replaces a good bit of the butter traditionally used to make this dessert. Soaking a vanilla bean in the oil adds deep, rich flavor; you'll never miss the butter.

Canola field during the springtime

Cake:
6 tablespoons canola oil
1 vanilla bean, split
  lengthwise
1¾ cups sugar
½ cup unsalted butter,
  softened
2 large eggs
12 ounces cake flour
  (about 3 cups)

2 teaspoons baking powder
½ teaspoon salt
1 cup nonfat buttermilk
Baking spray with flour

Glaze:
1 tablespoon unsalted butter
¼ cup sugar
2 tablespoons 2% reduced-fat
  milk
½ teaspoon vanilla extract

1. Preheat oven to 350°.
2. To prepare cake, combine oil and vanilla bean in a small skillet over medium-high heat, and bring to a simmer. Remove from heat. Let stand 10 minutes or until mixture cools to room temperature. Scrape seeds from bean, and stir into oil; discard bean.
3. Combine oil mixture, 1¾ cups sugar, and ½ cup butter in a large bowl; beat with a mixer at medium speed until well blended (about 5 minutes). Add eggs, 1 at a time, beating well after each addition. Weigh or lightly spoon flour into dry measuring cups; level with a knife. Combine flour, baking powder, and salt, stirring well with a whisk. Add flour mixture and buttermilk alternately to sugar mixture, beginning and ending with flour mixture.
4. Spoon batter into a 10-inch tube pan coated with baking spray, and spread evenly. Bake at 350° for 1 hour or until a wooden pick inserted in center comes out clean. Cool in pan 10 minutes on a wire rack, and remove from pan.
5. To prepare glaze, melt 1 tablespoon butter in a small skillet over medium heat; cook 2 minutes or until lightly browned. Remove from heat. Add next 3 ingredients (through vanilla), stirring until smooth. Drizzle glaze over warm cake. Serves 16 (serving size: 1 slice)

CALORIES 294; FAT 12.6g (sat 4.7g, mono 5.3g, poly 1.9g); PROTEIN 3.2g; CARB 42.8g; FIBER 0.4g; CHOL 44mg; IRON 1.7mg; SODIUM 149mg; CALC 60mg

LEMON-POPPY SEED BUNDT CAKE

HANDS-ON TIME: 21 MINUTES ★ TOTAL TIME: 2 HOURS

A favorite flavor combination—lemon and poppy seeds—enhances this version of the classic Bundt cake.

Cake:

1¼ cups granulated sugar

6 tablespoons unsalted butter, softened

¼ cup canola oil

2 large eggs

1 tablespoon grated lemon rind

2 tablespoons fresh lemon juice

1 teaspoon vanilla extract

10 ounces cake flour (about 2½ cups)

¼ cup poppy seeds

1½ teaspoons baking powder

½ teaspoon baking soda

¼ teaspoon salt

1 cup 1% low-fat buttermilk

Baking spray with flour

Glaze:

1 tablespoon unsalted butter

1 cup powdered sugar

3 to 4 teaspoons fresh lemon juice

Grated lemon rind (optional)

1. Preheat oven to 350°.

2. Place granulated sugar, 6 tablespoons butter, and oil in a large bowl; beat with a mixer at medium speed until well blended (about 5 minutes). Add eggs, 1 at a time, beating well after each addition. Beat in 1 tablespoon lemon rind, 2 tablespoons lemon juice, and vanilla. Weigh or lightly spoon flour into dry measuring cups; level with a knife. Combine flour and next 4 ingredients (through salt), stirring well with a whisk. Add flour mixture and buttermilk alternately to sugar mixture, beginning and ending with flour mixture.

3. Spoon batter into 12-cup Bundt pan coated with baking spray. Bake at 350° for 38 to 40 minutes or until a wooden pick inserted in center comes out clean. Cool in pan 15 minutes on a wire rack; remove from pan. Invert cake onto a plate.

4. To prepare glaze, combine 1 tablespoon butter, powdered sugar, and 3 teaspoons lemon juice in a medium bowl; stir until smooth, adding remaining 1 teaspoon lemon juice, if necessary, to reach drizzling consistency.

5. Spoon glaze over cake. Sprinkle with grated lemon rind, if desired. Cool completely before slicing. Serves 16 (serving size: 1 slice)

CALORIES 263; FAT 10g (sat 3.9g, mono 3.9g, poly 2g); PROTEIN 3.2g; CARB 40.5g; FIBER 0.8g; CHOL 37mg; IRON 1.6mg; SODIUM 141mg; CALC 79mg

NORTHWEST
Jammers
The Northwest's many berries and stone fruits make for some top-notch jams. In Portland, Oregon, breakfast mavens stop at Grand Central Bakery for jammers: generous-sized buttermilk biscuits with a thick, crunchy crust and tender, buttery interior, each oozing with a hefty dollop of the region's preserves.

AMERICA LOVES: BAKING
Lovin' from the country's ovens

WEST
Pineapple Upside-Down Cake
In 1925, the Hawaiian Pineapple Company sponsored a recipe contest, and nearly 2,500 of the 60,000 submissions featured pineapple upside-down cake. The company shared some of the recipes, establishing the cake's popularity. Although Southern versions often use canned pineapple, in Hawaii, this luau favorite always features fresh fruit.

SOUTHWEST
Texas Sheet Cake
Although the recipe for Texas Sheet Cake did not likely originate in Texas, proud Texans have adopted this classic cake as their own. It features a layer flavored with pecans and another of chocolate, all baked up as big and wide as the state of Texas.

NORTHEAST
Boston Cream Pie
While this classic dessert has "pie" in its title, it's actually two layers of sponge cake filled with vanilla cream custard and covered with a chocolate glaze. It was originally developed in the 19th century and in pie pans because they were more common than cake pans.

MIDWEST
Bundt Cake
In 1950, Nordic Ware introduced the Bundt pan, requested by a customer who wanted to make her German grandmother's *kugelhopf* recipe. The pan was originally called a "bund" pan (meaning "a gathering") but was later changed to "bundt" to trademark the name. Today, there are nearly 60 million Bundt pans in use across America.

EAST
Whoopie Pie
Whoopie pies consist of creamy frosting sandwiched between two palm-sized mounds of chocolate cake. They are thought to have originated as a lunchtime dessert for Pennsylvania Amish farmers. They were made from leftover cake batter, and likely got their name from the farmers' excited exclamations when finding the treat included in their lunch.

SOUTH
King Cake
In New Orleans, King Cake is a Mardi Gras tradition, baked in honor of the three kings who visited baby Jesus. A circle of twisted strands of cinnamon dough is covered with poured sugar tinted in traditional Mardi Gras colors and filled with custard. A small plastic baby (representing Jesus) hidden inside is said to bring good luck to whoever discovers it. The finder also wins the honor of bringing the cake for the next year's celebration.

SOUTHEAST
Lady Baltimore Cake
This classic white layer cake is topped with a boiled frosting combined with chopped nuts and dried or candied fruits. It was likely popularized by Lady Baltimore's Tea Room in Charleston, South Carolina, at the end of the 19th century, rather than Lady Baltimore (whose Irish husband inherited Maryland in the early 17th century), who never came to America.

TRIPLE-CHOCOLATE CAKE

HANDS-ON TIME: 50 MINUTES ★ TOTAL TIME: 1 HOUR 25 MINUTES

Chocolate lovers rejoice! This rich cake gives you a hit of chocolate in each element—the batter, filling, and glaze. And three kinds of chocolate are used: cocoa, bittersweet chocolate, and milk chocolate.

Cake:

1 cup boiling water

½ cup plus 1 tablespoon unsweetened cocoa, divided

2 ounces bittersweet chocolate, finely chopped

Cooking spray

1¾ cups granulated sugar

6 tablespoons butter, softened

1 teaspoon vanilla extract

3 large egg whites

½ cup fat-free sour cream

8 ounces cake flour (about 2 cups)

1½ teaspoons baking powder

½ teaspoon baking soda

½ teaspoon salt

Filling:

⅓ cup fat-free milk

1 tablespoon granulated sugar

1 tablespoon cornstarch

Dash of salt

4 ounces milk chocolate, finely chopped

¾ cup frozen fat-free whipped topping, thawed

Glaze:

½ cup powdered sugar

¼ cup unsweetened cocoa

3 tablespoons fat-free milk

2 teaspoons butter

⅛ teaspoon instant espresso granules

Dash of salt

1 ounce bittersweet chocolate, finely chopped

1. Preheat oven to 350°.

2. To prepare cake, combine 1 cup boiling water and ½ cup cocoa. Add 2 ounces bittersweet chocolate; stir until smooth. Cool to room temperature. Coat 2 (8-inch) round cake pans with cooking spray. Line bottoms of pans with wax paper; coat wax paper with cooking spray and dust pans with 1 tablespoon cocoa.

3. Place 1¾ cups granulated sugar, 6 tablespoons butter, and 1 teaspoon vanilla in a large bowl; beat with a mixer at medium speed 1 minute. Add egg whites, 1 at a time, beating well after each addition. Add sour cream; beat at medium speed 2 minutes. Weigh or lightly spoon flour into dry measuring cups; level with a knife. Combine flour, baking powder, baking soda, and ½ teaspoon salt in a bowl, stirring with a whisk. Add flour mixture and cocoa mixture alternately to sugar mixture, beginning and ending with flour mixture; beat just until combined.

4. Divide batter evenly between prepared pans. Bake at 350° for 30 minutes or until a wooden pick inserted in center comes out with moist crumbs clinging. Cool 10 minutes in pans on wire racks. Invert layers onto racks, and cool completely. Discard wax paper.

5. To prepare filling, combine ⅓ cup milk and next 3 ingredients (through dash of salt) in a saucepan over medium-low heat; bring to a boil, stirring constantly. Cook 1 minute or until thick, stirring constantly. Remove from heat. Add milk chocolate, stirring until smooth. Pour into a large bowl. Cover and chill. Uncover; fold in whipped topping.

6. To prepare glaze, combine powdered sugar and next 6 ingredients (through chocolate) in a saucepan over low heat. Cook 2 minutes, stirring frequently. Place 1 cake layer on a plate. Spread filling over cake, leaving a ¼-inch border. Top with remaining layer. Drizzle glaze over top of cake, spreading it out over edges. Serves 16 (serving size: 1 slice)

CALORIES 311; FAT 10.3g (sat 5.7g, mono 2.1g, poly 0.5g); PROTEIN 4.8g; CARB 50.6g; FIBER 1.8g; CHOL 49mg; IRON 2.2mg; SODIUM 224mg; CALC 66mg

A baker's essential

Vanilla extract—one of the most commonly used baking ingredients today—was invented in 1847 in Boston, Massachusetts, by Joseph Burnett, a druggist, chemist, and store owner. Burnett was known for purchasing expensive vanilla beans from New York. One day a wealthy customer entered the store and asked him to make a vanilla flavoring. After extensive testing in his laboratory, he shared the final product with the customer. She was so pleased with the quality that she urged him to make more and promised to introduce the extract to her aristocratic friends.

In 1855, he amicably sold his half of the store to his business partner and formed the Joseph Burnett Company. His new company went on to create other extract flavorings and introduced items like perfume, hair products, and lotions.

The South's celebration cake

Southern cooks have been using coconut since at least the 18th century, thanks to port cities like New Orleans, Louisiana; Charleston, South Carolina; and Savannah, Georgia, which all allowed the import of the fruit from the tropics. As the popularity of layer cakes grew in the 20th century, coconut cake arrived on the scene—and instantly became a Christmas tradition. Over the years, coconut cake became a popular Easter dessert as well, and today it's served to honor any truly special occasion. If you really want a special cake, use fresh coconut.

DOUBLE-COCONUT CAKE

HANDS-ON TIME: 50 MINUTES ★ TOTAL TIME: 1 HOUR 50 MINUTES

The light coconut milk in this recipe delivers richness, flavor, and moisture without all the extra saturated fat found in regular coconut milk.

Cake:

Cooking spray

1 tablespoon cake flour

9 ounces sifted cake flour (about 2¼ cups)

2¼ teaspoons baking powder

½ teaspoon salt

1⅔ cups sugar

⅓ cup butter, softened

2 large eggs

1 (14-ounce) can light coconut milk

1 tablespoon vanilla extract

Fluffy Coconut Frosting:

4 large egg whites

½ teaspoon cream of tartar

Dash of salt

1 cup sugar

¼ cup water

½ teaspoon vanilla extract

¼ teaspoon coconut extract

⅔ cup flaked sweetened coconut, divided

1. Preheat oven to 350°.

2. Coat 2 (9-inch) round cake pans with cooking spray; dust with 1 tablespoon flour.

3. To prepare cake, combine 2¼ cups flour, baking powder, and salt, stirring with a whisk. Place 1⅔ cups sugar and butter in a large bowl; beat with a mixer at medium speed until well blended (about 5 minutes). Add eggs, 1 at a time, beating well after each addition. Add flour mixture and coconut milk alternately to sugar mixture, beginning and ending with flour mixture. Stir in vanilla.

4. Pour batter into prepared pans. Sharply tap pans once on countertop to remove air bubbles. Bake at 350° for 30 minutes or until a wooden pick inserted in center comes out clean. Cool in pans 10 minutes on wire racks. Invert layers onto racks; cool completely.

5. To prepare frosting, place egg whites, cream of tartar, and salt in a large bowl; beat with a mixer at high speed until stiff peaks form. Combine 1 cup sugar and ¼ cup water in a saucepan; bring to a boil. Cook, without stirring, until a candy thermometer registers 238°. Pour hot sugar syrup in a thin stream over egg whites, beating at high speed. Stir in extracts.

6. Place 1 cake layer on a plate; spread with 1 cup frosting. Sprinkle with ⅓ cup coconut. Top with remaining cake layer; spread remaining frosting over top and sides of cake. Sprinkle ⅓ cup coconut over top of cake. Store cake loosely covered in refrigerator. Serves 14 (serving size: 1 slice)

CALORIES 298; FAT 7.9g (sat 5g, mono 1.7g, poly 0.3g); PROTEIN 3.4g; CARB 53.8g; FIBER 0.4g; CHOL 42mg; IRON 1.6mg; SODIUM 273mg; CALC 52mg

BIRTHDAY CAKE

HANDS-ON TIME: 36 MINUTES ★ TOTAL TIME: 3 HOURS

Buttery yellow cake with creamy chocolate frosting—what could be better on a birthday? I use baking spray with flour to prevent the cake layers from sticking to the pans.

My brother Evan and me on his birthday

Baking spray with flour
2 teaspoons cake flour
9 ounces cake flour (about 2¼ cups)
2½ teaspoons baking powder
½ teaspoon baking soda
½ teaspoon salt
½ cup unsalted butter, softened
1½ cups granulated sugar

3 large eggs
1 cup 1% low-fat buttermilk
2 teaspoons vanilla extract
¼ cup unsalted butter
4 ounces unsweetened chocolate, chopped
¾ cup 1% low-fat milk
1 teaspoon vanilla extract
4 cups powdered sugar
Candy sprinkles (optional)

1. Preheat oven to 350°. To prepare cake, coat 2 (9-inch) round cake pans with baking spray. Line bottoms of pans with wax paper or parchment paper; coat paper with baking spray. Dust each pan with 1 teaspoon flour. Weigh or lightly spoon 9 ounces flour (about 2¼ cups) into dry measuring cups; level with a knife. Combine flour and next 3 ingredients (through salt); stir well.

2. Place ½ cup butter in a large bowl; beat with a mixer at medium speed until creamy. Gradually add granulated sugar, beating until light and fluffy. Add eggs, 1 at a time, beating well after each addition. Add flour mixture and buttermilk alternately to sugar mixture, beginning and ending with flour mixture. Beat in 2 teaspoons vanilla. Pour batter into prepared pans.

3. Bake at 350° for 25 minutes or until a wooden pick inserted in center comes out clean. Cool in pans 10 minutes on wire racks. Invert cake layers onto racks; cool completely. Discard wax paper.

4. To prepare frosting, melt ¼ cup butter and chopped chocolate in a small heavy saucepan over low heat. Add low-fat milk, stirring with a whisk until smooth. Stir in 1 teaspoon vanilla. Remove from heat; transfer to a large mixing bowl, and cover surface of chocolate mixture with plastic wrap. Refrigerate until cooled completely and slightly thick, about 30 minutes.

5. Gradually add powdered sugar, beating with a mixer at medium speed until smooth and glossy. Place 1 cake layer on a plate; spread with ¾ cup frosting. Top with remaining cake layer. Apply a thin layer of frosting to entire cake. Allow frosting to set in the refrigerator about 30 minutes. Spread remaining frosting over top and sides of cake. Sprinkle edge with candy sprinkles, if desired. Let cake stand until frosting is set. Serves 20 (serving size: 1 slice)

CALORIES 306; FAT 11.9g (sat 6.5g, mono 3.1g, poly 1.5g); PROTEIN 3.6g; CARB 52g; FIBER 1.2g; CHOL 47mg; IRON 2.1mg; SODIUM 140mg; CALC 113mg

CARROT CAKE

HANDS-ON TIME: 33 MINUTES ★ TOTAL TIME: 1 HOUR 53 MINUTES

Warm spices and brown sugar add rich, caramelized flavors to this carrot cake. If you can't find fromage blanc, use more cream cheese.

Cake:

10.1 ounces all-purpose flour (about 2¼ cups)

2 teaspoons baking powder

1½ teaspoons ground cinnamon

¼ teaspoon salt

2 cups grated carrot

1 cup granulated sugar

½ cup packed brown sugar

6 tablespoons butter, softened

3 large eggs

1 teaspoon vanilla extract

½ cup 1% low-fat buttermilk

Cooking spray

Frosting:

6 ounces cream cheese, softened (about ¾ cup)

1 ounce fromage blanc

2 tablespoons butter, softened

½ teaspoon vanilla extract

⅛ teaspoon salt

3 cups powdered sugar

1. Preheat oven to 350°.

2. To prepare cake, weigh or lightly spoon flour into dry measuring cups, and level with a knife. Combine flour and next 3 ingredients (through salt) in a medium bowl, stirring with a whisk. Add carrot, tossing to combine.

3. Place granulated sugar, brown sugar, and 6 tablespoons butter in a large bowl. Beat with a mixer at medium speed until combined. Add eggs, 1 at a time, beating well after each addition. Stir in 1 teaspoon vanilla. Add flour mixture and buttermilk alternately to sugar mixture, beginning and ending with flour mixture. Spread batter into a 13 x 9–inch metal baking pan coated with cooking spray. Bake at 350° for 28 minutes or until a wooden pick inserted in center comes out clean. Cool cake completely on a wire rack.

4. To prepare frosting, place cream cheese and next 4 ingredients (through salt) in a medium bowl. Beat with a mixer at medium speed until fluffy. Gradually add powdered sugar, beating at medium speed until combined (don't overbeat). Spread frosting evenly over top of cake. Serves 20 (serving size: 1 piece)

CALORIES 284; FAT 9.7g (sat 4.9g, mono 2.8g, poly 0.8g); PROTEIN 3.6g; CARB 46.6g; FIBER 0.9g; CHOL 49mg; IRON 1mg; SODIUM 172mg; CALC 68mg

TEXAS SHEET CAKE

HANDS-ON TIME: 28 MINUTES
TOTAL TIME: 1 HOUR 45 MINUTES

Toasty nuts and fudgy cake topped with a thin, crackly glaze make this a deliciously moist, irresistible dessert.

Cooking spray
2 teaspoons all-purpose flour
9 ounces all-purpose flour (about 2 cups)
2 cups granulated sugar
1 teaspoon baking soda
1 teaspoon ground cinnamon
¼ teaspoon salt
¾ cup water
½ cup butter

½ cup unsweetened cocoa, divided
½ cup 1% low-fat buttermilk
1 tablespoon vanilla extract, divided
2 large eggs
6 tablespoons butter
⅓ cup fat-free milk
3 cups powdered sugar
¼ cup chopped pecans, toasted

1. Preheat oven to 375°.
2. Coat a 15 x 10–inch jelly-roll pan with cooking spray; dust with 2 teaspoons flour. Set aside.
3. Weigh or lightly spoon 9 ounces flour (about 2 cups) into dry measuring cups; level with a knife. Combine flour and next 4 ingredients (through salt) in a large bowl. Combine ¾ cup water, ½ cup butter, and ¼ cup cocoa in a saucepan; bring to a boil, stirring frequently. Pour into flour mixture. Beat with a mixer at medium speed until well blended. Add buttermilk, 1 teaspoon vanilla, and eggs; beat well. Pour batter into prepared pan. Bake at 375° for 17 minutes or until a wooden pick inserted in center comes out clean. Place on a wire rack.
4. Combine 6 tablespoons butter, fat-free milk, and ¼ cup cocoa in a saucepan. Bring to a boil, stirring constantly. Remove from heat. Gradually stir in powdered sugar; stir in 2 teaspoons vanilla and pecans. Spread over hot cake. Cool completely on wire rack. Serves 20 (serving size: 1 piece)

CALORIES 298; FAT 10g (sat 5.5g, mono 3.2g, poly 0.7g); PROTEIN 3.1g; CARB 49.8g; FIBER 0.5g; CHOL 44mg; IRON 1.1mg; SODIUM 188mg; CALC 25mg

The cake that keeps on giving

The tradition of making fruitcakes for special celebrations and holidays dates back to the 18th century, when the costs of materials were considered extravagant. Up until the 1940s, it was the top choice for a wedding dessert. How it became exclusive to the Christmas season and when it fell from grace is unknown. Today, people either love it or loathe it. Either way, it often gets a bad rap for being undesirable and is joked about throughout the holidays.

Some think the decline in popularity of fruitcake began when they were mass-produced for mail order. Those cakes tend be much drier than homemade. I'm personally a fan of homemade fruitcake. The flavor and the tenderness of the crumb are far superior to the prepared version. And what's not to like about a bourbon-laced cake made with nuts and butter?

SOUTHERN FRUITCAKE

HANDS-ON TIME: 40 MINUTES ★ TOTAL TIME: 27 HOURS 40 MINUTES

Ideally, fruitcake should be made at least a month before you plan to serve it, but it will last for several months when stored tightly wrapped in the fridge.

Cooking spray
2¼ cups chopped pecans
1⅔ cups chopped pitted dates
1½ cups raisins (you can use all dark or ¾ cup each dark and golden)
⅔ cup chopped candied orange peel
⅔ cup chopped candied pineapple
⅔ cup candied cherries, halved
9 ounces all-purpose flour (about 2 cups)
½ teaspoon ground cinnamon
½ teaspoon kosher salt
¼ teaspoon ground cloves
¼ teaspoon ground nutmeg
⅛ teaspoon ground ginger
¾ cup unsalted butter, softened
¾ cup sugar
4 large eggs
2 large egg whites
1 cup bourbon, divided
1 teaspoon vanilla extract
1 teaspoon almond extract

1. Preheat oven to 250°.
2. Coat 2 (8 x 4–inch) loaf pans with cooking spray; line bottom and sides of pans with parchment paper. Coat parchment paper with cooking spray.
3. Combine pecans and next 5 ingredients (through cherries) in a large bowl. Weigh or lightly spoon flour into dry measuring cups; level with a knife. Add 1 cup flour to pecan mixture, tossing to coat.
4. Combine 1 cup flour, cinnamon, and next 4 ingredients (through ginger) in a small bowl. Place butter and sugar in a large bowl; beat with a mixer at high speed 3 minutes or until light and fluffy, scraping sides of bowl occasionally. Add eggs and egg whites, 1 at a time, beating well after each addition. Add flour-spice mixture; beat at medium speed until blended. Add ¼ cup bourbon and extracts, beating at low speed until blended. Stir pecan mixture into batter.
5. Spoon batter into prepared pans, pressing firmly to pack. Press a piece of parchment paper onto surface of batter in each pan.
6. Add water to a 13 x 9–inch glass or ceramic baking dish to a depth of 1 inch; place on bottom rack in oven. Place loaf pans on middle rack in oven. Bake at 250° for 1 hour and 45 minutes to 2 hours or until a wooden pick inserted in center comes out clean.
7. Remove top piece of parchment paper. Immediately pierce cakes several times with a long wooden pick, and brush 2 tablespoons bourbon over each cake. Cool completely in pans on a wire rack. Remove from pans.
8. Cut 2 (18-inch) pieces of cheesecloth. Soak cheesecloth in ½ cup bourbon. Wrap a bourbon-soaked piece of cheesecloth around each cake, and place each cake in a large zip-top plastic bag; seal and store in a cool place at least 24 hours. Serves 24 (serving size: ½₂ of a loaf cake)

CALORIES 298; FAT 12g (sat 3.9g, mono 5.7g, poly 2.3g); PROTEIN 4.0g; CARB 42g; FIBER 2.5g; CHOL 43mg; IRON 0.9mg; SODIUM 80mg; CALC 26mg

ST. LOUIS BUTTER CAKE

HANDS-ON TIME: 24 MINUTES ★ TOTAL TIME: 3 HOURS 59 MINUTES

A beloved St. Louis dessert whose very name includes "butter" with fewer than 200 calories and 4 grams of saturated fat per luscious serving? Yes!

The St. Louis Arch the gateway to the West

3 tablespoons 1% low-fat milk, room temperature

2 tablespoons warm water (100° to 110°)

1¾ teaspoons dry yeast

¼ cup canola oil

3 tablespoons granulated sugar

2 tablespoons unsalted butter, softened

1 teaspoon salt

1 large egg

7.9 ounces all-purpose flour (about 1¾ cups)

Baking spray with flour

3 tablespoons plus 1 teaspoon light corn syrup

2 tablespoons water

2½ teaspoons vanilla extract

1½ cups granulated sugar

9 tablespoons unsalted butter, softened

½ teaspoon salt

1 large egg

5.2 ounces all-purpose flour (about 1 cup plus 3 tablespoons)

1 tablespoon powdered sugar

1. Combine milk and 2 tablespoons warm water in a bowl, stirring with a whisk. Dissolve yeast in milk mixture. Let stand 5 minutes. Place canola oil and next 3 ingredients (through salt) in a large bowl; beat with a mixer at medium speed until well blended (about 1 minute). Add egg, beating well. Weigh or lightly spoon 7.9 ounces (about 1¾ cups) flour into dry measuring cups; level with a knife. Add flour and milk mixture alternately to sugar mixture, beginning and ending with flour. Beat 5 minutes or until dough is smooth and pulls away from sides of bowl.

2. Pat dough into bottom of a 13 x 9–inch metal baking pan coated with baking spray; cover with a damp towel. Let rise in a warm place (85°), free from drafts, 2 hours or until doubled in size.

3. Preheat oven to 350°. Combine corn syrup, 2 tablespoons water, and vanilla in a bowl, stirring with a whisk. Place 1½ cups granulated sugar, 9 tablespoons butter, and ½ teaspoon salt in a large bowl; beat with a mixer at medium speed until fluffy (about 3 minutes). Add egg, beating well. Weigh or lightly spoon 5.2 ounces (about 1 cup plus 3 tablespoons) flour into a dry measuring cup; level with a knife. Add flour and corn syrup mixture alternately to sugar mixture, beginning and ending with flour mixture. Dollop topping over dough, and spread to edges of pan.

4. Bake at 350° for 35 minutes or until top is golden brown. Cool completely in pan on a wire rack. Sprinkle with powdered sugar, and cut into squares. Serves 24 (serving size: 1 piece)

CALORIES 196; FAT 8.2g (sat 3.7g, mono 3.1g, poly 1g); PROTEIN 2.3g; CARB 28.9g; FIBER 0.5g; CHOL 30mg; IRON 0.8mg; SODIUM 157mg; CALC 9mg

VANILLA CUPCAKES
WITH CREAMY VANILLA BUTTERCREAM

HANDS-ON TIME: 50 MINUTES ★ TOTAL TIME: 2 HOURS 30 MINUTES

Cupcakes of every imaginable flavor are all the rage these days, but it's hard to beat the rich simplicity of vanilla.

Cupcakes:

4 ounces cake flour (about 1 cup)

1¼ teaspoons baking powder

¼ teaspoon salt

3 tablespoons canola oil

1 large egg

1 large egg white

¾ cup plus 2 tablespoons granulated sugar

½ cup 1% low-fat buttermilk

2 teaspoons vanilla extract

Cooking spray

Buttercream Frosting:

6 tablespoons unsalted butter, softened

2 cups powdered sugar

2 tablespoons half-and-half

1½ teaspoons vanilla extract

Dash of salt

Sugar pearls (optional)

1. Preheat oven to 350°.

2. To prepare cupcakes, weigh or lightly spoon flour into a dry measuring cup; level with a knife. Combine flour, baking powder, and salt. Beat oil, egg, and egg white with a mixer at medium speed until combined. Add granulated sugar; beat until thick and pale. Add flour mixture and buttermilk alternately to sugar mixture, beginning and ending with flour mixture; mix after each addition. Stir in 2 teaspoons vanilla.

3. Place 12 paper or foil muffin cup liners in muffin cups; coat liners with cooking spray. Spoon batter into cups. Bake at 350° for 20 to 22 minutes or until tops of cupcakes spring back when pressed in center (they will not be brown.)

4. Cool in pan 10 minutes on a wire rack; remove from pan. Cool completely on a wire rack.

5. To prepare buttercream frosting, place butter in a bowl; beat with a mixer at medium speed until light and fluffy. Add powdered sugar; beat at low speed until blended. Add half-and-half, 1½ teaspoons vanilla, and dash of salt; beat at high speed until smooth and creamy. Top cupcakes with frosting. Sprinkle with sugar pearls, if desired. Serves 12 (serving size: 1 cupcake)

CALORIES 278; FAT 10g (sat 4.5g, mono 4g, poly 1.5g); PROTEIN 2.8g; CARB 43.3g; FIBER 0g; CHOL 47mg; IRON 0mg; SODIUM 149mg; CALC 48mg

Seeing red

While there's general agreement that red velvet cake is a Southern treat, the original recipe may actually have been born in New York. Some claim that the baker at New York City's Waldorf Astoria Hotel first introduced red velvet cake in the 1920s. A story goes that a guest of the hotel so loved the cake that she requested the recipe, which she subsequently passed to her network of friends.

During the Great Depression in the 1930s, the Adams Extract Company of Texas brought red velvet cake into public awareness by promoting their red food coloring on in-store posters and recipe cards. Some food historians attribute its recent rise in popularity to the 1989 movie *Steel Magnolias*, in which the groom's cake was red velvet (and also in the shape of an armadillo—nice touch!).

RED VELVET CUPCAKES

HANDS-ON TIME: 55 MINUTES ★ TOTAL TIME: 2 HOURS 33 MINUTES

The frosting takes this red velvet cupcake recipe from great to fantastic. The secret here: real butter and full-fat cream cheese—just less of it. The results are mouthwateringly good.

Cupcakes:

10 ounces cake flour (about 2½ cups)

3 tablespoons unsweetened cocoa

1 teaspoon baking soda

1 teaspoon baking powder

1 teaspoon kosher salt

1½ cups granulated sugar

6 tablespoons unsalted butter, softened

2 large eggs

1¼ cups nonfat buttermilk

1½ teaspoons white vinegar

1½ teaspoons vanilla extract

2 tablespoons red food coloring (about 1 ounce)

Cooking spray

Frosting:

5 tablespoons butter, softened

4 teaspoons nonfat buttermilk

1 (8-ounce) block cream cheese, softened

3½ cups powdered sugar (about 1 pound)

1¼ teaspoons vanilla extract

1. Preheat oven to 350°.

2. To prepare cupcakes, weigh or lightly spoon cake flour into dry measuring cups; level with a knife. Combine cake flour and next 4 ingredients (through salt) in a medium bowl; stir with a whisk.

3. Place granulated sugar and unsalted butter in a large bowl; beat with a mixer at medium speed until well blended (about 3 minutes). Add eggs, 1 at a time, beating well after each addition. Add flour mixture and 1¼ cups nonfat buttermilk alternately to sugar mixture, beginning and ending with flour mixture. Add white vinegar, 1½ teaspoons vanilla, and food coloring; beat well.

4. Place 30 paper muffin cup liners in muffin cups; coat liners with cooking spray. Spoon batter into cups. Bake at 350° for 20 minutes or until a wooden pick inserted in center comes out clean. Cool in pan 10 minutes on a wire rack; remove from pan. Cool completely on wire racks.

5. To prepare frosting, beat 5 tablespoons butter, 4 teaspoons nonfat buttermilk, and cream cheese with a mixer at high speed until fluffy. Gradually add powdered sugar; beat until smooth. Add 1¼ teaspoons vanilla; beat well. Spread frosting evenly over cupcakes. Serves 30 (serving size: 1 cupcake)

CALORIES 205; FAT 7.3g (sat 4.5g, mono 2g, poly 0.3g); PROTEIN 2.3g; CARB 33.5g; FIBER 0.3g; CHOL 34mg; IRON 0.9mg; SODIUM 168mg; CALC 35mg

SWEET AND SAUCY

Dress up a bowl of ice cream or slice of pound cake instantly.

MARSALA POACHED FIGS

 West

Combine ½ cup marsala, 1 (3-inch) cinnamon stick, 3 black peppercorns, and 1 tablespoon honey in a medium saucepan. Bring to a boil; cook 7 minutes or until syrupy. Add 6 halved fresh Black Mission figs (about 8.5 ounces); cook 1 minute or until thoroughly heated. SERVES 6 (serving size: 2 fig halves and 2 teaspoons sauce) CALORIES 72; FAT 0g (sat 0g); SODIUM 2mg

DARK CHERRY MERLOT SAUCE

 Midwest

Combine 2 cups pitted dark sweet cherries, 1 cup merlot, 2 tablespoons brown sugar, 1 teaspoon fresh lemon juice, and ⅛ teaspoon salt in a saucepan; bring to a boil. Lightly crush about half of cherries with a potato masher. Reduce heat, and cook until reduced to about 1 cup. Let stand 5 minutes. SERVES 8 (serving size: 2 tablespoons) CALORIES 33; FAT 0g (sat 0g); SODIUM 38mg

WARM BERRY SAUCE

 Northwest

Combine ⅔ cup raspberries, ⅔ cup blackberries, ½ cup water, ¼ cup sugar, and 2 tablespoons fresh lemon juice in a small saucepan. Bring mixture to a boil. Reduce heat to medium-low; gently boil 10 minutes or until sauce thickens. Stir in 1 tablespoon butter. SERVES 10 (serving size: 2 tablespoons) CALORIES 31; FAT 1.3g (sat 0.8g); SODIUM 10mg

CHILLED PINEAPPLE SAUCE

Southwest

Place 3 cups coarsely chopped pineapple, 2 tablespoons brown sugar, and ¼ teaspoon vanilla extract in a food processor; pulse 10 times or until finely chopped. Cover and chill. SERVES 14 (serving size: 2 tablespoons) CALORIES 24; FAT 0g (sat 0g); SODIUM 1mg

PEACH & BROWN SUGAR SAUCE

South

Melt 2 tablespoons unsalted butter in a large nonstick skillet over medium heat. Add 4 large pitted and sliced peaches to pan; cook 3 minutes, stirring occasionally. Add 2 tablespoons brown sugar and ½ teaspoon ground cinnamon to pan; cook 1 minute or until sugar melts, stirring occasionally. SERVES 8 (serving size: ½ cup) CALORIES 70; FAT 3g (sat 1.8g); SODIUM 26mg

FRESH BLUEBERRY SAUCE

 Northeast

Combine 1 cup water and ¾ cup sugar in a small saucepan over medium-high heat; bring to a boil. Cook 5 minutes or until sugar dissolves, stirring constantly. Add 1 cup blueberries, 1 teaspoon butter, 1 teaspoon lemon juice, ½ teaspoon vanilla extract, and ⅛ teaspoon ground nutmeg to pan; return to boil. Reduce heat to medium; cook 4 minutes or until berries pop, stirring occasionally. Remove from heat. SERVES 12 (serving size: 3 tablespoons) CALORIES 59; FAT 0g (sat 0g); SODIUM 2mg

APPLE & BRANDY SAUCE

 East

Melt 1 tablespoon butter in a small skillet over medium heat. Add 1½ cups sliced peeled apple; cook 5 minutes or until lightly browned, stirring frequently. Add 1 tablespoon sugar, 3 tablespoons brandy, ¼ teaspoon lemon juice, and ⅛ teaspoon ginger; cook over medium-low heat 2 minutes or until apple is tender, stirring occasionally. SERVES 6 (serving size: ¼ cup) CALORIES 43; FAT 2g (sat 1.2g); SODIUM 17mg

ORANGE-STRAWBERRY SAUCE

 *Southeast*

Peel and section 4 navel oranges (about 2 pounds) over a bowl, and squeeze membranes to extract juice. Set sections aside, and reserve ¼ cup juice. Discard membranes. Chop orange sections. Combine 1 tablespoon sugar and 1 tablespoon cornstarch in a 1-quart glass measure. Stir in reserved orange juice, ¼ cup fresh orange juice, and 1 tablespoon fresh lemon juice, and stir with a whisk until well blended. Stir in chopped oranges. Microwave mixture at HIGH 2 minutes and 45 seconds or until thick, stirring after 2 minutes. Stir in 2 cups sliced strawberries, ½ teaspoon vanilla extract, and ¼ teaspoon almond extract. SERVES 8 (serving size: ½ cup) CALORIES 56; FAT 0g (sat 0g); SODIUM 1mg

Fruit sauce tip Many traditional fruit sauces use an excess of sugar. Choosing fruits at their peak ripeness, when they are naturally sweet, will keep calories and sugar to a minimum.

OHIO BUCKEYES

HANDS-ON TIME: 33 MINUTES ★ TOTAL TIME: 1 HOUR 13 MINUTES

In this classic confection from the Buckeye State, peanut butter and chocolate combine to create an adorable replica of an Ohio tree nut.

2 cups powdered sugar

6 tablespoons unsalted butter, softened

2 ounces reduced-fat cream cheese, softened (about ¼ cup)

½ teaspoon kosher salt

1½ cups reduced-fat creamy peanut butter

¼ cup graham cracker crumbs

8 ounces dark chocolate (60–65% cocoa), chopped

1. Place first 4 ingredients (through salt) in a bowl; beat with a mixer at medium speed until creamy. Add peanut butter and crumbs; beat until blended.

2. Place chocolate in the top of a double boiler; place over simmering water, stirring until almost melted. Remove from heat; stir until smooth. Cool slightly.

3. While chocolate cools, cover a baking sheet with parchment paper. Shape peanut butter mixture by tablespoonfuls into 38 balls. Place balls on prepared baking sheet.

4. Place each ball on a fork, and dip ball in chocolate until partially coated; return to parchment paper to harden.

Serves 38 (serving size: 1 buckeye)

CALORIES 141; FAT 8.3g (sat 3.5g, mono 2.9g, poly 1.2g); PROTEIN 2.7g; CARB 14.7g; FIBER 1.1g; CHOL 6mg; IRON 0.6mg; SODIUM 95mg; CALC 6mg

BORN IN

OHIO

The state dessert

Unless you're native to the Midwest region around Ohio, you may not be familiar with this peanut butter and chocolate confection that's modeled after the nut of Ohio's state tree, the buckeye. The people of Ohio—also known as "Buckeyes"—are a proud community, passionate about their state symbols and their state recipes. One local joke goes, "You know you're from Ohio when you have four definitions for the word 'buckeye' and a recipe for at least one of them."

CLASSIC FUDGE-WALNUT BROWNIES

HANDS-ON TIME: 20 MINUTES ★ TOTAL TIME: 1 HOUR 15 MINUTES

Brownies were created in Chicago's Palmer House hotel in 1893. Bertha Palmer, a socialite and philanthropist, requested a dessert to be served in an upscale boxed lunch that would be easier to eat than a piece of pie and smaller than a layer cake. It wasn't until the early 1900s that the dessert was popularized by home cooks.

3.38 ounces all-purpose flour
    (about ¾ cup)
1 cup granulated sugar
¾ cup unsweetened cocoa
½ cup packed brown sugar
½ teaspoon baking powder
¼ teaspoon salt
1 cup bittersweet chocolate chunks,
    divided
⅓ cup fat-free milk
6 tablespoons butter, melted
1 teaspoon vanilla extract
2 large eggs, lightly beaten
½ cup chopped walnuts, divided
Cooking spray

1. Preheat oven to 350°.
2. Weigh or lightly spoon flour into dry measuring cups; level with a knife. Combine flour and next 5 ingredients (through salt) in a large bowl. Combine ½ cup chocolate and milk in a microwave-safe bowl; microwave at HIGH 1 minute, stirring after 30 seconds. Stir in butter, vanilla, and eggs. Add milk mixture, ½ cup chocolate, and ¼ cup nuts to flour mixture; stir to combine.
3. Pour batter into a 9-inch square metal baking pan coated with cooking spray; sprinkle with ¼ cup nuts. Bake at 350° for 22 minutes or until a wooden pick inserted in center comes out with moist crumbs clinging. Cool in pan on a wire rack. Cut into 20 pieces. Serves 20 (serving size: 1 piece)

CALORIES 186; FAT 9.1g (sat 4.2g, mono 2.2g, poly 1.7g); PROTEIN 2.8g; CARB 25.4g; FIBER 1.4g; CHOL 30mg; IRON 0.9mg; SODIUM 74mg; CALC 23mg

NUT BROWNIES

MAKES 16 BROWNIES

MEAS. AND SIFT TOGETHER.
1 CUP SIFTED FLOUR
1 TEASPOON BAKING POWDE.
5 TABLESPOONS COCOA
WORK WITH SPOON UNTIL SOFT.
1/2 CUP SHORTENING
1/2 CUP SUGAR
BEAT UNTIL LIGHT AND FLUFFY.
THEN ADD: 1 EGG -1TEASP. VANI
LLA. BEAT UNTIL WELL BLENDED
ADD.1/2 CUP DARK CORN SYRUP
GRADUALLY ADD SIFTED DRY
INGREDIENTS. AND ADD 1/2
CUP BROKEN WALNUTS MIX WELL
SPREAD MIXTURE INTO A
GREASED SQUARE PAN. BAKE IN A
SLOW OVEN(325F.) 30 MINUTES.
COOL-CUT IN SQUARES, STORE
IN BREAD BOX.

The original brownie recipe

There is some dispute about who printed the first brownie recipe. Some credit Fannie Farmer, who published her recipe in the 1906 *Boston Cooking School Cookbook*, while others credit Maria Willett Howard of Bangor, Maine, for her "Bangor Brownies," printed in *Lowney's Cook Book Illustrated in Colors* in 1907. Although the women lived in different states, their books were both published in Boston, Massachusetts. The recipes are almost identical, although Howard's recipe calls for an extra egg and an extra square of chocolate, which makes a fudgier brownie. Both recipes were a departure from a classic cake recipe.

BUTTER-CRUNCH LEMON BARS

HANDS-ON TIME: 45 MINUTES ★ TOTAL TIME: 9 HOURS 5 MINUTES

A buttery, crunchy pastry crust forms the base for a tangy lemon filling. You can substitute fresh orange juice and grated orange rind for lemon, if you wish. These are best served chilled.

Crust:
⅓ cup butter, softened
¼ cup packed dark brown sugar
¼ teaspoon salt
¼ teaspoon ground mace or nutmeg
4.5 ounces all-purpose flour (about 1 cup)
Cooking spray

Filling:
1 cup 1% low-fat cottage cheese

1 cup granulated sugar
2 tablespoons all-purpose flour
1 tablespoon grated lemon rind
3½ tablespoons fresh lemon juice
¼ teaspoon baking powder
1 large egg
1 large egg white
Powdered sugar (optional)

1. Preheat oven to 350°.

2. To prepare crust, place first 4 ingredients in a large bowl, and beat with a mixer at medium speed until smooth. Weigh or lightly spoon 4.5 ounces (about 1 cup) flour into a dry measuring cup, and level with a knife. Add flour to butter mixture, and beat at low speed until well blended. Press crust into bottom of an 8-inch square metal baking pan coated with cooking spray. Bake at 350° for 20 minutes.

3. To prepare filling, place cottage cheese in a food processor; process 2 minutes or until smooth, scraping sides of bowl once. Add granulated sugar and next 6 ingredients (through egg white), and process until well blended. Pour filling over crust.

4. Bake at 350° for 25 minutes or until set (the edges will get lightly browned). Cool. Cover and chill 8 hours. Sprinkle with powdered sugar before serving, if desired. Serves 12 (serving size: 1 bar)

CALORIES 187; FAT 6g (sat 3.5g, mono 1.7g, poly 0g); PROTEIN 3.5g; CARB 31g; FIBER 2.1g; CHOL 29mg; IRON 1.1mg; SODIUM 127mg; CALC 50mg

The milk that lasts

When cans of sweetened condensed milk were first sold by Gail Borden from his pushcart in New York City in 1856, the milk was introduced as an ingredient that could help prevent food poisoning related to lack of refrigeration. Eagle Brand became a household name during the Civil War when it provided the military with milk that would store well without spoiling.

Once families began enjoying the luxuries of the refrigerator, Eagle Brand became popular with home cooks—as a key ingredient in fudge and other desserts. In 1931, Borden Kitchens began offering homemakers $25 for recipes featuring sweetened condensed milk. The original Magic Cookie Bars recipe was one of over 80,000 submitted and was first published in the 1960s.

MAGIC COOKIE BARS

HANDS-ON TIME: 30 MINUTES ★ TOTAL TIME: 2 HOURS

These are also known as seven-layer bars. They take 30 minutes of hands-on prep and call for just eight ingredients, making them the perfect dessert for taking, well, just about anywhere!

1½ cups graham cracker crumbs
   (about 9 cookie sheets)
2 tablespoons butter, melted
1 tablespoon water
⅓ cup semisweet chocolate chips
⅓ cup butterscotch morsels
⅔ cup flaked sweetened coconut
¼ cup chopped pecans, toasted
1 (15-ounce) can fat-free
   sweetened condensed milk

1. Preheat oven to 350°.
2. Line bottom and sides of a 9-inch square metal baking pan with parchment paper; cut off excess parchment paper around top edge of pan.
3. Place crumbs in a medium bowl. Drizzle with butter and 1 tablespoon water; toss with a fork until moist. Gently pat mixture into an even layer in bottom of pan (do not press firmly). Sprinkle chips and morsels over crumb mixture. Top evenly with coconut and pecans. Drizzle milk evenly over top. Bake at 350° for 25 minutes or until lightly browned and bubbly around edges. Cool completely in pan on a wire rack. Serves 24 (serving size: 1 bar)
Note: These bars can create a sticky mess in the pan, so it's crucial to line it with parchment paper. Because the milk needs to seep into the graham cracker crumbs, don't pack the crumbs too tightly in the bottom of the pan.

CALORIES 123; FAT 4.4g (sat 2.3g, mono 1.3g, poly 0.6g); PROTEIN 2.1g; CARB 19.1g; FIBER 0.5g; CHOL 5mg; IRON 0.3mg; SODIUM 64mg; CALC 50mg

CHOCOLATE-PEANUT BUTTER BARS

HANDS-ON TIME: 10 MINUTES ★ TOTAL TIME: 2 HOURS 36 MINUTES

I distinctly remember making peanut butter bars (and sewing a pillow) in my middle school home economics class. Try this updated version of the bars, fit for modern palates, with your own young chef. Substitute light brown sugar for the dark if you are looking for a milder bar.

¾ cup granulated sugar

¾ cup packed dark brown sugar

6 tablespoons unsalted butter, softened

1 tablespoon canola oil

¾ cup reduced-fat creamy peanut butter

1 large egg

1 large egg white

4.5 ounces all-purpose flour (about 1 cup)

1 teaspoon baking powder

¼ teaspoon salt

Cooking spray

⅔ cup semisweet chocolate chips

1. Preheat oven to 350°.

2. Place first 4 ingredients in a large bowl; beat with a mixer at medium speed until well blended (about 2 minutes). Add peanut butter, beating well. Beat in egg and egg white.

3. Weigh or lightly spoon flour into a dry measuring cup; level with a knife. Combine flour, baking powder, and salt, stirring with a whisk. Gradually add flour mixture to peanut butter mixture, beating until blended (batter will be thick). Spread batter evenly in a 13 x 9–inch metal baking pan coated with cooking spray.

4. Bake at 350° for 26 to 28 minutes or until a wooden pick inserted in center comes out clean.

5. Place chocolate in the top of a double boiler set over slightly simmering water; melt chocolate chips, stirring until smooth. Spread chocolate evenly over top. Cool completely on a wire rack. Cut into bars. Serves 24 (serving size: 1 bar)

CALORIES 174; FAT 8g (sat 3.4g, mono 3.1g, poly 1.2g); PROTEIN 3g; CARB 23.9g; FIBER 0.9g; CHOL 15mg; IRON 0.7mg; SODIUM 92mg; CALC 20mg

My friends and me in home ec, Southside Middle School, Rockville Centre, NY

NO-BAKE CHOCOLATE PEANUT BUTTER DROPS

HANDS-ON TIME: 20 MINUTES ★ TOTAL TIME: 45 MINUTES

No-bake cookies make even the most oven-shy baker look like a hero. You'll see them at bake sales, fundraisers, and in millions of homes across the country as an after-school snack. I've cut out a lot of the unnecessary butter and added chocolate chips, providing firmness, texture, and a great gloss to these cookies.

1 cup sugar
⅓ cup butter
¼ cup unsweetened cocoa
¼ cup 2% reduced-fat milk
¼ cup dark chocolate chips

¼ cup reduced-fat creamy peanut butter
1 teaspoon vanilla extract
1½ cups uncooked quick-cooking oats

1. Combine first 4 ingredients (through milk) in a medium saucepan. Bring to a simmer over medium heat, stirring frequently. Cook until sugar dissolves, stirring gently (about 2 minutes). Remove from heat; add chocolate chips. Let stand 1 minute; stir with a whisk until chips are melted. Add peanut butter and vanilla; stir well with a whisk. Stir in oats. Cool slightly.
2. Drop mixture by tablespoonfuls onto wax paper; cool 15 minutes or until firm. Serves 30 (serving size: 1 cookie)

CALORIES 84; FAT 3.9g (sat 2g, mono 1.1g, poly 0.3g); PROTEIN 1.4g; CARB 12.3g; FIBER 1g; CHOL 6mg; IRON 0.5mg; SODIUM 33mg; CALC 7mg

OLD-FASHIONED SUGAR COOKIES

HANDS-ON TIME: 27 MINUTES ★ TOTAL TIME: 1 HOUR 9 MINUTES

This dough will work for slice-and-bake cookies or as a rolled dough for your favorite cookie cutters.

2 ounces ⅓-less-fat cream cheese, softened
¼ cup unsalted butter, softened
¼ cup canola oil
1 cup sugar, divided
1 tablespoon 2% reduced-fat milk
2 teaspoons vanilla extract
1 large egg
7.9 ounces all-purpose flour (about 1¾ cups)
¾ teaspoon baking powder
½ teaspoon kosher salt
Cooking spray

1. Place first 3 ingredients (through oil) and ⅔ cup sugar in a large bowl; beat with a mixer at medium speed until well blended. Add milk, vanilla, and egg. Beat until blended.
2. Weigh or lightly spoon flour into dry measuring cups; level with a knife. Combine flour, baking powder, and salt; gradually add to sugar mixture, beating until well blended. Cover and chill 30 minutes.
3. Preheat oven to 350°.
4. Place ⅓ cup sugar in a small bowl. Shape dough into 36 (1-inch) balls. Roll balls in sugar, and place 1½ inches apart on large baking sheets coated with cooking spray. Flatten cookies slightly with bottom of a glass.
5. Bake at 350° for 9 minutes or until set in center. Cool on pan 2 minutes. Remove from pan; cool completely on a wire rack. Serves 36 (serving size: 1 cookie)

CALORIES 77; FAT 3.4g (sat 1.2g, mono 1.4g, poly 0.5g); PROTEIN 1g; CARB 10.5g; FIBER 0.2g; CHOL 10mg; IRON 0.3mg; SODIUM 44mg; CALC 9mg

OATMEAL-RAISIN COOKIES

HANDS-ON TIME: 17 MINUTES ★ TOTAL TIME: 52 MINUTES

You'll find that this recipe is very similar to the famous recipe on the Quaker Oats package—only lighter. I cut the original amount of butter almost in half and added molasses to bump up the flavor.

½ cup packed brown sugar

½ cup granulated sugar

½ cup butter, softened

¼ cup canola oil

¼ cup molasses

1 teaspoon vanilla extract

1 large egg

1 large egg white

7.9 ounces all-purpose flour (about 1¾ cups)

1 teaspoon baking soda

1 teaspoon ground cinnamon

½ teaspoon salt

3 cups uncooked old-fashioned rolled oats

1 cup raisins

1. Preheat oven to 350°.

2. Place first 5 ingredients (through molasses) in a large bowl; beat with a stand mixer at medium speed until well blended (about 5 minutes). Add vanilla, egg, and egg white, beating well.

3. Weigh or lightly spoon flour into dry measuring cups; level with a knife. Combine flour and next 3 ingredients (through salt), stirring well with a whisk. Gradually add flour mixture to butter mixture, beating at low speed until blended. Stir in oats and raisins.

4. Drop dough by level tablespoons 2 inches apart onto ungreased baking sheets.

5. Bake at 350° for 12 minutes or until lightly browned. Cool on pan 2 minutes. Remove cookies from pan; cool completely on wire racks. Serves 48 (serving size: 1 cookie)

CALORIES 98; FAT 3.6g (sat 1.3g, mono 1.3g, poly 0.4g); PROTEIN 1.7g; CARB 15.3g; FIBER 0.8g; CHOL 7mg; IRON 0.6mg; SODIUM 68mg; CALC 12mg

PEANUT BUTTER COOKIES

HANDS-ON TIME: 20 MINUTES ★ TOTAL TIME: 1 HOUR 15 MINUTES

These are just like Grandma made, complete with the crosshatch pattern on top. It's easier than you think to make that pattern; just crisscross the tines of a fork and press gently into the top of each cookie before you bake.

Use a fork to make the classic crosshatch design

½ cup natural-style, reduced-fat creamy peanut butter

½ cup packed brown sugar

7 tablespoons unsalted butter, softened

½ teaspoon vanilla extract

¾ cup granulated sugar, divided

1 large egg

5.6 ounces all-purpose flour (about 1¼ cups)

½ teaspoon baking powder

½ teaspoon baking soda

¼ teaspoon salt

1. Preheat oven to 375°.

2. Place first 4 ingredients (through vanilla) and ½ cup granulated sugar in a bowl; beat with a mixer at medium speed until well blended (about 5 minutes). Add egg, beating well.

3. Weigh or lightly spoon flour into dry measuring cups; level with a knife. Combine flour and next 3 ingredients (through salt), stirring well with a whisk. Gradually add flour mixture to sugar mixture, beating well. Cover and refrigerate 15 minutes or until dough is firm.

4. Roll dough into 30 (1¼-inch) balls. Place ¼ cup granulated sugar in a small bowl. Roll balls in sugar, and place 2 inches apart on an ungreased baking sheet. Flatten cookies in a crisscross pattern with a fork. Bake at 375° for 10 minutes or until edges just begin to brown. Cool on pan 2 minutes. Remove from pan; cool completely on wire racks. Serves 30 (serving size: 1 cookie)

CALORIES 106; FAT 4.5g (sat 2g, mono 1.3g, poly 0.5g); PROTEIN 2g; CARB 14.1g; FIBER 0.4g; CHOL 13mg; IRON 0.4mg; SODIUM 64mg; CALC 10mg

Acknowledgements

a good book, which I believe this has turned out to be, is the result of a great deal of effort by many people. Thanks to Jim Childs, who helped conceive this book and gave me the permission to write it. To my sweet Southern-talking editor, Andrea Kirkland, and Leah McLaughlin for making it better. To Stacey Glick, my friend and agent, and to Scott Mowbray for bringing me into the *Cooking Light* editorial fold and writing the intelligent foreword.

Thank you David Thomsen for picking me as your host for *Blue Ribbon Hunter*, and Brian Hunt for the green light. To Sarah Lindland, my work wife, for being the heart of our show. To Sean Martin, Josh Simmons, Ryan Kuharic, Eric Branco, Brendan Banks, and Anthony Augello for taking the pictures, and Anna Robertson for letting us use them. To Blair Johnson, Gary Millus, and Paul Campione for listening. To Malia Hurwitz, Martin Goetz, Jennifer Needleman, and Joseph Orisino for bringing it together. To Dena Giannini for the glass slippers. To Michael Manus for waving your magic wand.

Thank you Susan Sherrill Axelrod and Julie Grimes for developing scrumptious recipes, and Sara Mae for testing them. To the Oxmoor House Test Kitchen staff in Birmingham, who gave each recipe the final review. To Felicity Keane for your art direction and to the photo team, who created such beautiful food photography: Hélène Dujardin, Mindi Shapiro, Mary Clayton Carl, Tori Cox, Catherine Steele, and Ana Kelly. Kathryn Millan and Keri Matherne for your attention to detail. Lisa Atwood, who helped me capture the great stories behind American cuisine.

And a very special thanks goes out to the Oxmoor House editorial and production teams, who worked tirelessly on this book—Melissa Brown, Claire Cormany, Maribeth Jones, Diane Keener, and Megan Yeatts.

Thank you Erin Clinton, Michelle Aycock, Allison Lowery, and The Door, for shouting from the rooftops.

Thank you Mom and Dad, Anne Gomes, Tara Spinelli, and Jen Kowal, for your help when the babies came early.

To Davida for setting the table and always trying a bite, even when it's spicy and you need a just-in-case glass of milk close by.

And thank you Aaron for telling me yes, you'd take care of everything when I left for the airport every other weekend for two years (and counting); for listening to my road stories; and for encouraging me to write this book.

Photo Credits

CONTRACT PHOTOGRAPHERS

Morgan & Owens: 5 Crow Farms; 77 holding lobster; 123 Lobster Pot Restaurant; 228 shucking corn; 247 holding pie; 265; back cover First Congregational Church; **Evan Sklar:** 10; **Kathryn Gamble:** 12 Allison with calf; 13 Allison eating butter on a stick, blue ribbon watermelon; 15 Allison with girls, fair; 53 Allison; 55 girl with gizmo tray; 66 Allison eating and man grilling; 91 Allison eating corn; 93 blue ribbon vegetables; 199 Allison with salad on a stick; 201 blue ribbon onions; 248 couple eating ice cream; 249 ice cream sculpture; **Quentin Bacon:** 13 burger; 18; 19 egg on a roll, espresso, pastry plate, waffles; 20 Aroma sign, mugs; 52 tacos; 53 burger, 55 salad; 90; 119; 124 Hamburgers sign; 125 matzoh ball soup pour; 198; 199 French fry sign; 247 sprinkles in jars; 269 cheesecake with fork; **Peter Frank Edwards:** 13 Seafood Market, tomatoes; 45 fishing, holding shrimp, marina; 53 waitress, sign; 55 serving line; 74 location; 91 market; 104 crabbing, crab in hand, crabs in net; 106 shrimp in hands; 122; 123 sign, family eating; 199 okra

COURTESY OF

Yahoo!: 11 Allison eating pizza; 13 apple pie; 15 Allison & chili, Allison at Varsity; 19 Allison at food truck; 25 kids chugging milk; 34 Allison, bacon socks; 53 fish taco truck; 87 location, Allison; 89 Allison; 93 Allison; 95 Allison; 117 Avocado Festival, Allison stirring, Allison with avocado; 123 Allison at chili-cook off; 124 Allison eating pizza; 125 Allison spinning pizza dough; 130 Memphis sign, meat on grill; 133 Dandelion winner; 137 meatball in hand; 156 Allison; 177 Tabasco sauce; 178 Fisherman's Wharf; 181 Allison cooking; 188 Allison, sign, Road Kill Festival; 220 Allison with trophy, Mac and Cheese, Festival; 235 Allison; 244 Allison at Varsity; 249 Allison with pies; 250 Allison; 256 Allison, peach festival, Allison eating; 267 Allison; **Allison Fishman Task:** 12 Zev and Abe; 110 in kitchen; 168 family shot; 204 sister-in-law; 219 Allison and babies; 280 Allison and brother; 303 Home Economics class; **Ted Axelrod:** 149; **Demetrisbbq.com:** 21; **Sunda New Asian, Chicago:** 40 Loco Moco; **Arcaderestaurant.com:** 41 Eggs Redneck; **Pat's King Of Steaks:** 59 location, sandwich; **Waldorf Astoria New York:** 79 location; **Lee and Jack Manfred:** 128; **Silver Palate Cookbook/ Workman:** 141; **Divan Parisien Restaurant/Chatham Hotel:** 143; **DeviNYC.com:** 144; **Minnesota Cultivated Wild Rice Council:** 193; **Adams Flavors, Foods & Ingredients:** 290 vintage red velvet cake

STOCK PHOTOGRAPHERS

Michael Persico: 19 Federal Donuts; 31 Federal Donuts exterior; 249 counter girl; **Jim Dow, courtesy Janet Borden, Inc.:** 19 Coffee sign; 54 EAT, diner counter; 55 Town Diner; 125 Abe's sign; 127 Pig sign; 150 Fish Fry; © **Jody Horton:** 53 gyro; 92 mussels; 200 green beans; 201 overhead dinner; © **Samuel Markey Photography 2013:** 21 Federal Donuts interior; **Kathryn Millan:** 21 Bakery window; 113 pimiento cheese; 161 pizza sign; **P. McDonald of redshallotkitchen.com:** 40 Hangtown Fry; **Restaurant-ingThroughHistory.com:** 57 Reuben's Restaurant; **Kimberly Davis:** 199 market; 201 carrots; 247 blackberries; 249 strawberries

STOCK AGENCIES

Corbis: 51 © Ocean/Corbis, granola jar; 64 © Macduff Everton/Corbis, baguettes; 146 © Radius Images/Corbis, pizza on grill; 164 © the food passionates/Corbis, pasta; 185 © Scrivani, Andrew/the food passionates/Corbis, split peas; 217 © Randy Faris/CORBIS; **Getty:** 14 John Elk; 38 Ron and Patty Thomas, foliage scene; 61 Danita Delimont, Greek sign; 71 Anne Rippy, French Quarter; 108 Lonely Planet; 113 Smneedham, cream cheese; 134 Panoramic Images, Longhorn sign; 155 Lew Robertson, chiles; 167 Richard Cummins, clock; 174 Huw Jones, handmade sign; 174 AdShooter, neon; 190 Village Production; 227 Andrew Dernie; 237 Mary Hope; 240 Bill Boch; 246 Daniel Loiselle, apple pie slice; 252 Dennis K. Johnson; 267 Preston Schlebusch, cranberry bog; 270 Sasha Radosavljevic; 273 Alexandra Grablewski; 274 Lauri Patterson, jammers; 274 Brian Hagiwara, pineapple upside-down cake; 275 Inti St. Clair, Boston Cream Pie; 275 James Baigrie, bundt cake; 277 Kurtwilson, vanilla; 278 Lara Hata, cake layers; 284 Brian Hagiwara, fruitcake and ribbon; 286 Andrea Pistolesi, St Louis Arch; 289 Adam Gault, cupcakes on rack; 295 Lynne Brotchie; 297 Linda Steward, recipe; 299 Danielle Wood; 308 Kirk Mastin; **iStock:** 255 sf_foodphoto, pumpkin pour; 275 sandoclr, King Cake; 306 Elenathewise; © **StockFood:** 22 Eising Food Photography, pecans; 41 Keller & Keller Photography, Eggs Benedict; 194 Richard Jung Photography Ltd., measuring flour; 197 Alain Caste-StockFood Munich, matzoh; 203 Paul Poplis Photography, Inc., sweet onions; 213 Mario Matassa-StockFood UK; 260 Greg Rannells Photography, Inc.

INDEX

Almonds, Honey-Glazed, 115
America Loves
Baking
East, Whoopie Pie, 275
Midwest, Bundt Cake, 275
Northeast, Boston Cream
Pie, 275
Northwest, Jammers, 274
Southeast, Lady Baltimore
Cake, 275
South, King Cake, 275
Southwest, Texas Sheet
Cake, 274
West, Pineapple Upside-
Down Cake, 274
Casseroles
East, Kugel, 211
Midwest, Spaghetti
Casserole, 211
Northeast, New Brunswick
Lobster Casserole, 211
Northwest, Walla Walla
Onion Casserole, 210
Southeast, Shrimp and
Grits Dressing, 211
South, Spoonbread, 211
Southwest, King Ranch
Casserole, 210
West, Cowboy Casserole,
210
Cheese
East, Philadelphia Cream
Cheese, 113
Midwest, Iowa Maytag
Blue, 113
Northeast, Vermont La
Luna, 113
Northwest, Oregon
Tillamook Cheddar, 112
South, Alabama Goat
Cheese, 113

Southeast, Pimiento
Cheese, 113
Southwest, Arizona Cotija,
112
West, San Francisco
Teleme, 112
Eggs
East, Pennsylvania Dutch
Pickled Eggs, 41
Midwest, Savory Egg
Muffins, 41
Northeast, Eggs Benedict,
41
West, Hangtown Fry, 40
West, Loco Moco, 40
South, Eggs Redneck, 41
Southwest, Huevos
Rancheros, 40
Fire
East, Steamed Crabs, 147
Midwest, Kansas City
Burnt Ends, 147
Northeast, Lobster Bake,
147
Northwest, Wood-Plank
Smoked Salmon, 146
South, Pig Pickin', 147
Southeast, Frogmore Stew,
147
Southwest, Texas Brisket,
146
West, Pizza on the Grill,
146
Soup
East, Pepper Pot, 83
Midwest, Cheddar Cheese
& Beer Soup, 83
Northeast, New England
Clam Chowder, 83
Northwest, Baked Potato
Soup, 82

South, Pot Likker Soup, 83
Southeast, Brunswick Stew,
83
Southwest, Tortilla Soup,
82
West, Green Chile Stew, 82

Appetizers. *See also* **Snacks.**
Blue Cheese Ball, 114
Clams and Mussels, Beer-
Steamed, 103
Clams, Baked, 102
Crab Cakes with Cajun
Rémoulade, 105
Deviled Eggs, 101
Dips
Artichoke-Spinach Dip,
119
Five-Layer Dip, 121
Guacamole, 116
Texas Caviar, 120
Fried Green Tomatoes with
Garlicky Rémoulade, 100
Lettuce Wraps, Thai, 108
Pigs in a Blanket, 97
Shrimp with Fiery Mango
Sauce, Coconut, 107
Artichoke-Spinach Dip, 119
Avocados
Guacamole, 116
Salad, Avocado & Orange,
230
Sandwich, B.L.A.S.T., 69

Bacon, Brussels Sprouts with,
225
Bacon-Corn Chowder with
Shrimp, 180

Banana Pudding, Roasted, 260
Barbecue. *See also* **Grilled.**

Hot Dogs, Memphis BBQ, 73
Pork Ribs, Barbecue, 131

Beans
Baked Beans, Vermont, 222
Black Beans, 231
Dip, Five-Layer, 121
Dirty Rice and Beans, Baked
Louisiana, 217
Enchiladas, Vegetarian, 156
Greens, Beans &, 233

Beef. *See also* **Beef, Ground;**
Sandwiches.
Burgoo, Kentucky, 189
Chili, 186
Hash, Red Flannel, 38
Steak with Milk Gravy,
Chicken-Fried, 135
Stew, Beef and Mushroom,
190

Beef, Ground. *See also* **Sandwiches.**
Meatballs and Spaghetti, 137
Meatballs, Sweet and Sour,
111
Meat Loaf, 139

Beverages
Alcoholic
Chicago Attack, 98
Long Island Iced Tea, 99
Mai Tai, 98
Margarita, 98
Mojito, 99
Montana Sky, 98
Old Fashioned, 99
Sazerac, 99
Smoothies
Bloody Mary Smoothies,
Spicy, 29
Blueberry Soy Smoothies,
29
Dark Cherry Smoothies, 28
Fresh Peach Smoothies, 29
Mango, Avocado & Lime
Smoothie, Creamy, 28
Mocha Java Smoothies, 28
POG Smoothies, 28
Ruby Slipper Smoothies, 29

Blueberries
Cake, Maine Blueberry, 32
Pancakes, Peach and
Blueberry, 27
Sauce, Fresh Blueberry, 293

Breads. *See also* **French Toast;**
Pancakes.
Biscuits with Sausage Gravy,
Alabama Cat Head, 46
Buns, Caramel-Pecan Sticky,
22
Donuts, Mini, 31
Monkey Bread, 24
Scones, Cranberry-Orange, 33
Broccoli-Cheddar Soup, 182
Brussels Sprouts with Bacon,
225
Burgoo, Kentucky, 189

Cabbage with Sausage &
Apples, Red, 231

Cakes
Birthday Cake, 280
Blueberry Cake, Maine, 32
Butter Cake, St. Louis, 286
Carrot Cake, 282
Cheesecake with Cherry
Topping, Vanilla, 268
Chocolate Cake, Triple-, 276
Coconut Cake, Double-, 279
Cupcakes, Red Velvet, 291
Cupcakes with Creamy
Vanilla Buttercream,
Vanilla, 289
Fruitcake, Southern, 285
Lemon–Poppy Seed Bundt
Cake, 273
Pound Cake with Brown
Butter Glaze, 270
Texas Sheet Cake, 283
Calabacitas, 234
Caramel-Pecan Sticky Buns, 22
Carrot Cake, 282
Carrots, Roasted, 224

Casseroles
Chicken Divan, 143

Dirty Rice and Beans, Baked
Louisiana, 217
Mac and Cheese, Truffled,
221
Onion Casserole, Sweet, 202
Potatoes, Funeral, 208
Shells, Stuffed, 169
Squash Casserole, 205
Strata, Mushroom, Bacon,
and Swiss, 35
Sweet Potato Casserole with
Marshmallow Topping,
206
Tuna Casserole, 153
Cauliflower, Roasted with
Mornay Sauce, 227

Cheese. *See also* **Sandwiches.**
Baked Mozzarella Bites, 94
Chicken Parmesan, 138
Fettuccine Alfredo, 171
Mac and Cheese, Truffled,
221
Pizza, Margherita, 163
Cherry Merlot Sauce, Dark,
292
Cherry Topping, Vanilla
Cheesecake with, 268

Chicken
Burgoo, Kentucky, 189
Dirty Rice and Beans, Baked
Louisiana, 217
Divan, Chicken, 143
Dumplings, Chicken and,
195
Gumbo, New Orleans, 176
Marbella, Chicken, 140
Parmesan, Chicken, 138
Pizza, Chicken & Cheddar,
163
Pizza, Chicken Pesto, 162
Pizza, Peach & Gorgonzola
Chicken, 163
Riggies, Chicken, 167
Salad with Green Goddess
Dressing, Cobb, 81

Soup, Chicken–Matzoh Ball, 196
Soup, Minnesota Wild Rice, 192
Tikka Masala, Chicken, 144
Chiles Rellenos, 155
Chili, 186
Chocolate
  Bars and Cookies
    Brownies, Classic Fudge-Walnut, 296
    Magic Cookie Bars, 301
    No-Bake Chocolate Peanut Butter Drops, 304
    Peanut Butter Bars, Chocolate–, 303
  Buckeyes, Ohio, 295
  Cakes and Tortes
    Birthday Cake, 280
    Texas Sheet Cake, 283
    Triple-Chocolate Cake, 276
  Chowder with Shrimp, Bacon-Corn, 180
  Cioppino, 179
  Clams and Mussels, Beer-Steamed, 103
  Clams, Baked, 102
  Coconut Cake, Double-, 279
  Coconut Shrimp with Fiery Mango Sauce, 107
  Collards, Quick, 232
Cookies
  Bars and Squares
    Brownies, Classic Fudge-Walnut, 296
    Butter-Crunch Lemon Bars, 299
    Chocolate–Peanut Butter Bars, 303
    Magic Cookie Bars, 301
    No-Bake Chocolate Peanut Butter Drops, 304
    Oatmeal-Raisin Cookies, 307
    Peanut Butter Cookies, 308
    Sugar Cookies, Old-Fashioned, 305

Corn
  Calabacitas, 234
  Chowder with Shrimp, Bacon-Corn, 180
  Creamed Corn with Bacon, 230
  Pudding, Corn, 207
  Succotash, 229
Crab Cakes with Cajun Rémoulade, 105
Crab Soup, She-, 85
Cranberry Crunch, 266
Cranberry-Orange Scones, 33

Dandelion Soup, Creamy, 89
Dandelion-Stuffed Pork Loin, 132
Desserts. *See also* **Cakes; Cookies; Pies and Pastries; Pudding.**
  Buckeyes, Ohio, 295
  Ice Cream with Fresh Strawberries, Vanilla Bean, 262
  Sauces
    Apple & Brandy Sauce, 293
    Berry Sauce, Warm, 292
    Blueberry Sauce, Fresh, 293
    Dark Cherry Merlot Sauce, 292
    Orange-Strawberry Sauce, 293
    Peach & Brown Sugar Sauce, 293
    Pineapple Sauce, Chilled, 292
  Trifle, 263
Donuts, Mini, 31
Dumplings, Chicken and, 195

Eggs
  Deviled Eggs, 101
  Hash, Red Flannel, 38
  Migas, Tex-Mex, 37
  Muffins, Savory Egg, 49

Roll, Egg and Cheese on a, 47
Scramble, L.E.O., 36
Shakshuka, 43
Enchiladas, Vegetarian, 156

Fennel, Sausage & Caramelized-Apple Stuffing, 213
Fettuccine Alfredo, 171
Figs, Marsala Poached, 292
Fish
  Catfish Classique, 150
  Cioppino, 179
  Salmon Burgers, Hoisin-Glazed, 158
  Sticks with Tartar Sauce, Oven-Fried Fish, 152
  Tacos, Chimichurri Fish, 68
  Tuna Casserole, 153
French Toast, Baked, 26
Fruit. *See also* **specific types.**
  Fruitcake, Southern, 285
  Sauce, Warm Berry, 292

Garlic
  Burgoo, Kentucky, 189
  Chicken Marbella, 140
  Chicken Riggies, 167
  Chicken Tikka Masala, 144
  Chili, 186
  Enchiladas, Vegetarian, 156
  Fish Tacos, Chimichurri, 68
  Jambalaya, 175
  Pasta Puttanesca, 172
  Pork Loin, Dandelion-Stuffed, 132
  Pork Ribs, Barbecue, 131
  Soup, She-Crab, 85
Granola, All-American, 50
Gravy, Alabama Cat Head Biscuits with Sausage, 46
Gravy, Chicken-Fried Steak with Milk, 135
Greens
  Beans & Greens, 233
  Collards, Quick, 232

Grilled
Brisket Burgers, 159
Fish Tacos, Chimichurri, 68
Hot Dogs
Chicago, 72
Coney Island, 73
Cuban, 73
Hawaiian, 72
Memphis BBQ, 73
Philly, 73
Seattle Cream Cheese, 72
So-Cal Baja, 72
Vegetables
Caprese with Pesto, Grilled
Vegetable, 84
Jalapeño Poppers, Grilled,
96
Okra & Tomatoes, Grilled,
231
Sweet Potato Salad, Grilled,
243
Grits, Cajun-Style Shrimp and,
44
Guacamole, 116
Gumbo, New Orleans, 176

Ham
Fried Rice, 218
Pizza, Peppered Prosciutto &
Parmesan, 162
Soup with Ham, Split Pea,
185
Hash, Red Flannel, 38
Hometown Taste
Cocktail Remix
Chicago Attack, Midwest,
98
Long Island Iced Tea, East,
99
Mai Tai, West, 98
Margarita, Southwest, 98
Mojito, Southeast, 99
Montana Sky, Northwest,
98
Old Fashioned, Northeast,
99

Sazerac, South, 99
Eat Your Veggies
Avocado & Orange Salad,
West, 230
Black Beans, South, 231
Creamed Corn with Bacon,
Midwest, 230
Grilled Okra & Tomatoes,
Southeast, 231
Jicama-Corn Salad,
Southwest, 230
Red Cabbage with Sausage
& Apples, East, 231
Roasted Acorn Squash,
Northeast, 231
Sour Cream & Onion
Potato Chips, Northwest,
230
Pizza That Delivers
Chicken & Cheddar, South,
163
Chicken Pesto, West, 162
Hawaiian Pepperoni, West,
162
Margherita, East, 163
Peach & Gorgonzola
Chicken, Southeast, 163
Peppered Prosciutto &
Parmesan, Midwest, 162
Roasted Beet & Goat
Cheese, Northwest, 162
Smoked Salmon & Dill,
Northeast, 163
Slurp-Worthy Smoothies
Blueberry Soy, Northeast,
29
Creamy Mango, Avocado &
Lime, Southwest, 28
Dark Cherry, Midwest, 28
Fresh Peach, Southeast, 29
Mocha Java, Northwest, 28
POG, West, 28
Ruby Slipper, East, 29
Spicy Bloody Mary, South,
29
Sweet and Saucy

Apple & Brandy Sauce,
East, 293
Chilled Pineapple Sauce,
Southwest, 292
Dark Cherry Merlot Sauce,
Midwest, 292
Fresh Blueberry Sauce,
Northeast, 293
Marsala Poached Figs,
West, 292
Orange-Strawberry Sauce,
Southeast, 293
Peach & Brown Sugar
Sauce, South, 293
Warm Berry Sauce,
Northwest, 292
Tasty Dogs
Chicago, Midwest 72
Coney Island, Northeast 73
Cuban, Southeast 73
Hawaiian, West 72
Memphis BBQ, South 73
Philly, East 73
Seattle Cream Cheese,
Northwest 72
So-Cal Baja, West 72
Hot Dogs
Chicago, 72
Coney Island, 73
Cuban, 73
Hawaiian, 72
Memphis BBQ, 73
Philly, 73
Pigs in a Blanket, 97
Seattle Cream Cheese, 72
So-Cal Baja, 72

Jambalaya, 175
Jicama-Corn Salad, 230

Lasagna, Mushroom and
Spinach, 164
Lentil Soup, 183
Lettuce Wraps, Thai, 108
Lobster Bake, Maine, 149
Lobster Rolls, 77

Mac and Cheese, Truffled, 221
Meatballs and Spaghetti, 137
Meatballs, Sweet and Sour, 111
Meat Loaf, 139
Microwave
  Almonds, Honey-Glazed, 115
  Mozzarella Bites, Baked, 94
  Sauce, Orange-Strawberry, 293
  Soup, Broccoli-Cheddar, 182
Migas, Tex-Mex, 37
Muffins, Savory Egg, 49
Mushrooms
  Lasagna, Mushroom and Spinach, 164
  Pork Chops, Smothered, 127
  Strata, Mushroom, Bacon, and Swiss, 35
Mussels, Beer-Steamed Clams and, 103

Oats
  Chocolate Peanut Butter Drops, No-Bake, 304
  Cookies, Oatmeal-Raisin, 307
  Granola, All-American, 50
Okra & Tomatoes, Grilled, 231
Okra & Tomatoes, Stewed, 238
Onions
  Onion Rings, 245
  Scramble, L.E.O., 36
  Sweet Onion Casserole, 202
Orange-Strawberry Sauce, 293

Pancakes, Peach and Blueberry, 27
Pasta. *See also* **Fettuccine; Lasagna; Spaghetti.**
  Chicken Riggies, 167
  Puttanesca, Pasta, 172
  Shells, Stuffed, 169
  Vodka Cream Sauce, Pasta with, 170
Peaches
  Pancakes, Peach and Blueberry, 27

Pie, Peach, 257
Pizza, Peach & Gorgonzola Chicken, 163
Sauce, Peach & Brown Sugar, 293
Peanut Butter
  Bars, Chocolate–Peanut Butter, 303
  Buckeyes, Ohio, 295
  Chocolate Peanut Butter Drops, No-Bake, 304
  Cookies, Peanut Butter, 308
Peas
  Field Peas, Southern, 223
  Split Pea Soup with Ham, 185
  Texas Caviar, 120
Peppers
  Cheesesteak, Philly, 58
  Chiles Rellenos, 155
  Hot Dogs, Philly, 73
  Jalapeño Poppers, Grilled, 96
Pesto, Grilled Vegetable Caprese with, 84
Pies and Pastries
  Apple Crisp, 265
  Apple Pie, Blue-Ribbon, 251
  Cranberry Crunch, 266
  Hoosier Pie, 259
  Key Lime Pie, 252
  Peach Pie, 257
  Pumpkin Pie with Vanilla Whipped Cream, 254
  Shoofly Pie, 258
Pineapple
  Hot Dogs, Hawaiian, 72
  Pizza, Hawaiian Pepperoni, 162
  Sauce, Chilled Pineapple, 292
Pizza
  Chicken & Cheddar, 163
  Chicken Pesto, 162
  Hawaiian Pepperoni, 162
  Margherita, 163
  Peach & Gorgonzola Chicken, 163

Peppered Prosciutto & Parmesan, 162
Roasted Beet & Goat Cheese, 162
Sausage and Mushroom, Spicy, 161
Smoked Salmon & Dill, 163
Pork. *See also* **Bacon; Ham; Sausage.**
  Bánh Mì, 64
  Chops, Smothered Pork, 127
  Lettuce Wraps, Thai, 108
  Meatballs and Spaghetti, 137
  Meat Loaf, 139
  Pulled Pork, Slow-Roasted, 128
  Ribs, Barbecue Pork, 131
  Scrapple, Philly, 42
  Stuffed Pork Loin, Dandelion-, 132
  Tenderloin Sandwich, Pork, 67
Potatoes. *See also* **Sweet Potato.**
  Chips, Sour Cream & Onion Potato, 230
  "Fries," Garlic-Parsley Steak, 242
  Funeral Potatoes, 208
  Hash, Red Flannel, 38
  Mashed Potatoes, 240
Pudding, Corn, 207
Pudding, Roasted Banana, 260
Pumpkin Pie with Vanilla Whipped Cream, 254

Red Flannel Hash, 38
Rice
  Dirty Rice and Beans, Baked Louisiana, 217
  Fried Rice, 218
  Wild Rice Soup, Minnesota, 192
  Wild Rice Stuffing with Dried Cherries & Toasted Pecans, 214

Salads and Salad Dressings
Avocado & Orange Salad, 230
Caprese with Pesto, Grilled
Vegetable, 84
Cobb Salad with Green
Goddess Dressing, 81
Green Goddess Dressing, 81
Jicama-Corn Salad, 230
Slaw, Classic, 239
Sweet Potato Salad, Grilled,
243
Waldorf Salad, 78
Sandwiches
Bánh Mì, 64
B.L.A.S.T. Sandwich, 69
Burgers, Brisket, 159
Burgers, Hoisin-Glazed
Salmon, 158
Burger, Shrimp, 74
Cheesesteak, Philly, 58
Egg and Cheese on a Roll, 47
Grilled Cheese, Tomato Soup
and, 86
Grinder, 63
Gyros, 60
Kentucky Hot Brown, 62
Lobster Rolls, 77
Po' Boy, Shrimp, 70
Pork Tenderloin Sandwich, 67
Reuben Sandwich, 57
Sauces. *See also* **Desserts/Sauces.**
Mango Sauce, Coconut
Shrimp with Fiery, 107
Mornay Sauce, Roasted
Cauliflower with, 227
Rémoulade, Crab Cakes with
Cajun, 105
Rémoulade, Fried Green
Tomatoes with Garlicky,
100
Tartar Sauce, Oven-Fried
Fish Sticks with, 152
Vodka Cream Sauce, Pasta
with, 170
Sausage
Burgoo, Kentucky, 189

Chili, 186
Gravy, Alabama Cat Head
Biscuits with Sausage, 46
Gumbo, New Orleans, 176
Jambalaya, 175
Pizza, Spicy Sausage and
Mushroom, 161
Red Cabbage with Sausage &
Apples, 231
Stuffing, Fennel, Sausage &
Caramelized-Apple, 213
Scrapple, Philly, 42
Shakshuka, 43
Shrimp
Burger, Shrimp, 74
Cajun-Style Shrimp and
Grits, 44
Coconut Shrimp with Fiery
Mango Sauce, 107
Jambalaya, 175
Po' Boy, Shrimp, 70
Snacks
Almonds, Honey-Glazed,
115
Mozzarella Bites, Baked, 94
Poppers, Grilled Jalapeño, 96
Soups. *See also* **Chowder; Stews.**
Broccoli-Cheddar Soup, 182
Chicken–Matzoh Ball Soup,
196
Dandelion Soup, Creamy, 89
Lentil Soup, 183
She-Crab Soup, 85
Split Pea Soup with Ham,
185
Tomato Soup and Grilled
Cheese, 86
Wild Rice Soup, Minnesota,
192
Spaghetti, Meatballs and, 137
Spinach Dip, Artichoke-, 119
Spinach Lasagna, Mushroom
and, 164
Squash
Acorn Squash, Roasted, 231

Butternut Squash Agrodolce,
237
Calabacitas, 234
Casserole, Squash, 205
Stews. *See also* **Burgoo; Gumbo;
Jambalaya; Soups.**
Beef and Mushroom Stew,
190
Cioppino, 179
Stuffing, Fennel, Sausage &
Caramelized-Apple, 213
Stuffing with Dried Cherries &
Toasted Pecans, Wild Rice,
214
Succotash, 229
Sweet Potato Casserole with
Marshmallow Topping, 206
Sweet Potato Salad, Grilled, 243

Tacos, Chimichurri Fish, 68
Tomatoes
Fried Green Tomatoes with
Garlicky Rémoulade, 100
Pasta Puttanesca, 172
Soup and Grilled Cheese,
Tomato, 86
Toppings. *See also* **Sauces.**
Cherry Topping, Vanilla
Cheesecake with, 268
Marsala Poached Figs, 292
Marshmallow Topping,
Sweet Potato Casserole
with, 206
Turkey
Kentucky Hot Brown, 62
Scrapple, Philly, 42

Vegetables. *See also* specific
types.
Grilled Vegetable Caprese
with Pesto, 84
Salad with Green Goddess
Dressing, Cobb, 81
Shells, Stuffed, 169

NUTRITIONAL ANALYSIS

How to Use It and Why

Glance at the end of any *Cooking Light* recipe, and you'll see how committed we are to helping you make the best of today's light cooking. With chefs, registered dietitians, home economists, and a computer system that analyzes every ingredient we use, *Cooking Light* gives you authoritative dietary detail like no other magazine. We go to such lengths so you can see how our recipes fit into your healthful eating plan. If you're trying to lose weight, the calorie and fat figures will probably help most. But if you're keeping a close eye on the sodium, cholesterol, and saturated fat in your diet, we provide those numbers, too. And because many women don't get enough iron or calcium, we can help there, as well. Finally, there's a fiber analysis for those of us who don't get enough roughage.

Here's a helpful guide to put our nutritional analysis numbers into perspective. Remember, one size doesn't fit all, so take your lifestyle, age, and circumstances into consideration when determining your nutrition needs. For example, pregnant or breast-feeding women need more protein, calories, and calcium. And women older than 50 need 1,200mg of calcium daily, 200mg more than the amount recommended for younger women.

In Our Nutritional Analysis, We Use These Abbreviations

sat	saturated fat	CARB	carbohydrates	g	gram
mono	monounsaturated fat	CHOL	cholesterol	mg	milligram
poly	polyunsaturated fat	CALC	calcium		

Daily Nutrition Guide

	Women ages 25 to 50	Women over 50	Men ages 24 to 50	Men over 50
Calories	2,000	2,000 or less	2,700	2,500
Protein	50g	50g or less	63g	60g
Fat	65g or less	65g or less	88g or less	83g or less
Saturated Fat	20g or less	20g or less	27g or less	25g or less
Carbohydrates	304g	304g	410g	375g
Fiber	25g to 35g	25g to 35g	25g to 35g	25g to 35g
Cholesterol	300mg or less	300mg or less	300mg or less	300mg or less
Iron	18mg	8mg	8mg	8mg
Sodium	2,300mg or less	1,500mg or less	2,300mg or less	1,500mg or less
Calcium	1,000mg	1,200mg	1,000mg	1,000mg

The nutritional values used in our calculations either come from The Food Processor, Version 10.4 (ESHA Research), or are provided by food manufacturers.

METRIC EQUIVALENTS

The information in the following charts is provided to help cooks outside the United States successfully use the recipes in this book. All equivalents are approximate.

Cooking/Oven Temperatures

	Fahrenheit	Celsius	Gas Mark
Freeze Water	32° F	0° C	
Room Temp.	68° F	20° C	
Boil Water	212° F	100° C	
Bake	325° F	160° C	3
	350° F	180° C	4
	375° F	190° C	5
	400° F	200° C	6
	425° F	220° C	7
	450° F	230° C	8
Broil			Grill

Liquid Ingredients by Volume

¼ tsp	=					1ml
½ tsp	=					2ml
1 tsp	=					5ml
3 tsp	=	1 Tbsp	=	½ fl oz	=	15ml
2 Tbsp	=	⅛ cup	=	1 fl oz	=	30ml
4 Tbsp	=	¼ cup	=	2 fl oz	=	60ml
5⅓ Tbsp	=	⅓ cup	=	3 fl oz	=	80ml
8 Tbsp	=	½ cup	=	4 fl oz	=	120ml
10⅔ Tbsp	=	⅔ cup	=	5 fl oz	=	160ml
12 Tbsp	=	¾ cup	=	6 fl oz	=	180ml
16 Tbsp	=	1 cup	=	8 fl oz	=	240ml
1 pt	=	2 cups	=	16 fl oz	=	480ml
1 qt	=	4 cups	=	32 fl oz	=	960ml
				33 fl oz	=	1000ml = 1 l

Dry Ingredients by Weight

(To convert ounces to grams, multiply the number of ounces by 30.)

1 oz	=	⅟₁₆ lb	=	30 g
4 oz	=	¼ lb	=	120 g
8 oz	=	½ lb	=	240 g
12 oz	=	¾ lb	=	360 g
16 oz	=	1 lb	=	480 g

Length

(To convert inches to centimeters, multiply the number of inches by 2.5.)

1 in	=			2.5 cm	
6 in	=	½ ft	=	15 cm	
12 in	=	1 ft	=	30 cm	
36 in	=	3 ft	= 1 yd	=	90 cm	
40 in	=			100 cm	= 1m

Equivalents for Different Types of Ingredients

Standard Cup	Fine Powder (ex. flour)	Grain (ex. rice)	Granular (ex. sugar)	Liquid Solids (ex. butter)	Liquid (ex. milk)
1	140 g	150 g	190 g	200 g	240 ml
¾	105 g	113 g	143 g	150 g	180 ml
⅔	93 g	100 g	125 g	133 g	160 ml
½	70 g	75 g	95 g	100 g	120 ml
⅓	47 g	50 g	63 g	67 g	80 ml
¼	35 g	38 g	48 g	50 g	60 ml
⅛	18 g	19 g	24 g	25 g	30 ml

ISBN-13: 978-0-8487-3959-1
ISBN-10: 0-8487-3959-0
Library of Congress Control Number: 2013946187
Printed in the United States of America
First printing 2013

Be sure to check with your health-care provider before making any changes in your diet.

Oxmoor House

Editorial Director: Leah McLaughlin
Creative Director: Felicity Keane
Brand Manager: Michelle Turner Aycock
Managing Editor: Elizabeth Tyler Austin

Cooking Light® Lighten Up, America!

Senior Editor: Andrea Kirkland, MS, RD
Assistant Designer: Allison Potter
Junior Designer: Maribeth Jones
Assistant Directors, Test Kitchen: Julie Christopher, Julie Gunter
Recipe Developers and Testers: Wendy Ball, RD; Victoria E. Cox; Tamara Goldis; Stefanie Maloney; Callie Nash; Karen Rankin; Leah Van Deren
Recipe Editor: Alyson Moreland Haynes
Food Stylists: Margaret Monroe Dickey, Catherine Crowell Steele
Photography Director: Jim Bathie
Senior Photographer: Hélène Dujardin
Senior Photo Stylist: Kay E. Clarke
Photo Stylist: Mindi Shapiro Levine
Assistant Photo Stylist: Mary Louise Menendez
Production Manager: Tamara Nall Wilder
Assistant Production Manager: Diane Rose Keener

Contributors

Writer: Lisa Atwood
Art Director: Claire Cormany
Project Editors: Melissa Brown, Megan Yeatts
Photographers: Quentin Bacon, Peter Frank Edwards, James Owens, Jessie Owens, Beau Gustafson, Evan Sklar, Daniel Taylor
Food Stylists: Erica Hopper, Ana Price Kelly
Photo Stylists: Mary Clayton Carl, Missie Crawford, Leslie Simpson, Caitlin Van Horn
Photo Editor: Kathryn Milan
Nutrition Analyst: Keri Matherne, RD
Copy Editors: Jacqueline Giovanelli, Erica Midkiff
Proofreaders: Rebecca Benton, Dolores Hydock

Indexer: Mary Ann Laurens
Interns: Frances Gunnells, Susan Kemp, Madison Taylor Pozzo, Jeffrey Preis, Maria Sanders, Deanna Sakal, Julia Sayers, April Smitherman
Makeup: Susana Canario
Hair: Danielle Romeo

Time Home Entertainment Inc.

Publisher: Jim Childs
VP, Brand and Digital Strategy: Steven Sandonato
Executive Director, Marketing Services: Carol Pittard
Executive Director, Retail & Special Sales: Tom Mifsud
Director, Bookazine Development & Marketing: Laura Adam
Executive Publishing Director: Joy Butts
Associate Publishing Director: Megan Pearlman
Finance Director: Glenn Buonocore
Associate General Counsel: Helen Wan

Cooking Light®

Editor: Scott Mowbray
Acting Creative Director: Dimity Jones
Executive Managing Editor: Phillip Rhodes
Executive Editor, Food: Ann Taylor Pittman
Executive Editor, Digital: Allison Long Lowery
Special Publications Editor: Mary Simpson Creel, MS, RD
Senior Food Editor: Timothy Q. Cebula
Senior Editor: Cindy Hatcher
Assistant Editor, Nutrition: Sidney Fry, MS, RD
Assistant Editors: Kimberly Holland, Phoebe Wu
Assistant Test Kitchen Director: Tiffany Vickers Davis
Recipe Testers and Developers: Robin Bashinsky, Adam Hickman, Deb Wise
Art Directors: Fernande Bondarenko, Shawna Kalish
Senior Deputy Art Director: Rachel Cardina Lasserre
Senior Designer: Anna Bird
Designer: Hagen Stegall
Assistant Designer: Nicole Gerrity
Photo Director: Kristen Schaefer
Assistant Photo Editor: Amy Delaune
Senior Photographer: Randy Mayor
Senior Prop Stylist: Cindy Barr
Chief Food Stylist: Kellie Gerber Kelley
Food Styling Assistant: Blakeslee Wright
Production Director: Liz Rhoades
Production Editor: Hazel R. Eddins
Assistant Production Editor: Josh Rutledge
Assistant Copy Chief: Susan Roberts
Research Editor: Michelle Gibson Daniels
Administrative Coordinator: Carol D. Johnson
Associate Editor/Producer: Mallory Daugherty Brasseale

To order additional publications, call
1-800-765-6400 or 1-800-491-0551.
To search, savor, and share thousands
of recipes, visit myrecipes.com